Boston A to Z

Boston
A to Z

Thomas H. O'Connor

HARVARD UNIVERSITY PRESS
CAMBRIDGE, MASSACHUSETTS
LONDON, ENGLAND
2000

Library of Congress Cataloging-in-Publication Data

O'Connor, Thomas H., 1922–
Boston A to Z / Thomas H. O'Connor.
p. cm.
Includes index.
ISBN 0-674-00310-1 (alk. paper)
1. Boston (Mass.)—History—Miscellanea.   I. Title.

F73.36 .O37 2000
974.4'61—dc21   00-036952

Illustration Credits

Boston Public Library: Boston Public Library, Mary Dyer, 54th Regiment, Boston Garden, "Honey Fitz," The Steaming Kettle, "The Rascal King," Union Oyster House

The Bostonian Society: Custom House, Emerald Necklace, Ice, Jordan Marsh, Louisburg Square, Boston Massacre, Old State House, Public Garden, Scollay Square, Trinity Church, Hotel Vendome, Phillis Wheatley

Massachusetts Historical Society: African Meeting House

Peter Vanderwarker: The "New Boston," Quincy Market

Sonja Rodrigue/Zoo New England: Franklin Park Zoo

Contents

Preface: Travels with my Aunt Nellie

*M*any years ago, when I was a little boy about 9 or 10 years old, my Aunt Nellie would regularly take me on the trolley from South Boston, where we lived, for visits to downtown Boston. Aunt Nellie was my mother's aunt, a maiden lady who resembled the wonderful English actress who plays the part of Miss Marple on the PBS series about Agatha Christie's slightly dotty but disarmingly clever detective—she even talked like her in that deceptively quiet and ruminating manner. It was probably Aunt Nellie who first got me interested in history. She gave me presents of two books a year, one for my birthday and one for Christmas, usually books about American history written for boys. I still have the copy of Ralph Waldo Emerson's *Essays* she gave me for Christmas when I was in the eighth grade.

Aunt Nellie was an avid reader of the morning newspapers and always knew all about what was happening in the city that day—celebrations, parades, visiting dignitaries, grand openings, special department store sales, and anything else that was mentioned in the daily columns. And so, after we emerged from the Park Street Station, looking up at the tall white spire of the Park Street Church, we would wander around town all day, with Aunt Nellie pointing out the historic spots, describing the interesting sights, and identifying the passersby. One morning as we were walking up School Street on our way toward Tremont Street, passing City Hall (the old one—the new one hadn't been built yet), I looked up and saw a tall and very distinguished gentleman walking toward us on his way from Beacon Hill to Washington Street. "That's Representative

Leverett Saltonstall," Aunt Nellie confided to me, leaning down. Then she raised her head, smiled, and said "Good morning." Mr. Saltonstall raised his gray fedora politely, smiled, nodded his head, said "Good morning" to the two of us, and continued on his stately way.

Our travels around the city took us to many different places. During the cold winter weeks between Thanksgiving and Christmas, we would walk through the slush and snow to the corner of Washington and Summer streets to enjoy the brilliantly lighted windows of the Jordan Marsh department store, with their colorful tableaus of the Bethlehem story, the visits of Santa Claus, scenes from Dickens's *Christmas Carol*, and other familiar images of the holiday season. In summer months, we would stroll hand-in-hand through the Public Garden, where Aunt Nellie described in great detail the various species of flowers, shrubs, and trees, before we bought our tickets for the obligatory ride on the Swan Boats. On cold winter days, when the pond was encased in ice, we would cross Arlington Street and end up on the second-floor gallery of Schrafft's, on Boylston Street, to enjoy a cup of hot chocolate—topped with real whipped cream!—with a packet of plain saltine crackers on the side. No two visits to Boston with Aunt Nellie were ever the same, and rarely did we see the same sights twice.

This book of essays about Boston has something of the perpetually perambulating and essentially serendipitous nature of my trips to the city with my Aunt Nellie. It is neither a dictionary nor an encyclopedia; it is certainly not a reference book or a tour guide. Instead, it is a stroll through a highly personal, completely subjective, and decidedly eclectic list of topics relating to Boston that I have chosen to write about as my fancy struck me. If a reader were to ask—as some invariably will—"Why did you include this topic?" or "Why didn't you include that topic?" I must admit that while I have no really satisfactory answer, I can perhaps suggest the kinds of remarkable changes in the city's history that brought many of the topics to mind.

Some thirty-five years ago, the eminent historian Samuel Eliot Morison wrote a delightful memoir called *One Boy's Boston*, recalling what it was like to grow up in the city at the turn of the twentieth century. His Boston generally encompassed the sedate areas of Beacon Hill and the Back Bay, home to the kinds of wealthy Brahmin families Oliver Wendell Holmes had described as enjoying "their houses by Bulfinch, their monopoly of Beacon Street, their ancestral portraits and Chinese porcelains . . ."

My Boston is a different place, in a different era. It is no longer a nineteenth-century town of gaslights, cobblestone streets, and horse-drawn carriages—although these can be readily found if you know where to look for them. Boston today is a bustling twenty-first-century urban metropolis, a sometimes bizarre mixture of the past and the present, where historic residences and colonial meeting houses are set against an incongruous backdrop of the high-rise buildings and modernistic skyscrapers that announced the arrival of the "New Boston." Standing on Washington Street, just beyond the cemetery at King's Chapel, you can actually see three centuries of Boston architecture at once: the eighteenth-century Faneuil Hall, the nineteenth-century Sears Crescent, and the twentieth-century City Hall—and perhaps catch a glimpse of Boston Harbor, where the ships of the first English settlers arrived in the early seventeenth century. It is this curious blend of the old and the new, the juxtaposition of the antique and the modern, that gives Boston perhaps its most distinctive flavor. While it is true that the rather calm and measured pace of an earlier time has been replaced by a noisier and much more frenetic way of life, Boston continues to offer the pleasures of a charming diversity to those who walk its winding streets and explore its historic trails.

My Boston also covers a much wider geographical area than Professor Morison's "tight little island" around Brimmer Street a century ago. It extends out from the central city into the various neighborhoods and reflects a much more varied population, whose social customs and cultural observances offer a sharp contrast with those of earlier generations of Bostonians. It makes for a curious and fascinating mixture. Here you will find nativists and newcomers; Boston Brahmins and Irish ward bosses; Puritan ministers and Catholic prelates; Revolutionary heroes and modern-day scoundrels; Back Bay matrons and African American activists; colonial dames and burlesque strippers; world-class surgeons and celebrated jazz art-

ists; college professors and short-order cooks; connoisseurs and
con men. Whether they are legends of the past or realities of the
present, they have all helped personalize the extraordinary character of a city that, in the course of the last century, acquired the sophisticated complexities of the modern age without losing touch
with its colonial heritage.

This book does not attempt a comprehensive and exhaustive list-
ing of every single person, place, and event related to Boston history—an impossible task in any event. Rather, it provides an alphabetical overview of a number of topics that I feel are *representative*
of the fascinating, distinctive, and unique character of Boston. Such
a book by another author would, I'm sure, have a completely different list. But this is mine, and in its attention to matters large and
small, sacred and profane, honorable and disreputable, I hope it
gives some sense of the rich rewards of the interest in the past and
present of Boston that my Aunt Nellie bequeathed to me, which has
sustained me through a lifetime of studying my native city.

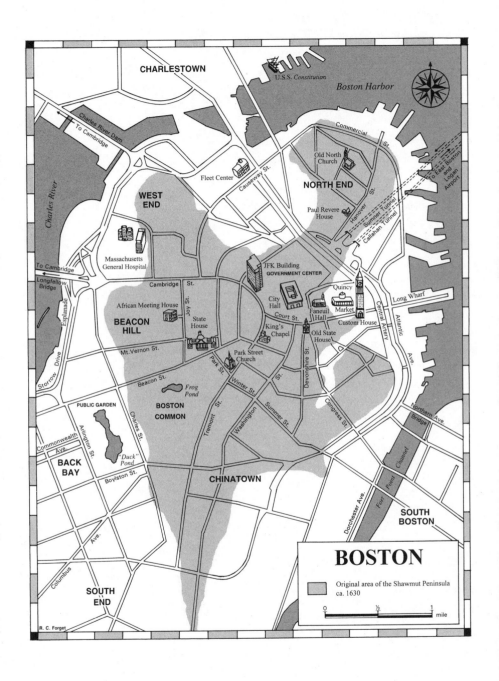

CHARLESTOWN

U.S.S. Constitution

Boston Harbor

Charles River Dam
To Cambridge

Fleet Center

Commercial St.

Old North Church

NORTH END

Paul Revere House

Hanover St.

Summer Tunnel

Callahan Tunnel

To East Boston and Logan Airport

Charles River

WEST END

Causeway St.

Massachusetts General Hospital

JFK Building
GOVERNMENT CENTER

To Cambridge

Longfellow Bridge

Cambridge St.

City Hall

Quincy

Long Wharf

African Meeting House

BEACON HILL

State House

Court St.

Faneuil Hall

Market

Custom House

Central Artery

Esplanade

Joy St.

King's Chapel

Old State House

Atlantic Ave.

Mt. Vernon St.

Park Street Church

Devonshire St.

Storrow Drive

Beacon St.

Frog Pond

Park St.

Winter St.

St.

PUBLIC GARDEN

BOSTON COMMON

Charles St.

Tremont St.

Washington St.

Summer St.

Congress St.

Northern Ave.

Bridge

Commonwealth Ave.

Arlington St.

"Duck" Pond

BACK BAY

Boylston St.

CHINATOWN

Dorchester Ave.

Fort Point Channel

SOUTH BOSTON

Columbus Ave.

SOUTH END

R. C. Forget

BOSTON

Original area of the Shawmut Peninsula ca. 1630

0   ½   1
mile

A

African Meeting House

✦

Abigail Adams

Abigail Smith was born in 1744, the second child of William Smith, a Weymouth minister, and Elizabeth Quincy, of the nearby town of Braintree. A highly intelligent young woman of strong Congregational convictions, Abigail never attended school because of poor health, but instead was instructed at home by her parents, her sister, and her grandparents.

On October 24, 1764, Abigail married a promising young lawyer from Braintree, John Adams, who had known her family for many years. While John spent most of his time traveling to court sessions in Boston, Abigail kept the house and produced five children, two of whom died in infancy. In 1768 John moved his family to Boston, where they rented a house in Brattle Square. Once again Abigail kept the home and concentrated on the upbringing of the children while John was off to Philadelphia to serve as a member of the Continental Congress.

Over the years, John and Abigail engaged in a long, lively, and loving correspondence involving serious issues of state as well as personal expressions of affection. Into the period of rebellion and throughout the Revolution, Abigail proved to be a faithful, brilliant, and perceptive correspondent, responding to her husband's activities and offering her wise and mature advice. She followed his involvement in the affairs of the Continental Congress, and in March 1774 advised him to think through the implications of the Declaration of Independence on which he was working. "I desire you would remember the ladies," she wrote, "and be more generous and favorable to them than your ancestors!" She later told him of how she first heard the Declaration of Independence proclaimed from the balcony of Boston's Old State House. The news from Philadelphia concerning the opening of hostilities found a response in her description of the Battle of Bunker Hill from a rooftop in Boston. She anxiously waited for John to complete his work in Paris on the final peace treaty so that at last her "dearest of Friends and the tenderest of Husbands" would return home.

When the Revolution was over, Abigail and some of the children joined John in London while he was serving as ambassador to Great Britain. When they returned to America they lived in New York City while her husband served as the first vice-president, under George Washington. In 1796 Abigail somewhat reluctantly supported John's decision to run for the presidency in his own right, fearing that on the national scene she might not have the "patience, prudence, and discretion" of Martha Washington, whom she had come to know and admire. Following John Adams's victory in 1796, the couple moved to the temporary capital at Philadelphia, but after two years Abigail decided to return home to Massachusetts. After a serious bout of illness that almost proved fatal, she once again returned to her husband, and became the first First Lady to occupy the newly constructed Presidential Mansion in Washington, D.C. John and Abigail did not remain in the White House very long, however, for in November 1800 John Adams was defeated by his rival, Thomas Jefferson, and the Adamses returned to Massachusetts for good.

Although Abigail Smith Adams had the pleasure of seeing her oldest son, John Quincy Adams, sworn into office as President James Monroe's Secretary of State in 1817, she did not live long enough to see him become president. After coming down with typhus, John Adams's loving wife of fifty-four years died on October 28, 1818, just before her seventy-fourth birthday.

Born in 1735 in the small farming community of Braintree, John Adams had Boston connections through his mother, Susanna Boylston, daughter of a Boston physician. Young John graduated from Harvard College in 1755, later studied law, and was admitted to the Massachusetts bar in 1758. In 1764 he married Abigail Smith of Weymouth, a loving union that was to have a significant influence throughout his life.

It was not long before John Adams showed signs of becoming involved in the increasingly tense relations between the American colonists and the British government. In 1765, only a year after his marriage, he wrote the "resolution and protest" for the town of Braintree and came out against the Stamp Act, which he opposed because the colonists had not consented to it. In 1768 he moved his family to Boston and successfully defended the merchant John Hancock against charges of smuggling. In 1700, after British soldiers killed five colonists during the so-called Boston Massacre, Adams agreed to undertake the unpopular task of representing the soldiers in court. Insisting that every accused person had the right to a fair trial, Adams successfully defended the soldiers and they were acquitted on the grounds of self-defense, although the outcome went against his personal political views.

Adams was less judicious in his reaction against the passage of the Tea Act, however, and in December 1773 wrote that the destruction of the tea during the Boston Tea Party was "the grandest event" since the trouble with Britain began. The following year he was selected to represent Massachusetts in the First Continental Congress, and did so in the second as well. Early in 1776 Adams came out publicly in support of separation, seconded Richard Henry Lee's motion for independence, and worked closely with Thomas Jefferson in the preparation of the Declaration of Independence. During the initial stages of the Revolution, he served on the Board of War as well as on several congressional committees, where his legal talents were extremely helpful.

Late in 1777 Adams was sent to Europe as a commissioner to France. Accompanied by his 10-year-old son, John Quincy, Adams arrived to find that France had already decided to extend recognition to the colonies as the United States of America and was in the process of working a treaty of alliance with the new nation. Adams continued to serve the interests of his country overseas until Great Britain finally agreed to peace negotiations after its defeat at Yorktown in 1781. Adams was dispatched to Paris to assist Benjamin Franklin and John Jay in working out a final treaty that recognized the independence of the United States of America and ceded the new nation all territory east of the Mississippi River.

In 1785 John Adams was appointed Ambassador to Great Britain, where he served for three years before returning to the United States in time to be chosen George Washington's first vice-president under the terms of the new Constitution. Always his own man, with his own strong and stubborn views, John Adams not only clashed with the leader of the opposition party, Secretary of State Thomas Jefferson, over national political and economic policies, but he also contested with Secretary of the Treasury Alexander Hamilton, a member of his own Federalist party, about the goals and direction of the party.

After George Washington had completed two terms of office, in 1796 John Adams was elected president of the United States, although he had to suffer the election of Jefferson as his vice-president. The most important controversy during his administration, however, was with his fellow Federalist Alexander Hamilton over the question of war with France. Relations between the United States and France had deteriorated so badly that a "quasi-war" was in process; French and American ships were already firing on one another on the high seas. Although Hamilton and his supporters argued strongly in favor of a declaration of war against the French Directory, Adams stubbornly held out for a peaceful negotiated settlement. To Adams's good fortune, young Napoleon Bonaparte came to power in 1800, overthrew the Directory, and agreed to negotiations with the United States.

Adams may have preserved the peace (something he regarded as his greatest accomplishment), but the split with the Hamilton wing of the Federalist party proved fatal to his political future. In the presidential election of 1800, Adams was defeated by Thomas Jefferson in a political victory that ushered in the Democratic party. Now out of office at the age of 65, Adams returned to Braintree, where he spent his time writing political essays, retelling the events of the Revolution, and watching the promising career of his son John Quincy Adams. His dear wife Abigail died in 1818, but Adams himself lived long enough to see his son elected president of the United States in November 1824. On the evening of July 4, 1826, John Adams died, only a few hours after Thomas Jefferson—the two Founding Fathers passing into history on the same date on which they had given to the world the Declaration of Independence.

Today, in the city of Quincy, some ten miles south of Boston, visitors can find two modest seventeenth-century wood-frame houses which are the birthplaces of John Adams and his son John Quincy Adams. Furnished with colonial period pieces and reproductions, the homes are open to the public and are cared for by the National Park Service.

About two miles away, at 135 Adams Street in Quincy, visitors will find a much larger and more elegant mansion into which John Adams, Abigail Adams, and their children moved in 1788. Known as the Old House, this handsome estate is surrounded by outbuildings, country gardens, and rolling greens. Filled with invaluable historic documents, books, portraits, and artifacts from the eighteenth and nineteenth centuries, this Adams National Historic Site offers tourists and visitors a fascinating insight into the personal lives of one of America's great families.

Sam Adams

There he stands—his arms folded, his legs planted firmly apart, his brow furrowed in a frown—in front of Faneuil Hall, looking across at City Hall and the city whose freedom he helped to forge.

Born in Boston in 1722, Samuel Adams was named for his father, a wealthy ship owner. Young Sam attended Harvard, studied theology and law, and wrote his senior thesis on the subject of resistance to political authority. After Sam's graduation in 1740, his father suffered financial reverses, and left to his son a brewery business that soon slipped into bankruptcy. Sam went into politics, held several minor offices, and in 1756 was elected town tax collector. He proved so ineffective at collecting taxes that delighted voters elected him to nine one-year terms. By 1760 Adams belonged to several political clubs, most notably the powerful Boston Caucus. After the end of the French and Indian War in 1763, he supported young James Otis in his attacks against the Writs of Assistance, which allowed British officials to search for unspecified cargo while looking for smuggled goods.

The passage of the Sugar Act in 1764 sent Sam Adams into a

frenzy. Although Parliament had the authority to use taxes to regulate trade, he argued that it could not use taxes to raise revenue: only the colonial assemblies could do that. With the backing of the Boston Caucus, Adams persuaded the Massachusetts assembly to adopt a petition calling for the repeal of the Sugar Act. But it was the passage of the Stamp Act in 1765 that propelled Adams to the leadership of the radical movement in Massachusetts. This new tax law united the patriot movement and provided the basis for new attacks against British authority. Adams supported mob violence against both the person of the local tax collector, Andrew Oliver, and the property of Lieutenant-Governor Thomas Hutchinson. Although the Stamp Act was repealed the following year, Adams continued to participate in the Sons of Liberty—a group of local farmers, shopkeepers, and apprentices united by their resistance to British rule—and formed a new group called the Loyal Nine that included such well-known patriots as John Hancock, Joseph Warren, and Sam's cousin from Braintree, John Adams.

The Townshend Act of 1767, which set up duties on a series of imported commodities, reactivated the radical movement in Boston, and provided Adams with more ammunition in his fight against British authority. Under his direction, the Massachusetts House of Representatives circulated a letter to other colonies denying Parliament's right to introduce such taxes. In response to this document, known as the Circular Letter, merchants in New York and Philadelphia organized non-importation associations. Smuggling increased and tensions heightened as Britain sent military reinforcements to Boston. The explosion finally came on the evening of March 10, 1770, with the so-called Boston Massacre, an event Sam Adams repeatedly exploited in his efforts to arouse opposition to the Crown.

For a short period of time, the repeal of the Townshend duties in March 1770 appeared to have deflated the radical movement. The passage of the Tea Act in 1773, however, granting the British East India Company a monopoly on tea, revived the patriot movement almost overnight. Opposition on the part of wealthy Boston merchants, in conjunction with anger among the general populace against more British taxes, led to the Boston Tea Party in December

1773, carried out by Adams and his supporters. The response of Parliament came in the form of the Coercive Acts, which closed the port of Boston, suspended the Massachusetts charter, and appointed General Thomas Gage as military governor, placing the colony under military rule.

Outrage at the British actions swept through the American colonies, and when the Massachusetts legislature met in session, it was Sam Adams who locked the doors of the council chamber so that General Gage could not dissolve the assembly. Despite Gage's formal announcement that the assembly was dissolved, the House remained in session and elected both Sam and his cousin John as representatives to the First Continental Congress, which was convening in Philadelphia. At the First and Second Continental Congresses, it was John Adams the lawyer rather than Sam Adams the politician who emerged as the revolutionary leader. Sam eventually retired from the Congress in 1779, just after he added his signature to the Articles of Confederation, and returned to work on the new Massachusetts Constitution of 1780.

Although Sam Adams recognized that there were serious flaws in the Articles of Confederation, he still hoped to keep the Articles as the permanent framework of government and thus came out early in opposition to the new Constitution of the United States that was created at Philadelphia in the summer of 1787. Adams greatly feared that his precious state sovereignty would vanish in the face of the strong central government proposed by the Constitution. Despite his reservations, at the ratification convention that was held in Boston in February 1778, Sam Adams finally agreed to support the new government. He worked with John Hancock to design a set of "Conciliatory Proposals" that would safeguard the rights of the states, and which were eventually included among the first ten amendments to the Constitution.

During the 1790s, Sam Adams succeeded John Hancock to serve three terms as governor of Massachusetts. In 1797, at the age of seventy-five, Adams announced his withdrawal from political life, and passed away quietly in 1803. A stubborn, inflexible, and self-righteous man, with a brilliant mind for politics and an uncanny skill for propaganda, Sam Adams laid the groundwork for the Revolutionary movement. He did not, however, possess either the personal temperament or the political flexibility for the complex constitutional process of establishing a new nation.

❖

African Meeting House

The African Meeting House is the oldest continuously operated black church in the nation. It is located on the north side of Beacon Hill, about halfway up Joy Street in Smith Court, in the area where most of Boston's black citizens made their homes during most of the nineteenth century.

During the colonial period, African Americans in Boston, many of them slaves, attended religious services in various white churches where they were discreetly hidden away in "Negro pews." When the Bay State emancipated slaves after the Revolution, most blacks withdrew from white churches and experimented with their own forms of worship. In August 1805 black leaders persuaded the white membership of the First and Second Baptist Churches to recognize the formation of the African Baptist Church. The following year, community leaders constructed a meeting house on Smith Court near Belknap (now Joy) Street, adopting the facade design from a work by the architect Asher Benjamin, and creating a building as fine as most neighboring white churches. On December 4, 1806, the Reverend Thomas Paul was installed as pastor, and the African Baptist Church functioned as the sole black Baptist church in Boston until 1840, when a number of parishioners, led by the Reverend George Black, broke away to form the Twelfth Baptist Church.

Throughout the antebellum period, the African Meeting House not only provided religious services for its members, preaching the Christian message and inspiring the congregation to maintain high moral standards, but also served as a social, economic, and religious center of African American life in Boston. The basement of the building housed the first black school in town, an operation later absorbed into the Abiel Smith School next door when, in 1854, the state legislature mandated integrated schools. The African Meeting House also served as a base for the programs and activities of such abolitionist leaders as William Lloyd Garrison, Wendell Phillips, and Frederick Douglass, and provided sanctuary for runaway slaves on their way north to Canada, as did many of the householders in the area.

Over the years, the original meeting house underwent considerable changes, both in ownership and in appearance. In 1964 the Museum of Afro-American History was founded and ten years later the meeting house was designated a National Historic Landmark. With assistance from the National Park Service, and after major renovations restored the African Meeting House to its 1854 appearance, the building was opened to the public in 1987. Today, the African Meeting House offers historical and educational programs, including exhibits, lectures, films, concerts, and workshops telling the story of the role African Americans have played in Boston's history.

❖

Ancient and Honorables

The Ancient and Honorable Artillery Company of Massachusetts is the oldest military body in the Western Hemisphere, receiving its first charter in 1637 from John Winthrop, the first governor of the Massachusetts Bay Colony. It was a New World version of the Honorable Artillery Company at London, England, which dates back to 1537—a century older than the Massachusetts group. Originally, according to one member, the Ancients formed the principal military organization for the protection of colonists in the New World.

The Governor of the Commonwealth of Massachusetts is the commander-in-chief of the Ancients, who serve as his honor guard on state occasions. On the first Monday of June each year, the governor commissions the incoming line officers—the captain commander, the first lieutenant, and the second lieutenant. On the day of the ceremony, called "June Day," the Ancients parade through Boston, hold a religious service at St. Paul's Cathedral on Tremont

Street in honor of their deceased comrades, and then conduct their commissioning ceremonies on Boston Common to the accompaniment of cannon fire.

The Massachusetts company at present has about 550 active members, as well as some 300 inactive members. It includes former members of all the military services, and its ranks have counted veterans from every war in which Americans have been involved for over 360 years. As a military attachment of the state, the Ancients hold a "Fall Field Day Tour of Duty" calling for some two weeks' service—often in different parts of the world—in commemoration of a chosen historic military occasion. In addition to their military activities, the Ancients also support a number of community affairs, such as the Easter Seal campaign and the Toys for Tots program. The present home of the Ancients is on the third floor of Faneuil Hall, where there is a meeting hall, a library, and a museum with a display of flags, uniforms, firearms, and other military artifacts.

Arnold Arboretum

Located along Boston's Jamaicaway, the Arnold Arboretum is a delightful link in the series of parkways that form Frederick Law Olmsted's "Emerald Necklace." This collection of living trees and shrubs is the largest in the world, and ranks in importance with Kew Gardens in England.

The Arboretum had its origins in 1868, when a wealthy New Bedford whaler and amateur horticulturist named James Arnold left $100,000 in his will for "horticultural improvements." Among friends of Arnold who supported his goals was Professor Asa Gray, the director of Harvard's Botanical Garden in Cambridge. Gray decided to use an estate of 210 acres of land in Jamaica Plain, donated back in 1842 by Benjamin Bussey to Harvard for use as an agricultural school, as the site for an arboretum. In 1872 Charles Sprague Sargent became the first director of the Arnold Arboretum, and worked with Frederick Law Olmsted to include the arboretum in his plans for the Emerald Necklace. In 1882 Harvard University turned over the Bussey lands to the City of Boston as part of the city's park system, and immediately leased them back for one thousand years at $1 per year, with an option to renew for another thousand years. Harvard continues to manage the collection of trees and shrubs; the City of Boston owns the land and maintains the roads.

In the Arnold Arboretum there are some fifteen thousand different species of trees and woody shrubs, most of which come from those parts of the world—North America, Europe, Asia—which share a temperate climate. Most specimens are carefully tagged with both scientific and common names, as well as the date when they were planted. Together with a large herbarium and library, now primarily located in Cambridge, the arboretum's living collections provide an important resource for botanical research. In the spring, the arboretum takes on the appearance of a nineteenth-century Victorian park. "Lilac Sunday" falls on the third Sunday in May, and usually attracts up to twenty thousand visitors. Memorial Day weekend marks the beginning of peak bloom for mountain laurels, azaleas, and other rhododendrons. By mid-June, the gardens of roses and their relatives are similarly spectacular, forming a picture library of non-hybrid rose types.

Athenaeum

An Athenaeum, the dictionary informs us, is a library or reading room named after a temple to Athena in ancient Athens frequented by poets and men of learning. This was undoubtedly what the leading men of Boston had in mind for an appropriate institution of literary and scientific learning in the heart of what they all regarded as the Athens of America.

The Boston Athenaeum is a proprietary library owned by shareholders, one of eighteen remaining membership libraries in the United States. At the present time it has 5,000 members, including 1,049 proprietors who own one share each, which until 1970 were traded on the Boston Stock Exchange.

The leaders of Boston's colonial society were voracious readers, whose intellectual interests were remarkably far-ranging. An insatiable curiosity led them to explore the latest treatises on political science and constitutional law, religious thought and ecclesiastical history, philosophical theories and scientific discoveries. In 1794 town leaders established the Boston Library Society, to which Charles Bulfinch donated space in the lower rooms over the arch in his Tontine Crescent buildings on Franklin Street. In 1807 the Boston Athenaeum was founded as a private library where gentlemen could permanently house their personal collections, and where they could read in peace, surrounded by good friends and elegant furnishings. In the 1820s the library moved into the Pearl Street residence of the wealthy merchant James Perkins, where an extension was added to house an ambitious art gallery.

In 1845 the trustees purchased the Phillips estate on Beacon Street, behind the Old Granary Burying Ground, as the site for a larger building. At that location, in 1849, they constructed an impressive three-story Italianate brownstone structure of neo-Palladian design, at the rather improbable address of 10½ Beacon Street, within sight of the State House. Designed by Edward C. Cabot, the building is set back from the street, with a modest stone balustrade along the sidewalk. The interior, with floors of lofty book-lined rooms, paintings, busts, and statues, overlooks the Old Granary Burying Ground as well as the white spire of the Park Street Church.

By the start of the twentieth century, even this new building seemed both too small and inadequately protected against fire. Talk about selling off the handsome structure and erecting a new building elsewhere was quashed by the vigorous efforts of such members as Katherine Peabody and Amy Lowell. Preliminary renovations were made in 1905 and a major expansion was launched in 1913, which fire-proofed the building and added a fourth and fifth floor to provide additional space.

Handsomely endowed, the Athenaeum is still a private library, reserved for the use of its own proprietors or shareholders, many of whose shares have passed down within the same family from generation to generation. Despite its private nature, however, the Athenaeum shares its invaluable historical resources with qualified scholars, writers, and researchers from all over the world. Its assortment of some 750,000 books includes many rare special collections, most of the personal library of George Washington, arguably the best collection of Confederate imprints in existence, and a magnificent art collection.

Crispus Attucks

One of the five men who died on King Street as a result of the so-called Boston Massacre on March 5, 1770, was a person of color named Crispus Attucks. Attucks and the other four victims were eventually buried together at the Old Granary Burying Ground. At the time of the Massacre, Attucks was working in Boston under the name of Michael Johnson. He had finished eating his supper on the evening of March 5, and was later described by one observer as walking toward the Custom House on King Street carrying a stick "about the width of a man's wrist."

It was later determined during the legal investigation after the Massacre that Attucks was a runaway slave belonging to William Brown of Framingham. In an advertisement in a local newspaper calling for his apprehension, Attucks was described as "a Mulatto fellow" named Crispus who was 6 feet 2 inches tall and had "short curled hair." While there seems no question that Attucks had been a slave, there is some question as to his racial origins. Some writers refer to him as a "Negro" of African extraction; others are convinced that Attucks may have been of Algonquin blood, a "Native Natick Indian." In the notes kept during the trial by John Adams, the defense counsel, Attucks is referred to as "the Indian" or "the Mulatto."

For many years, Crispus Attucks remained in the historical background, but his story appears to have been rediscovered by Boston's black community during the 1850s. According to the research of the historians James and Lois Horton, the new and oppressive Fugitive Slave Act of 1850 caused African Americans to seek out role models for their opposition to the new federal law and for their continued demands for emancipation. As a runaway slave, a fighter against tyranny, and a martyr who gave his life for freedom, Crispus Attucks was the ideal figure.

William Nell, a prominent leader of Boston's black community, wrote two books during the early 1850s on the heroic service of black Americans during the Revolutionary War. In each of these works, Attucks emerges not only as a leading figure of black liberation, but also as an African American—not an Indian. Historians have pointed out that in a popular and widely distributed lithograph of the Boston Massacre by J. H. Bufford in 1856, the figure of Crispus Attucks is clearly depicted as an African American.

It seems hardly a coincidence that on March 5, 1858, the anniversary of the Boston Massacre, and almost exactly one year after the promulgation of the Dred Scott decision, the first annual Crispus Attucks Day took place in Boston. The celebration was held in Faneuil Hall, the place where the body of Attucks had originally lain in state, and appropriate hymns were sung by the Attucks Glee Club, which had been founded to keep alive the name of "the first Boston martyr." Dr. John Rock, a highly respected black resident, appealed to history to illustrate the courage of such African American heroes as Crispus Attucks and suggested, as the clouds of war were on the horizon, that American slaves might soon have the opportunity to strike a blow for their own freedom. "Sooner or later," he declared prophetically, "the clashing of arms will be heard in this country, and the black man's service will be needed."

Boston Public Library

❖

Bathhouses

During the 1840s and 1850s, as the congested population of impoverished Irish immigrants produced epidemics of cholera and tuberculosis, personal hygiene became a subject of serious concern. Whether living in damp hovels along the waterfront or packed in squalid tenements in the neighborhoods, Irish laborers and their families had little opportunity to bathe. Many were lucky to have running cold water; most had no bathtubs, showers, or facilities for producing hot water.

A complete bath for the average immigrant family was at best a once-a-week affair—the familiar Saturday-night bath. At the end of the working week, a large galvanized washtub would be placed in the middle of the kitchen floor and then filled with water that had been heated in kettles on the large cast-iron stove. The children would take their baths first, and after that the grownups would have an opportunity to remove the dirt and grime of the week's labor.

Concerned about the lack of sanitary facilities in many homes, and convinced that moral purity and mental improvement were dependent on clean living, in 1860 the Boston City Council appointed a special committee to investigate the problems of public health. On the basis of this investigation, the committee resolved that the establishment of a series of public bathhouses would not only prove a beneficial health measure but also give poor working people an "inducement to self-respect and refinement."

Although the outbreak of the Civil War postponed further action, on March 5, 1865, only a month before the surrender of Lee at Appomattox, Mr. Israel Tafton submitted a report on public bathing that was immediately accepted by the Boston City Council, which then appointed a committee to determine appropriate sites for public bathhouses. The locations chosen for the first six bathhouses were in the most crowded immigrant sections of town, where filth was widespread and sickness rampant: at the Dover Street Bridge in the South End; at the West Boston Bridge, near Charles Street;

at the Warren Bridge, near the Fitchburg depot; at the Arch Wharf, at the end of Broad Street; in East Boston, at the sectional dock at Border Street; and in South Boston, at the foot of L Street.

The public bathhouses proved extraordinarily popular. Working people quickly availed themselves of the opportunity to take a hot shower two or three times a week in a public bathhouse, using their own soap and paying only one penny for the use of a towel. The Dover Street Bathhouse, located close to the heavily populated working-class Irish district between South Boston and the South End, served the largest number of people. It drew a summer attendance of 33,772—a high figure considering that the population of Boston in the late 1860s was only 200,000. By 1900 the L Street Bathhouse in South Boston had become such a popular and well-attended bath facility that a large new structure had to be built in the spring of 1901 to accommodate all those who wished to use it. City leaders were more than satisfied with the results of their project, and Mayor Josiah Quincy III proclaimed that if everyone would only bathe daily, homes would be much cleaner, and men and boys who were now spending their time in saloons "might then find their homes a fit place in which to spend an evening."

In the course of the twentieth century, however, the emphasis of the bathhouses slowly changed from cleanliness and godliness to exercise, physical fitness, and recreation. As more and more of the houses in the city were furnished with running water and modern plumbing, the bathhouses were used less to bathe and to shower, and more to swim, play competitive games, and enjoy the warm sands of the beach. This certainly was true of the L Street Bathhouse, which had been expanded and divided into three separate sections—one for women and girls, one for men, and one for boys. The recreational aspects of the L Street Bathhouse in South Boston became widely known, and the annual plunge of the so-called "L Street Brownies" into the frigid waters of Boston Harbor on New Year's Day has become the subject of national news coverage every year.

Beacon Hill

From all early accounts, the most noticeable feature of the original Shawmut Peninsula was a high rise of land with three distinct peaks, which gave Boston its first English name—Trimountain, eventually Tremont. On the water side, the easternmost peak was Pemberton Hill, popularly called Cotton Hill after the well-known Reverend John Cotton. The westernmost peak, sloping down to the Charles River, was known as Mount Vernon Hill, but often called by British soldiers "Mount Whoredom" because of the women of easy virtue to be found in the area. The central hill, and the highest (rising to about 138 feet above sea level), was originally known as Sentry Hill. Later it was called Beacon Hill, after a 65-foot-tall beacon pole, topped by a flame pot, was erected on its peak to be lighted in case of enemy attack.

Because the population of Boston was relatively small during colonial times (falling from 10,000 to 6,000 during the Revolutionary period), there was no great pressure to occupy the hills. In 1737 Thomas Hancock, a wealthy merchant, constructed a home on the southern slope of Beacon Hill, overlooking Boston Common, which was later occupied by his nephew, John Hancock. The painter John Singleton Copley purchased an extensive tract of pastureland, extending from Beacon Street down across what would later be Mount Vernon Street and Louisburg Square to Pinckney Street. Little effort, however, was made to develop this property, which was considered of small value at the time.

With the renewal of Boston's prosperity after the Revolutionary War, and with the rapid increase of the small town's population (from 18,000 in 1790 to 25,000 in 1800), a number of projects were undertaken to provide additional land upon which to build houses. Some developers bought up property across the channel in South Boston; others began to fill in the south side of Boston Neck. After the construction of the new state house by Charles Bulfinch on the crest of Beacon Hill, in 1795 a group of prosperous investors, incorporated as the Mount Vernon Proprietors, bought up Copley's colonial pastureland at a bargain price since Copley had gone off to England. After laying out a system of streets to accommodate townhouses, in the summer of 1799 they lopped off fifty or sixty feet from the top of the central hill to create more level ground for a fashionable residential area. With use of rails and what were called "gravity cars," they dumped the dirt and gravel into the Charles River and the tidal marshes of the Back Bay, extending the city's waterfront as well as improving the tax base.

Between 1806 and 1812 a total of fifteen red-brick houses, many of them designed by Charles Bulfinch, with bow fronts and white classic trim, were built on the old Copley property, giving the new community a distinctive appearance that remains little changed today. One of the first of these new houses was the second mansion Bulfinch designed for the prosperous lawyer Harrison Gray Otis—the first had been in the West End. Built in 1802 on Oliver Street (now 85 Mount Vernon Street), it is a free-standing Federalist townhouse of red brick with white trim, set back thirty feet from the street, with a lawn in front. In 1806 Mr. Otis had Bulfinch build him a third mansion, this time a four-story stately brick house on the downward slope of Beacon Hill overlooking Boston Common, where he lived and entertained distinguished company until his death in 1848.

In addition to the frequent use of the term "Beacon Hill" to mean the center of state government or the site of the Bulfinch State House, over the years Beacon Hill has also been home to many of Boston's most distinguished families. Its better-known residents have included such remarkable persons as Daniel Webster, Louis Brandeis, Julia Ward Howe, Nathaniel Hawthorne, Louisa May Alcott, John Singer Sargent, Oliver Wendell Holmes, Samuel Eliot Morison, and Henry James, who once described Beacon Hill's Mount Vernon Street as "the only respectable street in America."

The Big Dig

During the 1950s a six-lane elevated highway was built through the waterfront area of Boston. Known as the Central Artery, it was designed to permit motorists to travel from the South Shore to the

North Shore without driving through the notoriously crooked streets of the city. Two problems quickly emerged from this highway project: first, the Central Artery effectively cut off the waterfront area, as well as the historic North End, from the rest of the city of Boston. Second, by the time it was completed, the Central Artery was already obsolete. Originally designed to handle about 75,000 vehicles a day, the highway was eventually carrying more than 200,000, producing horrendous traffic jams through the heart of the city.

In an attempt to solve both these problems, during the 1980s transportation officials came up with an ambitious and extremely expensive project that became known to locals as the "Big Dig." It was decided to put the existing Central Artery underground, creating over the depressed artery an area of natural parks and walkways that will unify the oldest and most historic part of downtown Boston.

From the very outset of its original consideration, the Central Artery/Tunnel project was the subject of continuous political arguments and financial recriminations because of the time and money it would require. According to initial plans, the Big Dig, the largest civil-engineering construction job in United States history, was to take eighteen years to complete. It was projected for completion in the year 2004, and the total cost of construction was set at $11 billion. At first, the Reagan administration refused to allocate any federal funds at all for the project. Later, when the money was finally forthcoming, many unforeseen technical difficulties made the project seem impossible. Much of the original landfill in the old waterfront area, for example, proved much too soft to work with; and some of the existing bridges were too low to accommodate the huge construction machinery. These difficulties were further complicated by the fact that the 8-mile-long project had to be undertaken in the midst of a congested city that was expected to continue functioning around it.

The first phase of the extensive construction project, which tore up acres of land along the harborfront of South Boston and tunneled under Boston Harbor all the way to East Boston, was opened in December 1995. The Ted Williams Tunnel, named after the famous Red Sox home-run hitter, now provides new access under

Boston Harbor to Logan International Airport. Meanwhile, construction goes on, old roadways are closed, new access roads are built, road signs are changed, drivers are confused, traffic jams are endemic, delays are routine—but authorities assert that when the Big Dig is finally completed the results will make it all worthwhile. The overall cost of the massive project has grown dramatically since the initial estimates. In February 2000 Big Dig officials released yet another revised figure, prompting investigations into the project's finances at the state and federal levels. Nonetheless, the project's managers still insist it will be completed early in 2005.

❖

The Birth of a Nation

In early April 1915 the newspapers in Boston announced that local theaters would be showing D. W. Griffith's widely acclaimed silent motion picture *The Birth of a Nation*. Although this sweeping melodrama of American history received rave reviews from many theatergoers, opponents denounced its depiction of violence and corruption on the part of African Americans during the period of Reconstruction as dangerous racist propaganda. Black citizens and NAACP leaders from Los Angeles to New York City tried unsuccessfully to prevent the showing of the film; when it came to Boston similar efforts were undertaken.

Mayor James Michael Curley announced that he would hold a special hearing on the controversial movie before it opened at the Tremont Theater. Comfortable in the belief that Curley was "a democratic and very kindly Irishman," and that Boston had a heritage of liberal abolitionist sentiment, local black leaders expected a sympathetic hearing. Curley, however, indicated that his powers of censorship were narrowly defined, and would apply only to works that were either "indecent and immoral" or that tended to "corrupt public morals." The point of the hearing was to establish whether or not *The Birth of a Nation* fell into either of those two categories.

During the hearing, Curley listened to supportive testimony from the movie producers, including D. W. Griffith himself, as well as to opposition views expressed by Moorefield Storey, the Boston attorney who was the first president of the NAACP, together with William Monroe Trotter, a prominent black spokesman and publisher of *The Guardian.* The hearing ended inconclusively. Curley promised to use his influence to cut out some of the most offensive scenes, but stated that he was powerless to ban the film itself.

On the evening of April 17, 1915, the film opened at the Tremont Theater, with some minor changes that were hardly noticeable. Because rumors of a "Negro plot" to destroy the theater had circulated, dozens of plainclothes policemen were stationed inside, and when Trotter and a group of African American citizens showed up to buy tickets, the ticket window was shut abruptly. When the blacks protested, some two hundred policemen moved in with their billy clubs to clear the lobby. A total of eleven people were arrested for disturbing the peace, including Trotter. Not since the days of William Lloyd Garrison had Boston seen such racial tension.

The following day, an old-time "indignation meeting" was held at Faneuil Hall, sponsored by a surviving abolitionist, Franklin Sanborn of the Wendell Phillips Memorial Association. The crowd gave the speakers a wildly enthusiastic reception, particularly William Monroe Trotter, who complained bitterly about the betrayal of the black citizens of Boston by the city's mayor. "Where is the old Jim Curley of old," he asked, "the friend of the people—lovable Jim Curley, whom we colored people supported for the mayoralty against the advice of some of our white friends?" If this had been an attack on members of the Irish race instead, said Trotter to his supporters, Curley "would find a way pretty quick to stop it."

The following day, April 19, 1915, a crowd numbering from 1,500 to 2,000 assembled outside the State House on Beacon Street, singing "Nearer My God, to Thee" and asking to see Governor David I. Walsh. Although an audience with Walsh failed to produce any immediate results, the governor did introduce a bill into the state legislature (the Sullivan Bill) that called for a new Censorship Board, consisting of the mayor, the police chief, and the chief justice of the municipal court. This board could deny a theater's license for "any satisfactory reason." The Sullivan Bill passed on May 21 to great jubilation, but when the new board met it ruled that *The*

Birth of a Nation was "not at all objectionable" and that the Tremont Theater's license would not be revoked. Griffith's controversial masterpiece continued its Boston run for six-and-a-half months and 360 performances.

❖

William Blackstone

The first English person to claim settlement rights on the Shawmut Peninsula was a Church of England clergyman named William Blackstone (or Blaxton), a rather quiet and reflective soul who set up a house on the deserted peninsula near what would later become the Boston Common. In 1630 he invited the Puritans in Charlestown to join him on his side of the river, where ample supplies of fresh water were available. John Winthrop, governor of the Massachusetts Bay Colony, took advantage of Blackstone's invitation and negotiated a purchase of the land on which his people would settle.

The Reverend Blackstone was soon to regret his hospitality. More and more Puritans arrived and the population of the peninsula grew to such a size that he felt that his privacy had been endangered. Seeking a less crowded location and a more quiet atmosphere, in 1635 Blackstone packed up his books and belongings into saddlebags and moved south to the outskirts of Rhode Island—legend has it that he rode out of town on a white bull.

William Blackstone traveled south and settled near the little town of Rehoboth, Massachusetts, in what is now Cumberland, Rhode Island, to live the life of a cultured recluse, enjoying his library of 186 books and apparently at ease with the local Indians who were his neighbors. In 1659 he returned to Boston briefly and married a widow, Sarah Stevenson, whom he took back to his isolated home, where they had a son named John. Blackstone continued his quiet existence until his death about 1675. Later, during King Philip's War, his house and library were destroyed by fire.

Blue Hill Avenue

Before the Civil War, Boston had a small community of Polish and German Jews, who arrived during the 1850s following the political revolutions of 1848. In 1852 the Polish Jews established Congregation Ohabei Shalom in the South End, while those who followed the German rite established what eventually became Temple Israel.

During the 1880s and 1890s Jews began to arrive in much greater numbers from the ghettoes of Russia and Poland, escaping the pogroms that destroyed their homes and threatened their lives. The first waves of Jewish immigrants moved into Boston's North End, but later expanded into the West End. Within their tightly knit community, they established their own health clinics, orphanages, sewing circles, lending libraries, and labor groups, and even a baseball team. As time went on, some Jewish families moved across to East Boston while others moved into the South End. In 1910, when the city's Jewish population had grown to 80,000, Boston boasted seven Yiddish-language newspapers and a flourishing Yiddish theater in the vicinity of Dover and Washington Streets in the South End.

During the 1920s, as Irish families moved out of middle Roxbury and into larger homes in nearby Jamaica Plain, large numbers of working-class Jews moved in. By the 1940s more than 90,000 Jews lived within a 3-square-mile area that took in the neighborhoods of Roxbury, Dorchester, and Mattapan, making what became Ward 14 the most populous Jewish community in the city. The heart of this community was Blue Hill Avenue, which cut a four-mile swath through the Jewish district until it disappeared into the southern suburb of Milton.

Often derisively dubbed "Jew Hill Avenue" by members of other ethnic groups, it rivaled Manhattan's Lower East Side or the Bronx's Grand Concourse. Along both sides of the roadway were fish stores, food stalls, meat markets, delicatessens, pharmacies, credit unions, insurance companies, movie theaters, clothing stores,

Hebrew book stores, and a varied collection of shops that sold auto parts, heating equipment, and paints and wallpaper. The center of the community's political life was the G & G Delicatessen, halfway along Blue Hill Avenue, where the popular city councilor Julius Ansel, dapper in bow tie and sports jacket, held sway, and where residents of all ages met to eat deli sandwiches, cut deals, swap stories, talk with "Julie," and plan political campaigns. For some forty-five years, the G & G was a traditional campaign stop on election eve; politicians and followers flocked in by the thousands for corned beef, cheesecake, handshakes, and political banter. James Michael Curley, John W. McCormack, Henry Cabot Lodge, Franklin D. Roosevelt, Harry S Truman, and John F. Kennedy were among the political figures who spoke at the G & G over the years.

Every year, in the early fall, all commerce along Blue Hill Avenue came to a halt with the advent of Rosh Hashana, the Jewish New Year. On the High Holy Days, sidewalks would be cleared of business activity as men in dark suits and fedoras, women in silk dresses and fine hats, and boys and girls in new holiday outfits, would promenade slowly and proudly after services at the nearby synagogue. Jewish merchants and businessmen might go out early every morning into the Irish and Italian neighborhoods to operate meat markets, clothing stores, toy shops, variety stores, and restaurants, but they came home every evening to Blue Hill Avenue.

After World War II, with the assistance of the GI Bill, young Jewish war veterans and their families gradually began to move out of the old two- and three-decker houses along Blue Hill Avenue into new single-family homes in such nearby suburban towns as Milton, Randolph, and Canton, where larger lawns and better schools were available. This modest movement of Jewish families out of central Roxbury was suddenly accelerated in 1968 by a decision by Mayor Kevin White, supported by a consortium of twenty-two downtown Boston savings banks, to make low-cost housing mortgages available to more of the city's growing African American population. In the course of the next two years, some 4,000 black people entered Mattapan, moving down Blue Hill Avenue from Grove Hall to Mattapan Square. By 1972 the number of Jewish residents in the area had dropped to fewer than 2,500, and the subsequent flare-ups

of racial fears, panic selling, blockbusting, and redlining further accelerated the movement of older Jewish families out of the neighborhood. As a result, what once had been a predominantly Jewish
district was transformed into an almost all-black neighborhood. In
many ways, the transformation of Blue Hill Avenue and the entire
Mattapan area was an early and dramatic example of what would
eventually take place in almost all of Boston's traditional ethnic
neighborhoods. With the substantial increase in the city's African
American population after World War II, and with the influx of sizable numbers of Hispanic and Asian peoples during the 1960s and
1970s, the social, religious, and ethnic characteristics of Boston's
neighborhoods changed remarkably in the course of a single generation.

Boston, England

Boston, Massachusetts, was named after the town of Boston in
Lincolnshire, England. Legend has it that it was originally settled by
St. Botolph some 1,300 years ago, when he established a Roman
Catholic church there. "Botolph's Town" or "Botolph's Stone" was
later elided to "Boston."

Boston, England, located on the banks of the River Witham five
miles from where it empties into the North Sea, developed into a
very important trading port during the thirteenth and fourteenth
centuries. Sheep, wool, and other products came into Boston from
various parts of England to be shipped out to North Sea ports in
Flanders, Germany, and Scandinavia, as well as ports along the Bal-
tic Sea, while wines, fine cloth, furs, and other goods came in to
Boston from Europe. A sign of the town's wealth was the construction of St. Botolph's Church, started in 1309 on the ruins of a Nor-
man church. The distinctively ornate 282-foot tower, completed
about 1520, made the church a landmark for miles around.

With the coming of the Protestant Reformation in the sixteenth
century, King Henry VIII separated the English Church from
Rome; later his daughter Queen Elizabeth I established the sepa-

rate Church of England. Many English people felt that the new Anglican Church still retained too many of the old rituals of the Catholic Church, and set out to reform and purify the English church. By 1600 the area around Boston, England, became a hotbed of religious dissent, as Puritans removed the traditional altars, statues, holy-water fonts, and other decorations from the churches in favor of more simplified practices and ceremonies. In 1612 the well-known Puritan preacher John Cotton became vicar of St. Botolph's Church, where he proceeded to deliver lengthy sermons in the Puritan style.

Suffering persistent illness and embroiled in frequent controversy, in 1631 John Cotton left the pulpit of St. Botolph's Church. Two years later, after the death of his wife, he decided to move to the Massachusetts Bay Colony, taking a number of his more devoted Puritan followers with him. In this way, the strong Puritan ideals that had characterized Boston, England, were transported across the Atlantic to John Winthrop's new Puritan commonwealth, established a year earlier at Boston, Massachusetts.

Boston Accent

Persons in other parts of the United States insist that Bostonians speak with an accent that is both distinctive and amusing. Among other things, Bostonians are accused of retaining the British practice of dropping the "r" except between vowels, so that such phrases as "park the car" come out as "pahk the cah," and "Dorchester" becomes "Doahchestah." On the other hand, they customarily add an "r" to words that end in vowels, so that "Cuba," for example, comes out as "Cuber." Bostonians are also said to open their "o," as in "Bawston," and to broaden their "a" in pronouncing such words as "ahnt" (aunt) and "cahnt" (can't). When visiting their favorite seafood restaurant, Bostonians have a bowl of clam "chowdah" before settling down to a meal of succulent Maine "lobstah," and people from other parts of the country can't wait to have Bostonians tell them how they "pahk their cahs in Hahvahd

Yahd" (of course there is no actual parking in Harvard Yard!). If a friend happens to walk by, he is immediately welcomed with an affectionate "Hihahwahya?" ("Hi, how are you?")—the universal greeting among Boston politicians from the State House to City Hall.

Of course, there is no single Boston accent in a city of such diverse nationalities and cultures. There is the Beacon Hill accent, with its own clipped tones and distinctive nasal twang. There is the neighborhood accent, with its subtle hints of an Irish brogue here or an Italian inflection there. And there is the Kennedy accent, in which the sharp nasal tone, the Irish lilt, and the Harvard broad "a" combine to produce a unique dialect. For the most part, however, Bostonians themselves generally fail to acknowledge that they speak in anything but a proper manner. Indeed, when President John F. Kennedy came from Washington to Boston in 1963 to participate in the centennial of Boston College, he announced his great pleasure in returning to a city "where my accent is considered normal, and where they pronounce words the way they are spelled!"

Boston Associates

The War of 1812 between the United States and Great Britain was a disaster for the Bay State's mercantile economy. When the Royal Navy blockaded the Atlantic ports, American overseas trade became impossible. Boston ships lay rotting at the wharves, the region's specie was rapidly depleted, and Yankee merchants had no place to invest their idle capital.

A number of old Boston shipping families—the Cabots, Lees, Perkinses, Higginsons, and Amorys—diverted their capital into textile manufacturing as a temporary expedient. By the time the Treaty of Ghent officially ended the war in December 1814, the textile industry was proving remarkably profitable. The old seafaring families found themselves joined by such new industrial entrepreneurs as Francis Cabot Lowell, Abbott and Amos Lawrence, Nathan and

William Appleton, and James and Patrick Jackson in this new business.

By the late 1820s there developed a cohesive group of about forty Boston families that became known as the Boston Associates. Starting out with textile mills in Newton and Waltham, and then expanding to operations at Lowell and Lawrence, the Associates eventually took a commanding interest in virtually all the major textile industries in northern New England. By 1850 they controlled about one-fifth of all the cotton spindles in the United States.

Not content with simply making money in textiles and shipping, the Associates also invested extensively in real estate, insurance, banking, railroading, and other enterprises. All the Boston banks, for example, with the exception of the Commonwealth Bank, were managed by the Boston Associates. The same men also directed the Boston & Albany, the Boston & Maine, the Boston & Lowell, and all the other major railroad lines that radiated from Boston during the antebellum years. With their financial holdings and their extensive economic interests, it is no surprise that the Boston Associates also wielded extensive political influence. They dominated city government, controlled the State House, and saw their conservative Whig interests in Washington ably represented by the state's two senators, Daniel Webster and Edward Everett.

At the same time that they were assuming a leading role in the business affairs of the Bay State, the Boston Associates further enhanced their dominance through the powerful agency of kinship and marriage. When he first set out to establish the Boston Manufacturing Company, Francis Cabot Lowell turned for support to his Cabot relatives as well as to his wife's brothers, the Jacksons. Lowell himself married Patrick Tracy Jackson's sister. John Amory Lowell's son married Nathan Appleton's daughter; Nathan Appleton became Thomas Jefferson Coolidge's father-in-law; young Amos A. Lawrence married Nathan Appleton's niece. Partners in industry and colleagues in business, heirs to old shipping money and amassers of new factory money now became part of the same extended family circle, living in close proximity in their elegant mansions on Beacon Hill.

By diversifying their investments and buying into new enterprises, Robert Dalzell has observed in his *Enterprising Elite,* many of the Boston Associates found that manufacturing offered a much more stable income than the uncertainties of trade, affording them leisure time to patronize the arts and engage in philanthropic and humanitarian activities. They were able not only to furnish generous sums of money to such institutions as the Boston Athenaeum, the Massachusetts Historical Society, King's Chapel, and the Massachusetts General Hospital, but also to serve personally and actively as trustees and directors for colleges, boarding schools, asylums, libraries, museums, and other cultural institutions. For nearly two hundred years the descendants of the Boston Associates have maintained their preeminence in the financial affairs of the city and have also continued to devote much of their time, money, and talent to supporting those cultural, educational, and charitable institutions they believe make Boston such a distinctive city.

Boston Baked Beans

There is a very good reason why Boston is often referred to as "Bean Town." One part of colonial Boston's famous "triangular trade" brought valuable cargoes of rum and sugar to Boston from the West Indies. While most of the molasses was distilled into rum and then transshipped across the Atlantic to the west coast of Africa to be exchanged for slaves, enough of the molasses was available locally to become one of the essential ingredients for the distinctive food known as "Boston Baked Beans." The earthy, robust flavor of these beans, baked with mustard, onions, and thick molasses, achieved its succulent peak through many years of practice as the recipe was handed down from mother to daughter for generations.

During the colonial period, the Puritan Sabbath lasted from sundown on Saturday until sundown on Sunday, so baked beans provided the early Puritans with a dish that was easy to prepare beforehand, while the family was attending lengthy religious services. The large beanpot could be kept cooking over a slow heat in a fireplace so that beans could be served at Saturday night supper and again at breakfast on Sunday morning. As time went on, women who were too busy with other household chores could turn the baking of the beans over to a local baker. The baker would call each Saturday morning to pick up the family's beanpot and take it to the community oven, usually located in the basement of a nearby tavern. The free-lance baker would return the beans with a bit of brown bread—also made with molasses—on Saturday evening or early Sunday morning. "Brown bread and Gospel is good fare" was said to be a common refrain among Puritans.

In later years baked beans, because they were inexpensive, filling, and nutritious, became an important part of the Irish immigrant diet, especially during the mid-nineteenth century after the traditional staple of potatoes had failed. In most Boston neighborhoods, every Friday morning the Irish women would have their children bring their pots down to the local bakery, where, for a nickel, the beans would be slowly baked to perfection in the large bakery ovens. The next day, the featured meal of every working-class Irish neighborhood would be the traditional "Saturday night supper," consisting of Boston baked beans and brown bread. While baked beans may no longer be served as the main dish at a meal, the tradition has been kept alive with the well-attended annual championship hockey series among local colleges, known as the Beanpot Tournament.

Boston College

Boston College was founded in 1863 by members of the Society of Jesus, a Catholic religious order, in an effort to provide the sons of poor Irish immigrants with the benefits of a Catholic education. After some sixteen years of planning, working with the encouragement of Bishop John B. Fitzpatrick, the Reverend John McElroy, S.J., secured 65,000 square feet of property on Harrison Avenue and James Street in Boston's South End. In 1863 he obtained a state charter for the incorporation of his "college in the city." On

September 5, 1864, with three teachers and twenty-two students, Boston College opened its doors.

Boston College followed a traditional classical curriculum, known to the Jesuits as the "Ratio Studiorum," which emphasized scholarly research, intellectual excellence, and strong moral values. Enrollment remained small, but the changing environment in downtown Boston led the college president, the Reverend Thomas Gasson, S.J., to purchase land in the nearby suburb of Chestnut Hill for a new campus. After a $10 million fundraising effort and an architectural competition, on January 20, 1908, the grounds were dedicated as "University Heights."

With the completion of the central building, a handsome English Gothic structure called Gasson Hall, in 1913, students were moved from the old school in the South End to their new location at Chestnut Hill. By 1928 three additional buildings were erected, constituting one of the nation's outstanding complexes of Gothic architecture. Enrollment grew slightly during the 1920s and 1930s, to about 1,500 students, while the number of schools increased. In 1925 a graduate school of arts and sciences and a law school were created; in 1929 an Evening College was added; in 1936 a graduate school of social work came into being; and in 1938 a college of business administration became part of the curriculum.

After World War II, however, with the influx of returning veterans and the financing of the GI Bill, both the student body and the campus of Boston College expanded rapidly. In 1948 enrollment passed the 5,000 mark, and it has continued to rise ever since. Under the college president the Reverend Michael P. Walsh, S.J., the property was extended, new academic buildings were constructed, student dormitories were built, and a professional faculty was recruited. From a small, all-male, liberal arts commuter college, Boston College gradually evolved into one of the larger coeducational Catholic universities in the country.

In 1972 the Reverend J. Donald Monan, S.J., became the 24th president, and under his direction, Boston College streamlined its fiscal management, broadened its academic programs, attracted an enrollment of some 14,000 students from 40 states and 27 foreign countries, and established a national reputation for the college as well as for the Law School, the Carroll School of Management, and the School of Education.

Under its most recent president, the Reverend William P. Leahy, S.J., Boston College has expanded its academic interests into the international arena. Drawing on its Jesuit roots and its Irish heritage, it has established an Irish Studies Program that not only provides scholarly programs in Irish academic studies but also offers outreach programs to political, business, and educational leaders in the Irish Republic and in Northern Ireland.

Boston Cream Pie

During the nineteenth century, when men worked long hours at heavy tasks six days a week, it was not at all unusual for them to have pie at their hearty morning breakfasts. In many households, pies were a daily favorite, with apples, cherries, berries, squash, raisins, and mince pressed into service to vary the fillings.

According to a story told by the food historian Jerome Rubin, one Boston wife became bored with turning out the usual two-crust pies. She surprised her husband by baking a cake in a pie pan, slicing the layer in two, and putting a filling of cooked custard in between the two layers. The tasty concoction, with the addition of chocolate frosting, became known as Boston Cream Pie—although it was not a pie at all. Indeed, in some parts of the city it was known as Boston Cream Cake. Whatever its origins, by the late nineteenth century it had become a popular specialty at the well-known dining room of Boston's Parker House.

Boston Latin School

Just down the street from King's Chapel, set in the sidewalk pavement in front of Old City Hall on School Street, is a colorful mosaic designed and executed by the artist Lilli Ann Killen Rosenberg. This mosaic marks the original site of the famous Boston Latin

School. Its accompanying inscription reads: "School Street Boston. Site of the oldest public school in the United States, founded 1635."

Established on April 23, 1635, by order of the Town of Boston, the Boston Latin School is the oldest public school in America with a continuous existence. The establishment of the school was due in great part to the influence of the Reverend John Cotton, who sought to create in America a school like the Free Grammar School of Boston, England, where instruction in Latin and Greek was provided. The opening classes of the Latin School met in the home of the first master, Philemon Pormont, who was allotted by the town the sum of fifty pounds; his "usher" (assistant) Daniel Maude received thirty pounds. In 1638 Maude succeeded Pormont as master and conducted classes in his home until 1643, when the first school building was constructed on School Street. Morning sessions started at 7 o'clock in the summer and 8 o'clock in the winter; they ended at 11, after which the pupils would attend a nearby writing school. In winter the boys would bring their sleds with them, and when school was over they would climb Beacon Hill and coast down Beacon Street, across Tremont, and down School Street.

During the turbulent 1770s headmasters and pupils were caught up in the growing excitement of the crisis with Great Britain, and on the morning of April 19, 1776, the news of the first shots fired at Lexington caused the headmaster John Lowell to announce dramatically to his class: "War's begun and school's done; *deponite libros!*" (put away your books). After the Revolution was over and independence won, the Latin School continued to follow its classical models under a series of colorful and demanding headmasters. Benjamin Apthorp Gould became headmaster in 1814, and proceeded to institute the system of "misdemeanor marks" for misbehavior. He established the practice of public declamation to encourage the development of memory and to prepare students for public speaking. He also initiated a school library and issued regular reports to parents concerning their sons' standing in class. Later headmasters, such as Frederick Percival Leverett (author of *Leverett's Latin Lexicon*), Francis Gardner (editor of a series of Latin School textbooks), and Henry Pennypacker (a noted scholar and athlete) provided Boston Latin School with a staff of learned teachers who kept the standards high.

In 1922 Boston Latin School moved out of downtown and into the Fenway district, at an address on Avenue Louis Pasteur. This was the first of many changes that gradually altered the institutional character of the school, but not its reputation for scholarship. Traditionally, for example, Boston Latin School had always been a school exclusively for boys, but in 1877 a group of citizens petitioned the Boston School Committee to admit women. Although the petition was rejected, it was eventually decided to create a separate school for young women instead. On February 9, 1878, a separate Girls Latin School was opened nearby to provide girls with a preparation for college that would be equivalent to that provided by the Public Latin School for boys. In 1972, in response to the demand for equal educational opportunities for girls, it was determined to make Boston Latin School coeducational. Girls were admitted to Boston Latin School on the same competitive examination basis as boys.

During the 1960s and 1970s, in recognition of the growing racial diversity in the city and in response to the struggle over school desegregation, Boston Latin School instituted a system of admitting a greater number of students from minority families, despite lower grades on the entrance examination. In the mid-1990s, however, one white family complained that their daughter had been denied admission to Latin School while a number of minority students with lower examination grades had been admitted. A subsequent court decision ruled against the school's race-based admissions policy and forced the school to reexamine ways in which it could promote student diversity without establishing quotas.

In July 1999 Cornelia A. Kelley, a longtime teacher at the school, was appointed by the Boston School Committee as Boston Latin School's first female headmaster in the 365-year-old history of the institution.

Boston Marathon

In April 1896 the first modern Olympic games were held in Athens, Greece. Athletes from Boston made up the heart of the American team, which traveled to Athens and dominated the international games. James Brendan Connolly of South Boston, a member of the Suffolk Athletic Club, left Harvard during his freshman year so that he could join the American team. He became the first person to win an Olympic gold medal by winning the first event—the hop, step, and jump, later called the triple jump. This was followed by the victorious performances of Ellery H. Clark, T. E. Burke, T. P. Curtis, and W. W. Hoyt, all members of the Boston Athletic Association. The local athletes returned to a tumultuous greeting in Boston, a reception at Faneuil Hall, a formal greeting from Mayor Josiah Quincy, and the commissioning of a triumphal ode set to the strains of "Fair Harvard."

At these first Olympic games, the members of the Boston Athletic Association watched the marathon race, commemorating the legendary run by Phillipides in 490 B.C.E. from Marathon to Athens—a distance later standardized at 26 miles, 385 yards—to carry the news that the Athenian army had defeated the invading Persians on the plains of Marathon. When the Americans returned to Boston, they decided to duplicate the historic race in the United States. They settled upon Patriots Day, April 19, as the day for the race, and the first Boston Marathon took place in 1897, with only fifteen starters who ran the 25 miles from Ashland to the center of Boston. In 1924 the starting line was moved back to Hopkinton so that Boston could be considered an Olympic qualifying race of the official length established during the 1908 Olympics.

For a number of years the Boston Marathon received little fanfare and attracted few spectators. Public interest began to grow as certain favorite athletes emerged. Clarence De Mar first captured the gold medal in 1911; a decade passed before he won again in 1922. After that the Medford athlete was almost unstoppable, repeating his victory in 1923 and again in 1924. Against all odds, De Mar went on to take the Boston Marathon in 1927, in 1928, and for the seventh time in 1930. Another local favorite was Johnny Kelley, who won the race in 1935 and 1945 and came in second seven times in the fifty-eight marathons he completed during his long career. A bronze statue of the aged Kelley, running hand-in-hand with a younger version of himself, now stands at the 20-mile mark, at the foot of the hill in Newton known as "Heartbreak Hill." As the century went on, the Boston Marathon continued to be an informal event involving a relatively small number of local runners. Many top runners began to abandon Boston to run in other races where the competition was better and where prize money was available.

In response to this challenge, during the 1980s sole rights to the sponsorship of the Boston Marathon were signed over to the Boston lawyer Marshall Medoff, who proceeded to turn the race into a profit-making venture with financial prizes designed to attract an international field of professional runners. The John Hancock Insurance Company became the first major sponsor of the race, but over the years some seventeen other corporate sponsors have helped raise the Marathon's $15 million budget. With corporate sponsorship, the commercialization of products, the publicity of big-name runners, the official inclusion of women athletes in 1972 and wheelchair athletes in 1975, and greatly increased television coverage, the Boston Marathon became an international event that brought runners from all over the world. The number of entrants has grown substantially in recent years, reaching the figure of 38,708 runners who ran the Boston Marathon in 1997 on its hundredth anniversary.

Freed from work and school by the annual Patriots Day holiday, more than one million spectators line the route of the road race and cheer the runners along the course. Since the professionalization of the race, the winners are no longer local favorites such as Johnny Kelley, Bill Rodgers, and Joan Benoit Samuelson, but instead elite runners from Europe, Asia, and Africa. Indeed, there has not been an American winner since Greg Meyer and Joan Benoit won their respective divisions in 1983. Although the winners and frontrunners are usually highly trained professional athletes, however, most of the participants are still dedicated and enthusiastic amateurs whose greatest joy is to complete the 26-mile course and later boast that they "ran the Boston."

Boston Marriage

"There were, in my parents' circle of friends in Boston, several households consisting of two ladies," recalled Helen Howe, daughter of the well-known literary figure Mark A. De Wolfe Howe. "Such an alliance I was brought up to hear called a 'Boston marriage,'" she wrote, as recorded by Douglass Shand-Tucci in his *Boston Bohemia*. The practice of two unmarried women, unrelated by blood or by marriage, living together in a house or apartment as equal partners became so prevalent in Boston during the nineteenth century that the phenomenon was indeed generally referred to as a "Boston Marriage."

There were practical reasons for such arrangements. With the birthrate among old, upper-class Brahmin families dropping at an alarming rate, there often were not enough eligible bachelors whose family backgrounds, financial resources, and natural intelligence matched those of their female counterparts. In such cases, prominent Boston women found it preferable to live together in a household where they could manage their daily lives and participate in social affairs without entering into a marriage that would force them to lower their standards or compromise their values.

In other cases, the same-sex arrangements were the result of intimate romantic associations between unmarried women of similar tastes and reciprocal interests, who found fulfillment in living together in a permanent relationship. The women who entered into these relationships often referred to themselves in their writings as spinsters, celibate women, or women involved in a romantic friendship. Unless one or the other of the women had inherited family money, most women had to have some kind of professional career as a writer, artist, architect, teacher, or social worker to afford to live outside the traditional family unit.

The close relationship between Alice James, the sister of the novelist Henry James and the Harvard psychologist William James, and

Katharine Peabody Loring was perhaps one of the most celebrated of Boston marriages; Henry James used the women as a model for the feminists he described in his 1886 novel *The Bostonians.* After Annie Adams Fields's husband, James T. Fields, the well-known Boston publisher, died in 1881, Annie found personal fulfillment with Sarah Orne Jewett, a regionalist writer who was inspired by New England themes. The Irish-American poet, literary scholar, and daughter of the Civil War hero Patrick Guiney, Louise Imogen Guiney, had a long-term, loving relationship with the writer Alice Brown. Katharine Lee Bates met Katharine Coman at Wellesley College, where they began a lifelong relationship that ended only with Coman's death in 1915. Bates was a respected member of the English faculty who gained national recognition as the author of the lyrics for "America, the Beautiful," inspired by a visit to Pike's Peak. Amy Lowell, a flamboyant cigar-smoking writer who helped modernize American poetry, met the divorced actress Ada Dwyer Russell in 1909, and by 1914 they were living together in Lowell's Brookline mansion.

Out of these well-known relationships developed a network of Boston professional and artistic women whose lives did not center on husbands, children, family duties, or household responsibilities. Instead, they concerned themselves with the distinctive contributions they felt they could make to the Boston cultural and intellectual community. Through a round of friendships, dinner parties, musical evenings, and artistic exhibits in the rarefied atmosphere of the Back Bay, this "notable circle of women," as the architect Ralph Adams Cram described them, did much to preserve the "old and priceless quality of historical Boston."

Boston Massacre

Although Great Britain was forced to repeal the Stamp Act in March 1766 after protests against the tax by the colonists, the following year Parliament passed a series of laws known as the Townshend Acts placing duties on such imported products as glass, lead, paper, paint, and tea. Furious at this attempt to re-impose taxes on colonials who had no representation in Parliament, Americans boycotted English goods, devised local substitutes, smuggled products in from foreign countries, and formed associations with other colonies to insure the effectiveness of the boycotts. In Boston, political leaders like Sam Adams spoke out against the tyranny of the Crown, organized local demonstrations, and denounced the Townshend Acts as unconstitutional. When Governor Francis Bernard dissolved the Massachusetts Assembly, mobs of Bostonians moved into the streets to harass royal authorities and terrorize customs officials.

Convinced that Massachusetts was in the grip of anarchy, Lord Hillsborough, the British secretary of state, transferred English troops from Ireland to reinforce the local redcoats' establishment of law and order. On October 1, 1768, two regiments of infantry arrived in Boston, marched up King Street, and took up quarters at the State House and Faneuil Hall. The presence of nearly 4,000 armed redcoats in a small seaport town of only 15,000 civilian inhabitants made Boston a powderkeg ready to explode. One early sign of trouble occurred on Friday, March 2, 1770, when young Sam Gray, a local ropeworker, provoked a fight with a private of the 29th regiment named Kilroy that nearly led to a wholesale riot.

But the major eruption took place three days later, on March 5, 1770, a cold, snowy Monday night. About 8 o'clock, a mischievous youngster began making fun of a lone British sentry in his box outside the Custom House on King Street (now State Street), much to the delight of onlookers. When the soldier stepped out and cuffed the young man for his rudeness, the crowd began to press forward in a menacing manner. At that moment, the bell of the Old South Meeting House nearby began to peal, usually the signal for a fire, bringing more people out of their houses into the street. Standing alone, confronted by a hostile and growing crowd, the sentry shouted for help from the Main Guard, up the street. The duty-officer, Captain Thomas Preston, together with seven of his men, moved down the street with fixed bayonets, forced their way through the mob, and took up positions alongside the beleaguered sentry. The crowd pushed in upon the soldiers, and when the locals began striking at the soldiers, trying to take away their muskets, Captain Preston ordered his men to present arms. Then came the command: "Fire!" No one knows who gave the order, although everyone later agreed that it was not Captain Preston. When the smoke cleared, three Americans lay dead on King Street: Crispus Attucks, a laborer from Framingham; Sam Gray, the young man who had previously scuffled with Kilroy; and James Caldwell, a local seaman. Of eight other men wounded that night, two died a short time later: 17-year-old Samuel Maverick and Patrick Carr, an Irish tailor.

With the town in an uproar, Lieutenant-Governor Thomas Hutchinson sent the British regulars out of the town to Castle Island in order to avoid further bloodshed. Addressing the angry residents of the town from the balcony of the State House, he promised that the full course of justice would be pursued to determine responsibility for the night's tragedy. Paul Revere's engraving labeled "The Bloody Massacre Perpetrated on King Street," showing British troops drawn up in firing-squad formation, and their officer giving the command to fire, turned the incident into a major propaganda victory for the rebel patriots of Boston.

In many ways, however, the jury trial that followed the so-called massacre proved as significant as the event itself. When Captain Preston and his men were brought to separate trials for the murder of unarmed civilians, John Adams of Braintree agreed to serve as counsel for the defense—despite warnings from his friends that his career would be destroyed. As a result of Adams's vigorous and capable defense, Captain Preston was found not guilty of having given the command to fire. His men were later freed after Adams was able to use the self-defense argument to show that the soldiers fired only when they were convinced their lives were in danger. Upholding the English common-law tradition of trial by jury, the patriot lawyers had saved the lives of those responsible for the Boston Massacre. At the same time, patriot radicals, like John's cousin Sam Adams, were able to use the incident as further ammunition in their fight against the tyrannies of the English government.

Boston Public Library

Raised to believe in "the infinite capacity of human nature," the leaders of nineteenth-century Boston were determined to open new intellectual horizons to every citizen of Boston regardless of class or station. The scholarly George Ticknor, who possessed the greatest personal library in Boston, threw himself into the ambitious project of creating a circulating library that would be free and open to all citizens of the city. On several occasions he tried to persuade the Boston Athenaeum to make its private collections available to the public, but without success. Joining with Edward Everett, he was able to persuade the city administration to build a separate public library that would be dedicated to serving the "less favored" members of the community—not just scholars and specialists.

Founded in 1848 as the first large municipal library in America, the Boston Public Library originally shared rooms with the Massachusetts Historical Society above the archway in Bulfinch's Tontine Crescent in Franklin Place. In 1895 it moved to its present location in Copley Square, housed in a new building in the Italian Renaissance style designed by the architectural firm of McKim, Mead, and White and modeled after the Bibliothèque Ste. Geneviève in Paris. Appropriately enough, an inscription carved in stone above the main entrance of the library in Copley Square announces: "Free to All." The Boston Public Library was the first library to allow patrons to borrow books, first to institute a system of branch libraries, and first to have a children's room.

Raised on a low-stepped terrace, the handsome Italianate library is built around a central courtyard. The symmetrical granite facade, with a series of noble arched windows and entrance portals, overlooks Copley Square. Clusters of Strozzi-type lanterns with flaring spikes, inspired by those on the famous Florentine palazzo, flank the entrance. Carved panels by Augustus Saint-Gaudens, with the seals of the library, the city, and the commonwealth, as well as bronze doors executed by Daniel Chester French, enrich the exterior. On the front terrace are two colossal bronze figures, representing Science and the Arts.

The interior of the library is a repository of fine art as well as a storehouse for one of the nation's finest collections of books. A grand staircase of golden Siena marble, flanked by two great lions and surrounded by wall paintings by Pierre Puvis de Chavannes, leads to Bates Hall. This huge reading room (218 feet long) stretches the entire length of the second floor on the Copley Square side. On the Huntington Avenue side, a stately dark-paneled room forms the background for the well-known frieze paintings of *The Quest for the Holy Grail* by the British artist Edwin A. Abbey. The staircase leading to the third floor, where the Arts and Architecture departments are located, features murals by John Singer Sargent titled *The Triumph of Religion*. The Boston Public Library holds some 6.1 million books, with 250,000 new volumes added each year. In addition to books, the library stores some 3 million government documents, 120,000 musical scores, 75,000 prints and drawings, and 4.5 million units of microfilm.

To accommodate the growing number of books, as well as to provide an opportunity for extensive remodeling of the original McKim building, in 1972 the Boston Public Library engaged the architect Philip Johnson to design a new library building. Located on Boylston Street, adjacent to the main building, the so-called Johnson Building is an imaginatively modernistic version of the Renaissance original. Its open spaces, indoor bridges, and optimal sources of light make the new building better able to serve the general public, while the McKim building is more suited to house special collections and research materials. Not at all coincidentally, a significant part of the cost of the new addition came from a million-dollar trust fund established by John Defarrari. A penniless immigrant from Italy, Defarrari used the resources of the downtown Kirstein Branch of the Boston Public Library to study books on finance, invest his money wisely, and quietly make a fortune—which he ultimately shared with the Boston institution that had made it possible.

Boston Stock Exchange

As Boston capital began to accumulate during the 1830s, a combination of old money from shipping and new money from textiles, Boston entrepreneurs looked for new ways to expand their businesses and to participate in new enterprises. In 1834 Boston business leaders founded the Boston Stock Exchange, the third stock exchange in the United States. Located on State Street, the exchange provided a meeting place for local stockbrokers to trade their shares. Initially only the stocks of local banks and insurance companies were traded on the new Boston exchange; soon factory, railroad, utility, and canal stocks were added.

In 1878 the American Telephone and Telegraph Company was listed on the Boston Stock Exchange, only two years after Alexander Graham Bell had invented the telephone in his Boston workshop. In fact, capital raised in Boston funded many of the factories, mines, and railroads that fueled the economic expansion of the United States during the course of the late nineteenth and early twentieth centuries.

In 1908 a new home for the Boston Stock Exchange was constructed at 100 Franklin Street, just off Washington Street in downtown Boston. It has a neoclassical facade typical of turn-of-the-century Boston architecture, with a marble lobby and a magnificent central room on the ground that rises past the mezzanine level and houses the trading floor. The trading floor has massive windows, 40-foot-high ornately decorated columns, and coffered ceilings. The executive offices are located on the mezzanine level, where a visitor's gallery with educational exhibits overlooks the trading floor.

At the present time, the Boston Stock Exchange is an integral part of Boston's financial community, which is the third largest investment management center in the world, eclipsed only by New York and London. Boston, the birthplace of the mutual fund, is now arguably the "mutual fund capital" of the world, managing funds worth trillions of dollars.

Boston Stone

The Boston Stone is a ball-shaped stone that was brought over to Boston from England in 1635. It was originally used as a grinding stone by Thomas Child in his paint mill on the corner of Marshall Street and Creek Land. The stone would be rolled back and forth in a trough to pulverize pigments before they were mixed with linseed oil to make paint, which Child would use to do fancy house painting and interior decorating work.

In 1737 the round stone was salvaged from the old shop and embedded in a nearby stone wall, and visitors to the North End may see it still in place—where the Boston Stone Souvenir Shop is now located, not far from the Union Oyster House. The object became known as the Boston Stone, and for generations it was used as a reference point from which to mark distances from the center of the town.

Boston Strangler

From the late summer of 1962 to the early winter of 1964, a terrible sense of apprehension ran through the city of Boston as a result of a string of murders of single women. The "Boston Strangler" was on the loose; nobody knew who he was, or where he would strike next. The city was in the grip of terror. Gun stores sold out, locksmiths were kept busy installing deadbolts, local kennels saw a run on the sales of dogs, and the streets were almost empty after dark.

The circumstances of the murders were baffling. There were no signs of forcible entry. Around the necks of the thirteen female victims were knotted nylon stockings or some other article of personal apparel. Each woman had been sexually molested or assaulted. No clues were found; nothing had been stolen; no motive could be uncovered. At first, the victims were mostly middle-aged white women of modest means, who lived quiet and inconspicuous lives; the later victims were much younger. The women apparently let the murderer into their homes, only to be strangled to death without a struggle. The Boston police, the FBI, and other investigatory agencies used every standard means of detection, but also resorted to clairvoyants, "sensitives," those who claimed ESP powers, graphologists, and experts in pornography in their search to uncover the identity of the cunning and elusive serial killer. Not since Jack the Ripper had terrified nineteenth-century London had a city experienced such fear.

It was really by accident that the apparent identity of the murderer was discovered. A man named Albert de Salvo, a handsome, smooth-talking, borderline psychopath with serious sexual problems, was being held on a series of rape charges at the Center for the Treatment of Sexually Dangerous Persons at Bridgewater State Hospital. He confided to a fellow inmate that he was the Boston Strangler and was responsible for thirteen killings. This prisoner, George Nassar, reported the conversation to his Boston attorney, F. Lee Bailey, who spoke to the police about the details of the killings and then interviewed De Salvo himself. In the course of the interview, De Salvo confessed that he was the killer and revealed intimate details of the gruesome crimes which were known only to the authorities. He convinced the attorney and his interrogators that he was, in truth, the Boston Strangler.

Convinced that De Salvo was the murderer, but believing him to be insane, Bailey wanted him placed in a secure mental institution where his particular type of violent deviations and sexual aberrations could be scientifically studied. De Salvo was brought to trial, however, on a series of earlier charges, found guilty, and in January 1967 was sentenced to life imprisonment at Bridgewater State Hospital, a correctional facility. Angry that he was not sent to a different hospital where doctors would "cut out the corner of my brain that makes me do these things," on February 14, 1967, De Salvo escaped from Bridgewater, and instantly became the subject of an intensive manhunt until he turned himself in 36 hours later. At that point he was sent to the maximum security prison at Walpole where, on November 26, 1973, he was stabbed to death in his cell by another inmate. Although for all practical purposes the Boston Strangler was dead, there are still questions as to whether De Salvo was the killer. He never stood trial for the Boston stranglings, and never pled guilty to them. Many people still believe that George Nassar was the real murderer, but in 1999 Nassar offered to provide the Boston police with a sample of his DNA. Whether Nassar's DNA will be examined, and whether the body of Albert De Salvo will be exhumed so that samples of his DNA can be taken and a final identification can be made, remains to be seen.

The Boston Strong Boy

John L. (Lawrence) Sullivan was born on Roxbury's Harrison Avenue in 1858, the son of immigrants from Ireland. After attending local public schools, he completed his formal education at Boston College, which was still located in Boston's South End. While serving short stints at a variety of trades, Sullivan began to gain attention by boxing in exhibitions at local theaters. In April 1880 he defeated the English heavyweight champion, Joe Goss, so impressively that the *Pilot* prophesied that the 22-year-old fighter would someday be ranked "among the leading heavyweights of the country."

Five feet ten inches tall, weighing 190 pounds in peak condition, Sullivan had powerful arms and shoulders, a deep heavy chest, and short sturdy legs. Where other boxers of the period would begin a fight slowly, Sullivan rushed out at his opponent, swinging ferociously, and never let up. "He is a fighting man," remarked John Boyle O'Reilly admiringly.

By 1880 John L. Sullivan was eager for national recognition. After a year barnstorming all over the country, he took on the American champion, Paddy Ryan, in a bare-knuckle match scheduled for New Orleans in February 1882. Because the fight was illegal, however, the promoters moved it to nearby Mississippi City, where Sullivan knocked out Ryan and claimed the championship. Boston hailed the victory of the "Boston Strong Boy," the newspapers carried all the details of the match, and Sullivan was given a public reception on his return to the city.

For the next ten years, Sullivan fought his way through small towns and whistle stops all over the United States, as well as touring England, Ireland, France, and Australia, becoming a popular folk hero. On August 8, 1887, four thousand people crammed into the Boston Theater, with Mayor Hugh O'Brien and members of the Boston Common Council in attendance, to see Sullivan presented with a magnificent gold belt, studded with 397 diamonds, proclaiming him champion of the world.

Two years later Sullivan defeated Jake Kilrain for the heavyweight championship at Richburg, Mississippi, in a grueling bare-knuckle match that lasted seventy-five rounds. For the next three years Sullivan continued to dominate the field until September 1892, when he lost his crown to the boxing skills of young James Corbett. By that time, at the age of 34, Sullivan had become overweight and out of condition, slowed down from too much drinking and too little exercise.

Although the "Great John L." never regained the championship, he was still a hero to the Boston Irish who had seen one of their own rise from poverty and obscurity to become world-famous as a great athlete and a tribute to his people. His death in 1918 pushed the war news from the headlines, and as a testament to the high regard in which he was still held in Boston, Mayor James Michael Curley himself served as a pallbearer at his funeral.

❖

In 1773 the British ministry of Frederick Lord North passed the Tea Act, a measure designed to help the British East India Company escape bankruptcy after it had accumulated a huge surplus of unsold tea. Because the act would allow the Company to ship directly to the colonies and sell directly to the consumers, it was assumed that the measure would not only rescue the Company and thus secure Britain's interests in India, but also establish better relations with the Americans because of the low prices at which the tea could be sold.

Lord North had badly misjudged the colonial temper, however, and his Tea Act provided just the kind of provocation for which American radicals had been waiting. American merchants suspected a British plot to establish a monopoly on tea and thereby undermine their trade. Average colonists saw it as a British trick to seduce Americans into paying the detested Townshend duty on tea. Reactivating the committees of correspondence, Sam Adams and other radical leaders in seaport towns along the Atlantic circulated petitions, stirred up public opinion, and made preparations to prevent British tea from being brought ashore in America. Under orders from King George III, however, three ships loaded with cargoes of tea headed for the Massachusetts colony. The first to arrive was the *Dartmouth,* which sailed into Boston Harbor and docked at Griffin's Wharf on November 28, 1773. A second ship, the *Eleanor,* arrived on December 2; a third, the *Beaver,* was sighted on December 7. Their presence brought matters to a head.

During early December, local patriots held stormy meetings at the Old South Meeting House, demanding that the tea be shipped back to London. When Governor Thomas Hutchinson refused to order the tea ships to return to England, Adams and his supporters took matters into their own hands. On the night of December 16, 1773, after a packed meeting at the Old South Meeting House, a group of Bostonians, crudely disguised as Mohawk Indians to prevent identification, led a mob of inhabitants down Milk Street and off to Griffin's Wharf. Here the *Dartmouth* and the *Eleanor* were anchored, each carrying 114 chests of tea; anchored nearby was the *Beaver,* with 112 chests. Altogether the three vessels had over 90,000 pounds of dutied tea, worth about £9,000. The "Indians," numbering between thirty and sixty, were divided into three groups, with many of the men carrying hatchets. After boarding the ships and forcing the customs officers ashore, the patriots hauled the chests on deck, smashed them open, and poured the loose tea into the waters of Boston Harbor. All the while, a large crowd gathered along the waterfront and watched in silent approval. After the gang had completed its work, its members blended into the crowd as it straggled back to town.

British reaction to the Boston Tea Party was both immediate and decisive. It was one thing for colonials to defy the government in speeches, broadsides, and public demonstrations. It was quite another to lay violent hands on property aboard one of His Majesty's ships flying the royal standard. In the spring of 1774 Parliament passed a series of measures known as the Coercive Acts, singling out Boston as the chief center of resistance and moving to destroy the political and economic leadership of that troublesome town. The Boston Port Bill closed Boston Harbor to all commerce and trade; the Massachusetts Government Act brought in a military governor, established martial law, and moved the colonial capital from Boston to Salem. The Administration of Justice Act established that all British officials would henceforth be tried in English courts, and the Quartering Act allowed British troops to be quartered in private homes. What the Americans called the "Intolerable Acts" were to remain in effect at least until the loss of the valuable tea was paid for, and until the culprits responsible for the Tea Party were apprehended and punished. Defiance had turned to rebellion in Boston, and after the Tea Party things would never be the same.

Boston Terrier

A breed of dog developed from the bulldog, the French bulldog, the bull terrier, and the boxer, the Boston Terrier was first shown in Boston in 1870. Black in color, with white markings on its head, chest, and tail, the Boston Terrier stands 15 to 17 inches in height and weighs anywhere from 15 to 25 pounds. Its eyes are dark, large, and round; its ears are small and fine, carried erect. With short bright hair of fine texture, the breed has a broad chest and straight, muscular limbs.

Extremely alert and intelligent, the Boston Terrier is a reliable guardian of the house, yet affectionate with its owner and patient with children. The Boston Terrier, not at all coincidentally, is the official mascot of Boston University.

Boston University

The origins of Boston University go back to April 1839, when a school was founded as the result of a convention held in Boston by the New England Friends of Improved Theological Training. For the next 28 years, the small school had several New England locations; in 1867, it was relocated to Boston and called the Boston Theological Seminary. In May 1869 the Massachusetts legislature declared that President Isaac Rich and his fellow officers would constitute a "body corporate forever" under the title of the Trustees of Boston University.

During the institution's first decade as a university, five new schools and colleges—law, medicine, liberal arts, music, and a graduate school—were added to the original Department of Theology, which had become a school in 1871. Many other programs were added to the curriculum during the course of the twentieth century, until Boston University was able to offer degrees in sixteen schools and colleges as well as two independent programs.

First housed in a variety of buildings in Beacon Hill, Copley Square, and the South End, the university developed plans to bring together the schools and colleges in one central location. The Great Depression, followed by the difficult years of the Second World War, forced a delay, but by 1966 all schools and colleges were located along the Charles River, between Bay State Road and Commonwealth Avenue. The only exceptions were the School of Medicine and the School of Dentistry, which remained in their original downtown locations and eventually became members of the Boston University Medical Center.

In 1971, under its seventh president, Dr. John R. Silber, Boston University undertook a vigorous and sustained drive toward academic excellence that included bringing in distinguished teachers and scholars from all over the world. Today, Boston University stands as the fourth-largest independent institution of higher learning in the nation. Its student body of over 28,100 students—some 19,000 full-time and 9,100 part-time—come from every part of the nation and from more than 100 foreign countries.

Physical growth and expansion have kept pace with the extraordinary rise in Boston University's student population. In the ten years from 1971 to 1981, Boston University acquired by purchase or by gift a total of 96 new properties, most of which were used for student housing, while the remainder were put to academic and general use. Physical expansion continued, and early in 1982 Boston University began construction of a Center for the Sciences and Engineering. In 1983 Boston University also opened in nearby Kenmore Square the largest bookstore in New England.

Dr. Silber's leadership at Boston University has been stormy and controversial. His dynamic management style and confrontational approach have been described by many faculty members and students as both arrogant and intimidating. His right-wing political views and his conservative social positions attracted considerable debate when he ran for governor, and later when he became chairman of the Massachusetts Board of Education. There is no question that John Silber greatly improved the academic standing of Boston University by raising admission standards as well as by attracting internationally known scholars and prize-winning academics to the faculty. In the process, critics argue, he also increased the indebtedness of the institution by such things as risky investments in Seragen, a private pharmaceutical research firm, and the construction of a costly School of Management. Despite such concerns, Boston University is currently building an $80 million dormitory complex next to Nickerson Field, which it expects to follow with an ambitious athletic-recreational center.

The Bostonian Society

In 1879 a small group of distinguished but indignant Bostonians formed the Boston Antiquarian Club to prevent the city of Chicago from purchasing the dilapidated Old State House, tearing it down brick by brick, and transporting it to the shores of Lake Michigan as a national shrine "for all America to revere." After the Bostonians had succeeded in rescuing the Old State House from the clutches of the Westerners, the Antiquarian Club dissolved, but its members soon reincorporated as a new organization called The Bostonian Society. The name was carefully chosen so that the new group would not "excite the jealousy or interfere with the objects of any existing society." The stated purpose of the new organization was "to promote the study of the history of Boston and the preservation of its antiquities."

Since then the Bostonian Society has continued to collect materials pertaining to Boston history and to foster knowledge about the city's history. From 1881 the Society has leased the Old State House from the City of Boston, for twenty-year periods to assure the Society the stability for making long-range plans. The Society has been the only institution in the city with a museum of Boston history, located, appropriately enough, in the Old State House—the building it was originally organized to save and preserve. In addition to the museum and a series of rotating exhibits, the Society maintains a library that specializes in Boston materials, and offers public educational programs dealing with Boston history.

Anne Bradstreet

Anne was born to Thomas Dudley, Steward to the Earl of Lincoln, in England in 1612. Dudley provided his young daughter with an extensive education and an appreciation of literature that led her to experiment with writing in various poetic forms. During her seventeenth year, Anne suffered a bout of smallpox, but shortly after her recovery she married Simon Bradstreet in a happy union she later immortalized in her poetry.

A year after her marriage, Anne Bradstreet's husband and her parents left their comfortable homes in England and set off for the "wilderness" of New England. Her father had brought his 300-volume library with him to America, thus providing his daughter with an unusual opportunity for her to continue her reading and to develop her remarkable intellect. He eventually succeeded John Winthrop as governor of the Massachusetts Bay Colony.

Anne Bradstreet proved to be both a fervent Puritan and a strong-minded woman, with a superior intellect and an exalted social position that allowed her to accommodate both aspects. In one particularly bold poem, she praised the late Queen Elizabeth for having "wiped off the aspersions of her sex / that women wisdom lacked / to play the Rex." Despite the quiet objections of Governor John Winthrop, who did not approve of women reading and writing when they should be attending to household affairs, Anne Bradstreet continued with her writing. A collection of her early poems was published in London in 1650 without her knowledge by her brother-in-law, under the title *The Tenth Muse, Lately Sprung Up in America*. Anne Bradstreet and her sister, Mary Woodbridge, are the only two women to be listed among the many known American poets of the seventeenth century. Bradstreet and her family eventually left Boston, crossed the Charles River, and lived for several years in a Cambridge house located in present-day Harvard Square.

Brahmins

It is generally agreed that it was Dr. Oliver Wendell Holmes, the celebrated author of *The Autocrat of the Breakfast Table,* who first applied the term "Brahmins" to the elite members of Boston's mid-nineteenth-century social aristocracy. In his novel *Elsie Venner,* Holmes describes a young Bostonian: "He comes of the Brahmin caste of New England. This is the harmless, inoffensive, untitled aristocracy." Expanding upon this description, Holmes refers to the "Boston Brahmins" with their "houses by Bulfinch, their monopoly of Beacon Street, their ancestral portraits and Chinese porcelains, humanitarianism, Unitarian faith in the march of the mind, Yankee shrewdness, and New England exclusiveness."

As a new wealthy class emerged in Boston after the War of 1812 as a result of investments in the textile industry, their children began to marry into the older Beacon Hill families which had made their money during the colonial period in maritime enterprises and commerce. As the Lowells, the Lawrences, and the Appletons joined with the Cabots, the Higginsons, and the Russells in profitable financial arrangements, the association of the "wharf" and the "waterfall," as the historian Samuel Eliot Morison described it, became even more intimate through marriages between their children. A new generation emerged on Beacon Hill which not only had financial security and social status, but also took a leading role as patrons of the arts and arbiters of good taste.

Like the priestly caste of the Hindus of India who perform the sacred rites and set the moral standards for their people, the new leaders of Boston society emerged as the self-styled "Brahmins" of a new caste system in which they were clearly and indisputably the superior force. While their numbers may have diminished somewhat, and their financial dominance is no longer what it used to be, the Brahmin class continues to have a remarkable influence on the city's cultural and benevolent institutions. As active and conscientious trustees of hospitals, universities, libraries, and museums, as well as of numerous musical, artistic, and historical associations, they continue to preserve a legacy of excellence and good taste.

Bridges

Looking at the city today, it's easy to forget that Boston was originally almost completely surrounded by water. Located on the Shawmut Peninsula, with the Charles River on the northern side and the Fort Point Channel along the southern side, the colonial town had only one overland path to the mainland—the so-called Boston Neck that led to Roxbury—and even this path could be underwater at high tide. Connections with towns like Cambridge across the Charles or with Dorchester Neck (later South Boston) across the Channel had to be by boat.

The first changes in this pattern of relative isolation came shortly after the War of Independence, with the completion of the Charles

Street Bridge in 1786. As early as April 27, 1720, a town meeting had considered a proposal to "promote the building of a Bridge across the Charles River at the place where the Ferry hath been usually kept." Nothing came of this proposal, however, until an act was passed on March 9, 1785, incorporating John Hancock, Thomas Russell, and eighty-two others in a private enterprise to build a toll bridge across the Charles River, connecting Boston's North End with Charlestown. At the time the bridge was considered "the greatest that had ever been projected in America," with a total length of 1,503 feet, a width of 42 feet, and a construction cost of £15,000. Some twenty thousand spectators assembled on June 17, 1786, for the bridge's dedication, which included a formal celebration, the pealing of church bells, and the firing of thirteen cannon.

Besides being a marvel of engineering and an influence on the changing patterns of social life in Boston, the Charles River Bridge also figured prominently in American constitutional law. In 1828 the state legislature voted to charter the Warren Bridge Corporation to build a second north-south bridge to Charlestown. The corporation proposed to charge the same tolls as the Charles River Bridge, but only for six years; after that, the new bridge would be free. The Charles River investors were furious at what they saw as a violation of their exclusive contract, and hired Daniel Webster and Lemuel Shaw to sue the proprietors of the Warren Bridge Company. The Charles River Bridge case eventually made its way to the United States Supreme Court, where the newly appointed Chief Justice Roger B. Taney, in what conservatives regarded as a "radical" decision, chose to allow "the happiness and prosperity of the community" to supersede contractual obligations. The Warren Bridge was constructed, and a new constitutional doctrine that allowed the government to involve itself in economic issues opened the door to the rapid expansion of transportation projects and manufacturing enterprises for the rest of the nineteenth century.

Other bridges connected Boston with other places on the north side of the Charles River. A toll bridge across the Charles from the west end of Cambridge Street in Boston to the opposite shore in Cambridge, called the West Boston Bridge, was an even greater undertaking than the first bridge: it was 3,483 feet long, stood on 180 piers, and cost about £23,000. After opening on November 23, 1793, the new bridge contributed greatly to the development of Boston's West End, offering the most direct route to Cambridge and Harvard College. In 1907 a new and much more elaborate bridge replaced the old West Boston Bridge, named the Longfellow Bridge in 1927 in honor of the poet Henry Wadsworth Longfellow, who used to walk across the old bridge from Cambridge when he was courting his wife, Frances Elizabeth Appleton, in Boston. The new bridge also acquired the nicknames of the "salt-and-pepper bridge" or the "pepperpot bridge" because of the salt-cellar shape of its towers, whose design was actually adapted from a bridge in St. Petersburg, Russia.

In 1891 the Harvard Bridge (sometimes referred to as the Massachusetts Avenue Bridge) was constructed, extending Massachusetts Avenue from Boston all the way to Harvard Square in Cambridge. In 1958, as a fraternity initiation, a group of MIT students used Oliver R. Smoot, MIT '62, to measure the bridge. By laying young Smoot down end-to-end across the bridge, the students were able to arrive at the scientific conclusion that the bridge is exactly 364 "smoots"—plus one ear—in length. When the bridge was rebuilt in 1990, state engineers agreed to accept and repaint the Smoot measurements. They were able to determine that a "smoot" was exactly 66 inches long; MIT officials, however, refused to reveal the exact length of Smoot's ear.

In 1927 a new bridge was constructed across a bend in the Charles River, connecting Cambridge to a point near the border of Boston and Brookline. Originally it was called the Brookline Street Bridge, the Essex Street Bridge, or the Cottage Farm Bridge. As Boston University extended its main campus westward along Commonwealth Avenue, a group of students petitioned the state legislature to rename the bridge the Boston University Bridge. On May 7, 1949, B.U. President Daniel Marsh and the sponsoring senator marched at the head of a crowd of students and a motorcade of "pretty Boston University coeds" in a ceremonial procession across the structure.

At the same time that these north-south bridges were spanning the Charles River, other entrepreneurs were busy connecting the southern edges of the town with the peninsula across the Fort Point

Channel. After Dorchester Neck was annexed by the Town of Boston in 1804 and renamed South Boston, investors seeking to promote investment in the relatively unoccupied district set out to provide a convenient crossing from the Boston side. In 1805 construction was completed on a toll bridge that extended across the channel from Boston's South End, at what would later become Dover Street (today called East Berkeley Street) to a point at the western end of the South Boston peninsula. This new South Bridge did not prove very successful in attracting new settlers. A bridge closer to the center of town—somewhere near Summer Street, Federal Street, or Wind Mill Point—was needed to enable working-class people living along the waterfront to cross over to South Boston. After nearly twenty years of litigation and delay, in 1826 a charter was granted for the construction of a free bridge from the foot of Federal Street. This North Free Bridge proved such a popular route that in 1832 the investors in the original South Bridge had to sell off their properties to the city, although the bridge itself would continue to function well into the twentieth century.

In 1892 the L Street Bridge was built over the South Boston Reserved Channel, making it possible for people to cross directly from the center of the South Boston peninsula to the center of Boston at South Station and Summer Street. Additional access to downtown Boston was provided by the reconstruction of the Broadway Bridge over the Fort Point Channel in 1904, from West Broadway in South Boston to the lower end of Washington and Tremont streets in the city.

One of the last major efforts to allow travelers to reach the North Shore without either using the harbor tunnels or driving through the congested streets of Chelsea and Revere came with the construction of the Mystic River Bridge. A large steel span with two decks—the lower level going north, the upper level heading south—the bridge crosses the Mystic River with the Boston Harbor on one side and the Charles River Basin on the other. The state legislature officially renamed the bridge to honor the memory of Maurice J. Tobin, mayor of Boston from 1938 to 1944, and later Secretary of Labor in the Truman administration. It is now known as the Tobin Bridge.

Over the course of a century, therefore, Boston became a city of bridges. The Shawmut Peninsula sprouted tentacles on either side, connecting it with communities on the north side of the Charles River as well as those on the south side of the Fort Point Channel. These connections would allow Boston to maintain its own separate and distinctive life-style, while at the same time allowing associations that would prevent it from becoming too parochial or xenophobic.

With the progress of the Big Dig, and especially with the extensive development of the waterfront district across the channel in South Boston, it seems almost inevitable that additional bridges will be constructed to tie the central city to the expanding centers of finance and population. In October 1999, a four-lane span across the Charles River, called the Leverett Circle Connector Bridge, opened on schedule, taking traffic out of Boston from the Leverett Circle to Route I-93 north. A much larger ten-lane bridge is under construction that will give the North End, the Sumner Tunnel, and the Government Center area direct access to Route I-93 north. The widest cable-stayed bridge in the world, it will have 300-foot towers to provide the fulcrum for cables that anchor the weight of the main span of the bridge to land-based back spans. On a smaller scale, there has been considerable controversy about whether to save the old turn-of-the-century "swing" bridge that opens directly from downtown Boston and onto the entire length of Northern Avenue, or replace it with the new Evelyn Moakley Bridge (named after the deceased wife of Congressman Joseph Moakley of South Boston), which unfortunately has no access for pedestrians.

❖

The Brink's Robbery

On January 17, 1950, at about 7 o'clock in the evening, seven men wearing Navy pea coats and rubber Halloween masks walked quietly into the garage belonging to the Brink's Armored Car Company, just off Hull Street in Boston's North End, in the shadow of Copp's Hill. They pulled guns, tied up five employees, proceeded to stuff their bags with $2.8 million in cash, checks, and securities (some $17 million in today's currency), and then disappeared. It was the biggest armed robbery in U.S. history—dubbed "the crime of the century" by the FBI.

Because the thieves seemed to have keys to everything in the building and showed a familiarity with the layout of the garage and the routine of the security guards, the police assumed from the start that it was an inside job, carried out by professional bank robbers. But the thieves were actually a small gang of local Irish and Italian thieves, organized by a small-time crook named Tony Pino. They had spent months visiting the building, rifling through the files, observing routines from the rooftop of an adjoining building, familiarizing themselves with the company's procedures, and staging small robberies at locations where the Brink's trucks dropped off their payrolls.

Early in 1950 Pino decided it was time for the "big score" at the new Brink's garage and offices in the North End. The operation went like clockwork; the getaway truck was cut up into pieces that were dropped in several rivers; the loot was divided up and hidden away. With no clues, no leads, and no suspects, all indications were that the crime would never be solved. But six years later, in January 1956, just weeks before the statute of limitations was to have run out, one member of the gang named Joseph "Specs" O'Keefe, in jail for other crimes, broke down, confessed, and named the members of the gang. In August 1956 a highly publicized trial ended with life sentences for Pino and the other living gang members. However, not a cent of the bank loot was ever recovered. The story of this bizarre robbery was made into a motion picture in 1978, called *The Brink's Job,* directed by William Friedkin and starring the actor Peter Falk.

Broad Street Riot

As Irish immigrants began coming to Boston in the early nineteenth century in large numbers, resentment against these newcomers became louder and more violent. Native workers feared that before long immigrant laborers would be taking away their jobs and cutting into their salaries. Firemen and policemen were particularly concerned that immigrants would eventually want their share of the well-paying jobs that had been regarded as the exclusive province of native-born Americans.

The hard feelings between firemen and Irishmen were painfully demonstrated on a hot Sunday afternoon, June 11, 1837, when a company of Yankee firemen returning from a call came across a Catholic funeral procession that was moving along Broad Street in the opposite direction. Both sides began a heated argument over which should be given the right of way. In a matter of minutes, the argument had mushroomed into a full-scale riot. As fire bells sounded the alarm, engine companies in the city rushed to assist their comrades, while friends and relatives of the Irish mourners spilled out of their lodgings into the streets to help their countrymen. For more than two hours the battle raged up and down the streets of the lower part of the city where the immigrants lived, with a crowd estimated at ten thousand people watching eight hundred men fight it out with sticks and stones, bricks and cudgels.

The so-called Broad Street Riot finally came to an end only when Mayor Samuel Eliot brought in a military force, headed by the National Lancers and followed by some eight hundred of the state militia with fixed bayonets, to disperse the rioters and restore order to the city. Fourteen Irishmen and four native Bostonians were eventually brought to trial; not a single Yankee was found guilty, while three of the four Irishmen were given jail sentences for their part in the riot.

❖

The Broadcloth Mob

Boston has acquired the reputation of a liberal city that took the lead in freeing African Americans from the bondage of slavery. In fact, however, the Abolition movement that began in Boston in 1831 remained a small and isolated movement for nearly two decades, its leaders and supporters socially ostracized and physically abused.

While many Bostonians found the institution of slavery degrading and distasteful, they were perfectly willing to let it flourish below the Mason-Dixon line, where the plantation system could continue to supply raw cotton for their textile mills. The association between the "Lords of the Lash" and the "Lords of the Loom" was a long and profitable one.

Bostonians who felt moved to restrict the expansion of slavery or help ameliorate some of its more brutal conditions generally supported one of the antislavery societies that had grown up during the early 1800s. These associations supported slow, gradual, and nonthreatening programs of partial emancipation. During the 1820s and 1830s, for example, the American Colonization Society was joined by members of some of Boston's more prominent families. Purchasing the freedom of slaves and sending them back to Africa appealed to Northern gentlemen as a sensible way to emancipate some slaves, help Christianize Africa, and, in the process, gradually restore America as a "white man's country."

The appearance of William Lloyd Garrison and the publication of *The Liberator* in January 1831 completely changed the dynamics of the antislavery movement. By declaring slavery to be a moral evil, and by insisting that all slaves be freed immediately and without compensation, Garrison presented a clear and present danger to the social and financial interests of the city. Some Bostonians believed that Garrison, with his outspoken views on racial equality, was "poisoning the waters of community life" by flying in the face of social tradition and Biblical teaching. Abolitionists were generally viewed as agitators and troublemakers. "They do not go to work like Christian gentlemen," complained one local pastor, while another churchman agreed that the only thing they did was stir up "bitter passions and fierce fanaticism."

Other Bostonians were concerned that Garrison and his Abolition movement would seriously endanger good relations with their "Southern brethren." Outraged cotton planters were already threatening economic reprisals unless Northerners put an end to Abolitionist activities. "Grass will grow in the streets of Lowell," warned one Southern periodical, if strong measures were not taken against those "fanatical wretches."

Local frustration came to a head at 3 o'clock on the afternoon of October 21, 1835, when an angry mob burst into a meeting of the Boston Female Antislavery Society that was taking place in a small hall adjoining Garrison's office at 46 Washington Street. After breaking up the ladies' meeting, the mob went in search of Garrison, who escaped through a rear window. The shouting mob caught up with the Abolitionist leader, pummeled him severely, threw a rope around him, dragged him triumphantly through the streets, and then hauled him toward Boston Common, where they threatened to lynch him. Fortunately, he was rescued by constables, who placed him in protective custody for the night and put him on a train for Providence the next day.

Of the nature of the mob that had attacked him, Garrison had no doubt. "It was planned and executed," he insisted, "not by the rabble or the workingmen, but by 'gentlemen of property and standing from all parts of the city.'" Garrison's colleague Wendell Phillips, who had witnessed the event, later gave the classic description of the assault as being conducted by the gentlemen of the city—in "broadcloth and in broad daylight." A visitor from Baltimore described the members of the mob as "Merchants and bankers of Boston, assembled on Change [the Exchange] in State Street." There is little doubt that many of Boston's leading merchants and businessmen had taken time out of their financial activities to publicly demonstrate their goodwill toward their Southern brethren by attacking the leader of the movement to emancipate slaves. The "Broadcloth Mob" was only one of many bloody episodes during the mid-1830s that revealed the violent and deeply felt anti-Abolition sentiment in the North.

❖

Brook Farm

During the 1830s advocates of Transcendentalist philosophy were promoting ideas of naturalism and individualism throughout New England. A scholar and humanist named George Ripley decided to create an organized community based on these ideas that would be free from competitive influences, and that would create a wholesome, cultured, and harmonious environment for all its members. Known as Brook Farm, and located in what was later called West Roxbury, a suburb of Boston, the new community was designed to insure "a more natural union between intellectual and manual labor than now exists." Ripley, his wife, and a few friends were the first to come to live at Brook Farm in the spring of 1841; by July thirty people were living and working at the community. Although in the course of a year probably no more than one hundred people lived there, Brook Farm received as many as a thousand curious visitors.

The Transcendental nature of Brook Farm was perhaps most apparent in its approach to education. There were three schools on the site: an infant school for children under six; a primary school for children under ten; and a six-year preparatory school for college-bound students. Teaching methods at Brook Farm were very progressive, encouraging open discussion between students and teachers, while the approach to discipline was based on reason and explanation. Formal school hours were never set, but varied to accommodate time for work on the farm. Students usually took classes in the morning and did manual work in the afternoon. Boys would often hoe the fields, while girls would customarily do dishwashing and household chores.

Although many of the farmers at Brook Farm were amateurs, they were successful in producing most of the food consumed by the community. When they attempted to sell their surplus farm products for income, however, they were confronted with some practical difficulties. The soil around Brook Farm, for example, was rocky and sandy, producing poor-quality hay that did not bring a very high price. The farm also attempted to put the ideals of Transcendentalism into practice in its organization of labor. Women received the same pay as men and were given equal opportunities for jobs on the farm. It was also decided that everyone who worked on the farm would receive free room and board. When Brook Farm allowed its agricultural workers to set their own working hours, however, many workers objected to the fact that some people who worked fewer hours received the same pay as those who worked longer hours.

During its halcyon days, Brook Farm attracted the attention of numerous writers, intellectuals, and members of the local literati.

Ralph Waldo Emerson admired the intellectual environment of the experiment and persuaded his friend Henry David Thoreau to visit the community. Nathaniel Hawthorne invested some money in Brook Farm and actually lived there for a short period of time, although he finally found that the farm work interfered with his writing.

The summer of 1843 marked the beginning of the end of the communal experiment, when advocates of a new movement called Fourierism began to introduce what they considered more efficient methods and a more scientific approach to the operations of the community. Organized now as a "phalange," the site was centered on a phalanstery containing housing space, a dining hall, an educational area, and work spaces. According to the plans of Albert Brisbane, an advocate of the new system, people would work at a variety of jobs, and children would be educated according to what interested them individually.

Gradually people at Brook Farm became dissatisfied with the new order's emphasis on efficient social planning and divisions of labor in the farming operations. They were also becoming disturbed about growing expenses and the increasing financial problems facing the community. An outbreak of smallpox in November 1845 forced the school at Brook Farm to shut down permanently, and the following month a lawsuit brought by Nathaniel Hawthorne, charging that he had lost $530 on his original $1,000 investment, badly crippled the farming operations. The final blow to Brook Farm came on March 3, 1846, with the burning of a costly new phalanstery building on the final day of its construction, after which the community disbanded.

Charles Bulfinch

After the United States achieved independence from Great Britain in 1783, the town of Boston renewed its maritime activities, augmented its commercial prosperity, and increased its population. Proud of their independent status, Bostonians dramatized the role their town had played in the Revolution. Main Street became Washington Street, King Street was renamed State Street, and Queen Street was changed to Court Street. Citizens also wanted to replace the old British Town House with a State House of their own. Having selected a site on Beacon Hill for the new state capitol, state authorities chose the 24-year-old Charles Bulfinch to undertake the assignment.

Charles Bulfinch was the son of Dr. Thomas Bulfinch, a highly respected local physician. After graduating from Harvard College in 1781, Charles made the obligatory Grand Tour of Europe, where the artistic and architectural inspiration he found in France and England persuaded him to take up designing buildings when he returned to Boston. In only a short time, the young architect began to put his stamp on the postwar metropolis.

Bulfinch's first efforts came as wealthy merchants moved their homes out of the overcrowded waterfront section into the more open spaces of the West End. In 1792 he constructed a three-story brick house for his relative Joseph Coolidge, who had moved into the Bowdoin Square area; four years later, he built a handsome three-story house for Harrison Gray Otis on the corner of Cambridge and Lynde Streets that is operated today as a historical site by the Society for the Preservation of New England Antiquities. In 1815 the young man designed a pair of double houses between Cambridge and Green Streets for Samuel Parkman.

Bulfinch was also involved with the construction of churches. After building the Hollis Street Church, with its two domed towers and domed ceiling, in 1800 he designed, free of charge, the first Roman Catholic church in Boston, on Franklin Street. In 1804 he constructed a red-brick church on Hanover Street in the North End for the New North Religious Society, a structure that eventually became St. Stephen's Catholic Church. (During 1964–65 it was carefully renovated by Cardinal Richard Cushing.) In 1805 Bulfinch enlarged the original two-story Faneuil Hall to its present form by doubling the width of the building, adding a third story, and moving the cupola from the center to the front.

With his early buildings on display, and with some of Boston's wealthiest citizens as his patrons, Bulfinch became a natural choice for the construction of a new State House. In May 1795 a special committee authorized the purchase of the old Hancock property on the slope of Beacon Hill. The cornerstone was laid, appropriately enough, on July 4, 1797. Drawing upon what he had learned during his European travels, Bulfinch provided the Commonwealth with an impressive red-brick building on the crest of Beacon Hill with white marble trim, a long flight of steps, and an imposing dome that was subsequently gilded and that remains a distinctive landmark.

In addition to his skills in designing individual houses, churches, and public buildings, Charles Bulfinch was also an imaginative entrepreneur who developed expansive complexes of apartments and townhouses that in the twentieth century might well be described as condominiums. On Franklin Street, for example, he planned and built what became known as the Tontine Crescent—named after an English scheme of selling shares of stock in an enterprise, known as a "tontine." The Crescent included sixteen individual brick houses designed as a single unit along Franklin Street in a graceful curve, with an archway in the center (later called Arch Street), and eight more houses across an oval grass plot with trees and bushes. Although he was an imaginative architect, Charles Bulfinch was not always a successful businessman, and when subscriptions for this project did not come in fast enough to meet the bills, in 1796 he went bankrupt. Despite his financial reversals, in 1799 he was elected to the unpaid position of town selectman, and in May 1799 he was appointed Superintendent of Police at an annual salary of $600, which helped pay off his debts.

Unfazed by his money problems, in 1810 Bulfinch undertook the development of another impressive complex, this one known as the Colonnade, a series of nineteen elegant houses extending along Tremont Street from West Street to Mason Street. For many years this was a fashionable residential complex from which residents could look out their windows across Boston Common to the distant water, hills, and sunsets in the western skies. Once again, however, Bulfinch's bills grew faster than his income, and he spent the month of July 1811 in the local jail for debt.

Thanks to Charles Bulfinch, the old wooden colonial seaport town of Boston was rebuilt in elegant brick and granite, marking its transition into a stately federal metropolis of business, commerce, and banking. There are few individuals who have had such a profound influence on the design of their own city. As the eminent historian Walter Muir Whitehill has expressed it: "Few men deserve to be held by the citizens of Boston in more grateful remembrance than Charles Bulfinch."

Bunker Hill Monument

Two months after they had been forced to retreat to their barracks in Boston following the bloody encounters at Lexington and Concord, the British made plans to turn the tables on the American rebels. Using the fleet assembled at Boston, the British prepared to land forces on the opposite peninsula of Charlestown, place troops and artillery on its two strategic hills—Breed's and Bunker's—and destroy the rebel forces entrenched around Boston Neck. Warned in advance of these plans, on the evening of June 16, 1775, a force of Americans headed by General Israel Putnam and Colonel William Prescott moved in from the land side and fortified Breed's Hill, the foremost hill overlooking the beaches where the British troops would come ashore. The next day, June 17, confident of their own prowess and contemptuous of the abilities of American fighting men, the British regulars landed and marched boldly up the hill in close-order formation, only to be cut down by the withering fire of the Americans in their redoubts at the top. After a second assault failed, General William Howe brought over 400 marines from Boston and finally overran the defenders, who had run out of ammunition. Although the Battle of Bunker Hill (which was misnamed at the time—it was actually fought on Breed's Hill) was technically a British victory, it certainly was a Pyrrhic one, with British casualties outnumbering American two to one.

Perhaps the most prominent Bostonian to fall on the field of battle that day was Dr. Joseph Warren, a highly respected physician, orator, writer, and organizer for the patriot cause. In 1794 the King Solomon's Lodge of Masons erected an 18-foot pillar atop Breed's Hill in memory of Dr. Warren, a member of the Masons. As the fiftieth anniversary of the Revolutionary War approached, however, the Bunker Hill Monument Association was formed to commemorate the event with a larger and more impressive monument. The cornerstone was laid at a dedication ceremony in 1825, although construction wasn't completed until eighteen years later. The granite for the new Bunker Hill Monument came from a quarry in the nearby town of Quincy. It was brought in 12-foot blocks to the Neponset River on horse-drawn railroad cars ("the first commercial railroad in America"), and then taken by barge to the Charlestown site. The entire undertaking was very costly; a succession of fairs, cake sales, and other fundraising activities organized by Boston women, together with public subscriptions and private contributions, finally provided the funds to complete the project.

On June 17, 1843, the 221-foot, 6,700-ton granite monument, an Egyptian-style obelisk designed by Solomon Willard, was finally dedicated. The event was highlighted by an oration by Daniel Webster and the presence of thirteen elderly veterans of the battle. In 1845 a 9-foot model of the original 1794 monument was installed at the base of the ventilation shaft of the newly completed obelisk.

In 1919 the Bunker Hill Memorial Association turned the Bunker Hill Monument over to the City of Boston; in 1976, during the Bicentennial observances of the American Revolution, the city transferred ownership to the National Park Service. Fifteen feet square, the monument has 294 winding stairs and no elevator. Outside the historic site stands a statue of the defiant figure of Colonel William Prescott, sword in hand, telling his men: "Don't fire till you see the whites of their eyes." Members of the National Park Service maintain the Bunker Hill Monument and recreate the story of the battle using a series of dioramas located in the monument lodge.

Busing

During the mid-1970s the use of school buses to transport white children to black schools and black children to white schools in an effort to integrate Boston's public school system ignited racial conflict and neighborhood confrontations that changed the city forever.

Despite the 1954 Supreme Court ruling in the case of *Brown v. Board of Education of Topeka,* which outlawed racial segregation in public schools, black citizens of Boston complained that the public schools of Boston remained *de facto* segregated. Members of the Boston School Committee, however, refused to admit that any form of deliberate segregation existed in the public schools. The racial makeup of the schools, it insisted, was simply the result of parents' sending their children to the closest neighborhood school. In spite of constant pressure from the Massachusetts Department of Education, the Boston School Committee refused to come up with a plan for orderly and gradual integration.

Frustrated black parents joined the NAACP in a class-action suit against the Boston School Committee. Early in 1972 the case was assigned by lot to Federal Judge W. Arthur Garrity, Jr., a highly respected member of the Massachusetts bar. On June 21, 1974, after two years of study, Judge Garrity handed down his decision, charging the Boston School Committee with having "knowingly carried out a systematic program of segregation" that had produced "a dual system." Garrity ordered a program to take effect the coming September that would bus some 18,000 schoolchildren in order to achieve a balanced mixture of white and black students in the public schools.

White ethnic neighborhoods like Charlestown, South Boston, and East Boston exploded in anger, encouraged by many mem- bers of the Boston School Committee as well as by members of the Boston City Council. Strikes, boycotts, and outright violence marked the start of the city's busing program in September 1974. Hundreds of city and state policemen had to patrol the streets, monitor the schools, and protect the yellow buses that carried black and white children to schools in each others' neighborhoods.

Despite the noise and tumult, Judge Arthur Garrity refused to be deterred from carrying out his ruling. A year later, he produced a new plan calling for the busing of 3,000 more students, to take effect in September 1975. Although the U.S. Supreme Court refused to review Garrity's original decision, neighborhood opposition became even more vocal and violent. During the next two years, Boston saw a series of ugly racial incidents including stonings, beatings, firebombings, and even shootings.

The public turmoil over busing gradually subsided over the course of the next ten years as some of the major figures died, protesters grew weary, and families moved away. And yet, court-ordered busing had long-term effects upon trends in the city's demographics. The 1980 census reported that 12 percent of Boston's population—about 80,000 people—had left the city since 1970. One-third of the white families with children under the age of 18 were gone. While demographers can show that this "white flight" had actually been in process since the 1950s, city officials point out that the percentage of white students in the Boston public schools dropped from 49 percent to only 19 percent during that twenty-year period of court-ordered busing.

The busing crisis left behind a sad legacy of expressions of racial hatred that were a permanent embarrassment to a city once heralded as the "Cradle of Liberty." Now it had acquired the dubious distinction of being what the Celtic basketball star Bill Russell called "the most racist city in America."

On September 3, 1985, eleven years after the first yellow buses rolled up to South Boston High School, and the day Dr. Laval Wilson took office as Boston's first black superintendent of schools, Judge Arthur Garrity closed the file in the desegregation case. He subsequently returned control of the schools to the Boston School Committee, although he retained standby jurisdiction to insure continued racial equality. But if there were those who thought that the passage of time had put the busing crisis to rest, or that the emotional feelings about desegregation had died away, public reaction to the news of Judge Garrity's death in 1999 demonstrated otherwise. In a flurry of editorials, special articles, letters to the editor, radio reports, and television features, advocates representing both sides came out to resume the battle as fiercely as ever. Some praised Judge Garrity for his personal integrity and moral courage in forcing the city to desegregate its schools; others condemned him for destroying family values and causing irreparable damage to the Boston school system. Although twenty-five years had passed since court-enforced busing started, it was quite clear, to use the title of J. Anthony Lukas's classic study of the crisis, there still was no Common Ground.

Custom House

Melnea Cass

For over sixty years Melnea Cass fought vigorously and successfully for the improvement of services and the expansion of resources for Boston's African American community. Born in Richmond, Virginia, on June 16, 1896, Melnea Agnes Jones was the eldest of three daughters. Her parents brought the family to the South End of Boston to improve their employment opportunities and provide an education for their children. After Melnea's mother died at the age of 32, Melnea attended school in Newburyport, Massachusetts, and Rock Castle, Virginia, where she graduated in 1914 as the valedictorian of her class. She then returned to Boston.

Melnea worked at the Hyannis Inn on Cape Cod until she married Marshall Cass in 1917, just before he went into the army. She went to live with her mother-in-law, Rosa Brown, while her husband was in the service, and gave birth to a son in 1919. After Marshall returned from the service, they moved into their own house, where her two daughters were born. While raising her family at home, Melnea Cass became involved in community activities through the influence of her mother-in-law, who was a church leader and a member of the NAACP, the Equal Rights League, and the Women's Service Club. Melnea also joined the NAACP, became involved in the club movement, and helped Mrs. Brown raise money to help William Monroe Trotter publish his newspaper, *The Guardian*. In 1930 Melnea Cass and her husband moved from the South End to Roxbury. When her husband lost his job during the Depression, Mrs. Cass worked as a live-in housekeeper to keep the family fed and sheltered until he could finally find work with the General Services Administration.

Through her involvement with her own school-age children, Melnea Cass helped establish a Kindergarten Mother's Club at the Robert Gould Shaw House. Soon the need for expanded nursery school services led Mrs. Cass and the other women at the Shaw House to reorganize as the Friendship Club, which conducted fundraising activities, choral groups, and athletic events. Melnea

Cass also was involved in community activities beyond the school. She became vice-president of the Harriet Tubman Mothers' Club, an organization in which members tried to "mother" young women who had just arrived in Boston from the South. Mrs. Cass also served as secretary to the Sojourner Truth Club, a civic-minded organization of middle-class black women, named after the nineteenth-century advocate of abolition and women's suffrage. She was also active at St. Mark's Congregational Church.

As Boston's African American population grew larger and better organized during the 1940s, residents like Melnea Cass became more vocal and active in their demands for racial justice and civil rights. During the Depression years, Mrs. Cass had helped A. Philip Randolph in his work with the Brotherhood of Sleeping Car Porters in Boston. During World War II, Randolph called upon her again to help organize the 1941 National March on Washington to press for black jobs in America's defense industries. Along with Muriel and Otto Snowden, Mrs. Cass was among the sixteen cofounders of Freedom House in 1948, an organized effort to keep Roxbury an integrated, multicultural neighborhood, with clean streets, good lighting, adequate police and fire protection, and effective parental supervision of children. As the demand for civil rights became more intense, Mrs. Cass took a leadership role in public protests and demonstrations. During the 1940s she resigned from her position on the YWCA board because African Americans were not allowed to use the swimming pool, but would live to see the Clarendon Street YWCA named in her honor in 1976. During the 1950s she marched at the head of a picket line at Woolworth's Five & Ten Cent Store on Washington Street. A longtime member of the NAACP, Mrs. Cass became president of the Boston branch from 1962 to 1964, during the time of protests, sit-ins, and boycotts surrounding the desegregation of Boston's public schools.

Toward the end of her life, Mrs. Cass received many honors and awards for her years of work. In 1966 the Roxbury community celebrated her many achievements by establishing Melnea Cass Day; in 1970 the Eastern Chapter of the National Association of Social Workers honored Cass for her "outstanding lay contribution to social welfare." In 1976 Mayor Kevin White included Melnea Cass in his list of seven distinguished "Grand Bostonians," and during the Bicentennial celebrations that same year the First Lady of Roxbury, as she had become known, was among the local dignitaries introduced to Queen Elizabeth II when the English monarch visited Boston.

As society changed, and as Melnea Cass matured, her interests expanded to include the needs of the aged. She served several years on the Roxbury Council of Elders, which developed educational, nutritional, and social programs for the elderly. Although she was in her late seventies, she accepted an appointment as chair of the Mayor's Advisory Committee for the City of Boston Elderly, and was later appointed to the National Council of Senior Citizens. A few years after her death in 1978 at the age of 82, Melnea Cass was honored with a new thoroughfare bearing her name. In 1981 Melnea Cass Boulevard was officially opened in lower Roxbury. This boulevard had the unusual distinction of being exempt from the traditional City regulation that any street crossing Washington Street must change its name in honor of the first president. Previously, only Massachusetts Avenue and Columbus Avenue had been exempted from that provision.

Castle Island

Just off the shoreline of a peninsula that in colonial times was called Dorchester Neck (now South Boston) was a small knob of land in Boston Harbor named Castle Island. In July 1634 Governor Thomas Dudley authorized the erection of a small fortification on the island, funded by the General Court. As the years went by, the fort fell into disuse, until, in the early 1700s, English military engineers tore down the old structure and put up a new fortress they called Castle William. By the time of the French and Indian War in 1754, Castle William was recognized as one of the most strategically important forts in British North America.

Castle William remained in British hands until the royal forces were forced to evacuate Boston in 1776. General George Washington took possession of the fortress and hired Paul Revere to repair the damage done by the enemy when they abandoned the garrison. When the Revolutionary War was over, Governor John Hancock took possession of the fort until March 1795, when the state legislature turned the structure into a prison. In 1798, when the United States became involved in the "quasi-war" with France, the national government took custody of the fort for military purposes. The following year, President John Adams came to Boston and attended a ceremony at which the name was officially changed to Fort Independence.

The work of rebuilding the old structure was assigned to Lieutenant Colonel A. Louis Tousard, and when reconstruction was completed Nehemiah Freeman, commander of the fort, named each of the five new bastions after a well-known New Englander. The northeast bastion was named Winthrop, in honor of the first governor of the Massachusetts Bay Colony; the southeast bastion was named Shirley, in honor of the colonial governor William Shirley; the bastion on the southwest corner was named for John Hancock, the first governor after independence; the north bastion was called Dearborn, in honor of Secretary of War Henry Dearborn of New Hampshire; and the bastion at the corner of the fort was named Adams, after President John Adams.

Standing like a lonely sentinel in the silent gray waters of Boston Harbor, the old fort went on to have a romantic and often eerie history, with legends of duels, murders, suicides, strange voices, and ghostly noises. The story of a young officer entombed alive in the dungeon became the basis for "The Cask of Amontillado" by Edgar Allan Poe, who, as an army private, was stationed at Fort Independence for a brief period of time.

Later in the nineteenth century, as part of his string of public parks known as the "Emerald Necklace," Frederick Law Olmsted proposed building a causeway that would link the mainland at City Point with Castle Island and help create a protected bay that could be used for recreational purposes. Construction of such a causeway was held up for many years, however, because even though the City of Boston owned City Point, the U.S. Government held title to Castle Island and Fort Independence. After Congress finally gave

Boston the use of Castle Island in 1890, a wooden bridge was constructed that allowed tourists, visitors, and "promenaders" to enjoy the pleasures of Castle Island.

During World War I, the federal government took back control of Castle Island for a brief period, but after the war a permanent causeway replaced the old wooden bridge. During the Depression years, the construction of a new concrete boulevard to Castle Island furnished work for many South Boston residents. When World War II broke out, fears of espionage and fifth-column activities caused the War Department to close off access to Castle Island. Armed guards were stationed in a small guardhouse at the beginning of the causeway, and during the night additional guards were posted at 200-yard intervals along the causeway running from City Point to Castle Island.

In October 1970 Castle Island and Fort Independence were placed on the Register of National Historic Places, prompting a group of interested local residents to form the Castle Island Association. Volunteers from the association have worked with the Metropolitan District Commission in upgrading the ancient fort, maintaining the grounds, and preserving the history of the island by giving guided tours in period costume.

The Cathedral

During the last stages of the Revolution, a small handful of Roman Catholics in Boston slowly began to coalesce. They met together for religious services in a small abandoned Huguenot chapel on School Street. Mostly French and Irish, they employed the services of an occasional French chaplain and a succession of itinerant priests until Father François Matignon arrived from France as a permanent curate. He was joined in 1796 by young Fr. Jean-Louis de Cheverus, one of Matignon's former students from the seminary in Paris.

As the small congregation of Catholics grew too large for the little chapel, the priests decided it was time to build a church of their own. Fundraising was difficult for people with limited resources, but with plans provided free of charge by Charles Bulfinch and generous contributions from their Protestant neighbors, the Catholics were able to complete a small church on Franklin Street in downtown Boston. The structure was formally dedicated on September 29, 1803, and named the Church of the Holy Cross. After Cheverus was appointed first bishop of the newly created diocese of Boston in April 1808, the church became the town's first Roman Catholic Cathedral.

For the next half-century, the small church on Franklin Street served as the center of the Boston diocese and the seat of Boston's first four bishops. Cheverus remained until he returned to France in 1823; Benedict Fenwick, a Jesuit from Maryland, presided as the second bishop until his death in 1846. It was the third bishop, John Bernard Fitzpatrick, a Boston-born graduate of the Latin School, who decided that Boston's Catholic population had grown large enough by the late 1850s to need a new and more spacious cathedral. Observing that many of the city's well-to-do residents were planning to move into the recently developed South End, he considered this area to have the best prospects. Selling off the old Franklin Street property in 1860, he engaged the services of the New York church architect Patrick C. Keely to design the new cathedral.

When the Civil War broke out, plans for Boston's new cathedral had to be put aside indefinitely. For the next fifteen years, services were conducted at a number of temporary locations. After Fitzpatrick's death in 1866, his successor, Bishop John Williams, met with the architect, reaffirmed the original plans, and in June 1866 laid the foundation for the new cathedral. Supported by annual collections, private contributions, and a series of successful "Cathedral Fairs," the building project was finally completed in 1875—the same year Williams was elevated to the rank of Archbishop.

Boston's magnificent new Cathedral of the Holy Cross, built in an early English Gothic style, was almost as large as Notre-Dame in Paris or St. John Lateran in Rome. According to the original plans, the structure was supposed to have two lofty towers, but the short-

age of funds made that impossible. In the basement of the new cathedral was a large chapel containing the high altar from the old
Franklin Street cathedral.

Unfortunately, the elegance of the new Back Bay quickly eclipsed
the South End as Boston's most desirable residential address. By
the end of the century, the South End had become a rundown and
neglected neighborhood. Its handsome brick mansions had been
converted into boarding houses, inexpensive apartments, and
shabby businesses. When Archbishop Williams began building an
Archdiocesan Seminary in 1881, he located it not in the South End,
but in the rural suburb of Brighton. A generation later, Cardinal
William O'Connell moved the Chancery out of the South End to
offices near Brookline's Cottage Farm; he later constructed his palatial residence near St. John's Seminary in Brighton. The Cathedral
remained in the South End, but the stately building stood amid narrow and congested streets, all but obscured by the dark ugly scaffolding of the elevated railway that ran along Washington Street
with a deafening clatter that drowned out sermons and interrupted
devotions.

In recent years, Cardinal Bernard Law has done much to restore
the original beauty and splendor of the Cathedral of the Holy
Cross. The removal of the overhead elevated structures has created
much more open space in that area of the South End, and urban renewal programs have done much to provide upgraded housing,
wider streets, and a more gentrified population in the old neighborhood.

Cemeteries

One of the permanent markers of the age of a village or town is usually the local cemetery. The Old Towne of Boston, as evidence of its
own ancient origins, offers at least four old burying grounds that
date from the Puritan community's early years.

The King's Chapel Burying Ground was the first cemetery in colonial Boston. The original site was laid out in 1630 on a lot belong-

ing to Sir Isaac Johnson, who requested that he be buried on his own plot of land. For the next thirty years, this was the site of the oldest burying ground in the town, located on present-day Washington Street, alongside King's Chapel. Here are buried some of the town's first founders and earliest residents. John Winthrop, the first governor of the Massachusetts Bay Colony, has his grave here, together with two sons and other members of his family. Thomas Dudley, the first deputy governor; John Endicott, a later governor; and William Saltonstall are representative of the town's ruling class, while Reverend John Cotton is symbolic of the Puritan influence in town affairs. William Dawes, the patriot rider who brought to Lexington the news of the British redcoats, is also buried in the graveyard beside King's Chapel, as is Mary Chilton, who gained fame as the first Pilgrim to touch Plymouth Rock.

The Old Granary Burying Ground is the next-oldest cemetery in Boston. As the town of Boston grew, it became necessary to find more room for departed residents. An area called the Old South Burying Ground was laid out in 1660 for that purpose. Because it was originally located beside the old Town Granary, a long wooden building used for storing the colonists' grain supply, the cemetery later became better known as the Old Granary Burying Ground. Among the well-known colonial figures buried here are Judge Samuel Sewall, Peter Faneuil (written as "Funel" on his tombstone), Benjamin Franklin's parents, the five victims of the Boston Massacre, and such Revolutionary patriots as James Otis and Sam Adams. When Paul Revere died in 1818, he became one of the last of the Revolutionary heroes laid to rest in the downtown graveyard. Also buried here is Elizabeth Foster Goose (or Vergoose), reputed to be the original Mother Goose of fairytale fame.

Tourists and visitors to Boston are almost always captivated by the variety of markers and headstones in the Old Granary Burying Ground. During the Puritans' early years in Boston, life was harsh and earnest, and their view of death tended to be bleak. Hence the death's heads, the winged skulls, the crossbones, and the effigies of souls in flight which appear on so many of the earliest headstones and tombs. In later years, as life in Boston became easier, the stonecutters' symbols began to include the faces of cherubs and scenes of harvest time, while urns and willows—classical Greek and Roman motifs—emerged during the Republican period that followed the Revolution. The Old Granary Burying Ground offers a corner of calm and peace in the midst of the city, situated between the sheltering shadows of the Park Street Church on one side and the Boston Athenaeum on the other.

The Copp's Hill Burying Ground came next. A suitable plot was laid out atop Copp's Hill (sometimes called Snow Hill or Mill Field) in the North End of Boston. According to legend, the local graveyard was established on a piece of pastureland belonging to a shoemaker from England named William Copp. Copp's Hill Burying Ground has many early gravestones with quaint inscriptions, as well as a series of armorial markers arranged along the west wall. The tombs of two of Boston's famous ministers, Increase Mather and his son Cotton Mather, are located on Copp's Hill, along with the graves of the witch-trial judge, Samuel Sewall; Edmund Hartt, the builder of the *Constitution;* and Robert Newman, sexton of the Old North Church. The same old burial ground is the resting place for about one thousand freed slaves who made their homes in colonial Boston, including Prince Hall, a freed slave who founded a black Masonic Lodge in Boston.

The Central Burying Ground, laid out in 1756 in the southwest corner of the Boston Common, along Boylston Street, was the last of the four distinctive colonial graveyards. This cemetery has many interesting tombstones and wall tombs, and contains the remains of a number of British soldiers who died during the Revolutionary War. Although Gilbert Stuart had been born in Rhode Island, in 1806 the artist who became famous for his painting of George Washington came to live permanently in Boston, and lies buried in the Central Burying Ground.

Children's Hospital

Appropriate medical care for most children in early nineteenth-century Boston was haphazard at best; for children of the poor and disadvantaged it was almost nonexistent. An 1872 health commission report stated that in a city of 200,000 to 300,000 people, nearly half of all deaths occurred among infants and children. This led one doctor to recall the words of Lemuel Shattuck that children in the Irish districts of Boston "seemed literally born to die."

In 1848 Dr. William R. Lawrence, supported by funds from his father, Amos Lawrence, the well-known textile magnate, started a Children's Infirmary to care for the sick and destitute children of the city. Most of these children were newly arrived from famine-stricken Ireland, suffering from "ship fever and extreme prostration" as a result of their long and arduous ocean voyage. The infirmary lasted less than two years, however. Dr. Lawrence believed that the hospital's closing was due not so much to the lack of resources as to the "backwardness of the poor," who hesitated to entrust the health of their children to those native Bostonians "whose motives they had never learned to fathom."

In the decades following the Civil War, there was a renewed interest in medicine, surgery, and what would become known as orthopedics. Disabled veterans demonstrated that they could lead productive lives as a result of new medical and technical advances. These successes rekindled concern for more adequate care and treatment of children. Two Harvard-trained physicians who had served in the Civil War, Dr. Francis Henry Brown and Dr. William Ingalls, took up the idea of creating a hospital exclusively for the medical and surgical treatment of childhood ailments. Despite objections from the Massachusetts General Hospital, whose president insisted that existing institutions were capable of providing adequate care for children, the two doctors pushed ahead with their proposal, and appealed to the general public for charitable support. On July 21, 1869, newspapers reported that the Managers of the Children's Hospital had purchased a house at No. 9 Rutland Street in the South End, and were prepared to receive young patients for treatment. A 7-year-old girl named Ellen McCarthy, of Cove Street, was admitted with a fractured femur; the next day, the son of Mr. Andrew Carr, of 45 Second Street, South Boston, was treated for a similar injury.

The first Children's Hospital quickly proved much too small for the number of patients seeking admission, and between 1881 and 1890 a new and impressive red-brick structure went up in stages along Huntington Avenue. Generously proportioned and carefully designed, the new hospital deployed two wings, containing a total of 96 patient rooms, on either side of a tall administration block. In order to insure maximum sunlight and fresh air, which physicians regarded as essential to the treatment of children, a series of glass-enclosed balconies was constructed along the Huntington Avenue facade, and the ceilings in most of the wards went up to a height of 17 feet. Under the direction of Dr. Edward Hickling Bradford, a direct descendant of the governor of the Plymouth Colony, Children's Hospital made remarkable advances in the treatment of children with orthopedic problems.

The demands on the hospital continued to outstrip the size of its accommodations, however, and in 1914 Children's Hospital moved to its present location on Longwood Avenue, near Brookline, the first of the group of hospitals that relocated to surround the Harvard Medical School. Over the years, Children's Hospital made some remarkable advances in the treatment of children. In 1929, for example, in cooperation with the Harvard School of Public Health, the hospital developed the iron lung that was to become critical in the care of polio patients. Dr. William Ladd established the surgical service of the Children's Hospital as a separate unit, greatly facilitating progress in the surgery of infants and young children. And in 1938 Dr. Robert Gross opened the door to pediatric cardiovascular surgery when he successfully operated on a 7-year-old child to correct a congenital heart defect. The Enders Building, a 14-story pediatric research center, is named in memory of Dr. John Enders, who, with his colleagues, cultured the polio virus in 1949 and the measles virus in 1954, paving the way for the development of vaccines for both diseases.

In 1946 Children's Hospital entered into a federation with several other institutions that specialized in the health care of children to form the country's first Children's Medical Center. In 1976 the Children's Cancer Research Center, which had grown out of the Children's Hospital Medical Center, was renamed to honor its founder, Dr. Sidney Farber, who had served on the staff of Children's Hospital from 1929 to 1970. The two institutions have remained separate, but enjoy a cooperative relationship.

Today one enters the main entrance of the Children's Hospital Medical Center from Blackfan Street, off Longwood Avenue. The building's lobby is lively and colorful, with a cafeteria and a gift shop nearby and a great number of children moving through. Many young patients can be seen maneuvering about in what are called G-Carts, which have been used at the hospital since 1915. Originally rather unwieldy wooden contraptions, they have been greatly modernized and stabilized, with brakes, safety belts, and holders for IV poles. From the lobby, an array of windows looks out onto the Prouty Garden, a gift from Olive Prouty in memory of her two daughters. This courtyard, surrounded by the buildings of the medical center, has a fountain, flowering trees, restful benches, and a beautifully landscaped garden that do much to soften the institutional atmosphere of the hospital. The Children's Hospital Medical Center has achieved an international reputation for the quality of its care, the expertise of its staff, and its advanced research on childhood diseases.

Chinatown

Boston first developed commercial relations with the Chinese mainland in the early nineteenth century, and for many years carried on a lucrative China trade that created personal fortunes for many Yankee sea captains and merchants. It was not until the 1890s, however, that the city had its first permanent Chinese community.

During the 1850s and 1860s many workers from China came to the West Coast of the United States, where they served as a source of inexpensive labor, first during the California gold rush and later during the building of the transcontinental railroads. Once the railroads were completed, however, the Chinese began drifting to the big cities of the East Coast in search of work. In 1875 one group of Chinese were brought in to break a strike at a shoe factory in the town of North Adams. After the strike was settled, the Chinese workers lost their temporary jobs and continued on to Boston. Arriving in a low-rent district near South Station, they settled in a cluster of tents in a strip they called Ping-On Alley.

By about 1890 the whole South Cove area, a district running along Kneeland Street and encompassing Beach, Oxford, Tyler, and Hudson Streets, was established as a settlement of some 200 Chinese residents, in a neighborhood that was soon called Chinatown. Although the population gradually increased to about 1,200 residents, until well into the twentieth century the Chinese Exclusion Act of 1882 restricted the total number of immigrants. With the repeal of various immigration laws in 1943, the Chinese population grew much faster. While some of the older and more well-to-do Chinese families followed the general demographic patterns of the 1950s and 1960s by moving to the suburbs, Chinatown retained its national flavor and continued to attract new young immigrants from China as well as more recent refugees from Vietnam, Cambodia, Thailand, and other parts of Southeast Asia.

Today, Boston's Chinatown is the third-largest Chinese settlement in the nation, after San Francisco and New York City. The distinctive oriental design of the Chinese Merchants Association Building on Hudson Street and the pagoda-shaped telephone booths on the sidewalks make the district immediately recognizable to visitors and tourists. The neighborhood boasts a number of excellent restaurants, while shops along Kneeland Street offer jade and porcelain pieces, brocade jackets and dresses, and selections of teas and spices. Many people come into Chinatown to watch the colorful dragon dances and exciting fireworks displays during the Chinese New Year festivities in February or the Festival of the August Moon in the summer.

Because of Chinatown's location—adjacent to the city's business and theater districts, in the heart of the garment district, and next to the expressways that enter and leave downtown Boston—the Boston Redevelopment Authority, the Tufts–New England Medical Center, the Massachusetts Turnpike Authority, and the Department of Public Works have been among institutions and agencies vying for valuable space in this district. Through the efforts of business and professional leaders, the Chinese community has exerted pressure to save its territorial boundaries and preserve its integrity from "outside" developers. By establishing community associations to create social-service programs for such local issues as health care, adult education, and elderly housing, Boston's Chinese American citizens have been able to retain much of their cultural identity while making valuable contributions to the life of the city.

Christian Science Church

The magnificent church with the impressive dome on Massachusetts Avenue, near Huntington Avenue and across from Symphony Hall, is the Christian Science Church. Constructed in 1904, it is officially known as the Mother Church Extension, although it is actually much larger than the original Mother Church to which it is attached, and which was built in 1894.

The Christian Science religion was begun in 1879 by Mary Baker Eddy of New Hampshire, based to a large degree on doctrines developed in her book *Science and Health, with a Key to the Scriptures.* "It is our ignorance of God, the divine Principle," she wrote, "which produces apparent discord, and the right understanding of Him restores harmony." In 1893 Mrs. Eddy had a modest stone church constructed in Boston, virtually a chapel with stained-glass windows, that she called "our prayer in stone" and that members refer to as the Mother Church. The religion spread rapidly, particularly in New England, having a special appeal to Americans of the middle and upper classes as an antidote against the materialism of modern industrial society.

The First Church of Christ, Scientist, designed by the Boston architect Charles Brigham, was constructed between 1904 and 1906. A grandiose structure whose auditorium was inspired by Hagia Sophia in Istanbul, its central dome incorporates elements of the dome of St. Peter's in Rome and the Duomo in Florence. The church is built of granite from New Hampshire, the home state of Mrs. Eddy, and houses one of the largest Aeolian Skinner organs in the world. The Christian Science Publishing House, a long, pillared building next to the Mother Church, is the home of the highly regarded daily international newspaper *The Christian Science Monitor* and also houses the Mapparium, a 30-foot walk-through globe of the world executed in stained glass.

For many years, these impressive church buildings could not be fully appreciated in what was a congested section of the city until the entire complex was imaginatively redesigned under the direction of the architect I. M. Pei from 1968 to 1973, during the period of Boston's general redevelopment. By creating an expansive new limestone entrance plaza on Massachusetts Avenue, adding an adjoining world headquarters building as an extension of the church buildings, and extending a 700-foot-long reflecting pool along Huntington Avenue, Pei provided the entire Christian Science complex with a new unity and visibility.

Citgo Sign

The bright red triangle of the Citgo sign in Boston's Kenmore Square is a modern landmark for many Bostonians and a favorite sight from the bleachers of nearby Fenway Park. Erected by the Citgo (formerly Cities Service) gasoline company in 1940 and modernized in 1965, the sign uses 5,878 neon-filled glass tubes to advertise its product.

During Boston's period of urban renewal in the 1960s, a number of Bostonians thought that the sign was too cheap and garish and called for its removal. A majority, however, felt that the sign had become a familiar part of the Boston scene and voted to have it retained as a historic site. Baseball fans (and players) can still look beyond the right-field fence to see the flashing red triangle and the rippling blue lights of the Citgo Sign in the distance.

City Hall

What most native Bostonians still refer to as "Old City Hall" is located on School Street in downtown Boston, halfway between the city's two major thoroughfares, Tremont and Washington Streets. During the 1860s, despite the pressures and sacrifices of the Civil

War, Bostonians went ahead with their plans to fill in the Back Bay and create a fashionable neighborhood that would rival the expansive boulevards and magnificent buildings of Paris. "Boston suddenly surrendered to a passion for things French," writes the historian Douglass Shand-Tucci.

The Parisian influence was not restricted to the Back Bay, however. In 1862 the Boston architect Gridley J. Fox Bryant, whose father had designed the Granite Railway a generation earlier, provided Boston with a new City Hall. Inspired by the Tuileries and the Louvre while studying at the Ecole des Beaux Arts in Paris, Bryant and his associate, Arthur Gilman, created a stately building in Concord granite. Very much in the Second French Empire style, it had coupled columns and pilasters on the facade and was topped with a signature mansard roof of wood covered with copper.

For the next hundred years, the stately old structure on School Street served as the center of city government for a procession of mayors who served one-year terms and circulated through the office with a certain regularity. After the city charter was revised in 1909, John F. Fitzgerald was the first Boston mayor to serve a four-year term. Under Mayor James Michael Curley, whose first term began in 1918, the corridors and stairways of the old building teemed with constituents looking for jobs, favors, and appointments, while armies of contractors, suppliers, and vendors paraded through the executive office at all hours of the day and night.

In his ambitious plans for a "New Boston" during the 1960s, Mayor John F. Collins envisioned a major Government Center in the heart of the city that would combine state and federal offices with a new City Hall, dramatizing Boston's progress. After a national architectural competition, three members of the Columbia University architecture school—Gerhard Kallman, Noel McKinnell, and Edward Knowles—were chosen for their prize-winning design. The model of the new City Hall was officially unveiled on May 3, 1962, before a select audience at the Museum of Fine Arts. When the curtain was lifted, the assemblage saw a strikingly modernistic design, low and huge, with what Walter Muir Whitehill has described as "Mycenaean or Aztec overtones" in its soaring, stepped massiveness, borrowing heavily from the concepts of the Swiss architect Le Corbusier. Reactions were strongly mixed. No one seemed to be neutral—people either loved the new building enthusiastically or hated it passionately. Some praised the modern design as a fitting tribute to Boston's new future; others denounced it as an architectural disaster.

Despite the storm of controversy, Mayor Collins pushed ahead with his plans for a new City Hall and Government Center. Work on the building was nearing completion by the time Collins's second term was coming to an end in 1967. Unable to resist the opportunity to become the first tenant in his new City Hall, on December 18, 1967, he spent the entire day in his new office, going over work, visiting with friends, and speaking with his successor, Kevin H. White. Unfortunately, the unfinished construction and the absence of a heating system caused Collins to come down with a serious case of pneumonia that kept him bedridden for weeks. Kevin White was inaugurated as Mayor of Boston on Monday, January 1, 1968, but further delays in construction caused him to remain in the old School Street building for the remainder of the year. When he was satisfied that the new City Hall was fully operational, he scheduled a week-long series of events in February 1969, officially opening the new building.

Although more than thirty-five years have passed since the first model of the new City Hall was unveiled, the structure is no less controversial today. Critics continue to complain that the design is inappropriate for the city's heritage, that its sprawling brick plaza is a windswept wasteland, and that its interior structure is lacking in both beauty and efficiency. There are those who call for the entire structure to be razed to the ground. Under the administration of Mayor Thomas Menino plans are under way to modify the plaza, erect more buildings, establish additional green space, and create a harmonious relationship with the surrounding environment. Bostonians wait to see whether these ambitious plans will ever come to pass.

Clubs

Perhaps because of its English antecedents and its continuing Anglo-Saxon associations, Boston has long been regarded as a "club" town. Several well-known lunch-and-dinner clubs have offered prosperous Bostonians a private retreat in the city, a place apart from their Beacon Street homes or their suburban estates. Here, "gentlemen of property and standing" could meet to enjoy pleasant surroundings, a good dinner, an excellent brandy, a fine cigar, and an evening of stimulating conversation before retiring to an upstairs guest room.

The Somerset Club, the city's oldest and most distinguished social club, started out as the Travelers Club, and changed its name to the Tremont Club when in 1846 its quarters were located on Tremont Street. In 1852 it moved to the corner of Beacon and Somerset streets, near the State House, and took its present name from that location. According to local legend, on May 18, 1863, the conservative members of the Somerset Club closed the curtains of the club to shut out the sight of Colonel Robert Gould Shaw and his black troops of the 54th Massachusetts Regiment marching toward the State House. Members have always insisted that they were merely closing the drapes against the brightness of the sun. In 1872 the club moved to a new location, the stately mansion of white Rockford granite at 42 Beacon Street which Alexander Parris had built for Colonel David Sears. Boasting some 560 members, the club regularly provides breakfast, lunch, and dinner. Initiation fees range from $2,500 to $5,000, with yearly dues of $1,000 to $1,700.

The Union Club was founded in 1863, at the height of the Civil War, when the businessman John Murray Forbes led a group of friends out of the Somerset Club because of its less than enthusiastic support of the Lincoln administration. To demonstrate their commitment to preserving the Union, Forbes and his associates formed the Union Club and purchased the Park Street residence of the late Abbott Lawrence for their clubhouse, where members could dine in comfort in rooms that looked out onto the Boston

Common. A favorite of lawyers, thanks to its location close to the state and local courthouses as well as the headquarters of the Boston Bar Association, the Union Club tends to draw younger members of the city's legal and political circles.

The Tavern Club was founded in 1884 in downtown Boston, tucked away in a modest location at 4 Boylston Place, across from the south side of the Boston Common. Organized by a group of young Bostonians of artistic bent, over the years its members have included William Dean Howells, Charles Eliot Norton, Owen Wister, and Barret Wendell. In 1933 *Fortune* magazine described the Tavern Club as "the city's pleasantest male retreat, where the more Continentally minded members of Boston's great families hobnob with occasional Chicago poets in an atmosphere of canary-colored waistcoats, first names, and a round oak table." With a membership slightly under 200, the Tavern Club continues to maintain a slightly Bohemian character in comparison with the other clubs in town. Mascot toy bears adorn every nook and cranny of the dark-paneled and dimly lighted building, which still conveys the atmosphere of an "old boys club" that is interested in promoting literature, drama, and the arts throughout the city.

The Algonquin Club, located in the Back Bay at 219 Commonwealth Avenue, was founded in 1886 by General Charles H. Taylor, the swamp Yankee who resurrected the old Democratic newspaper the *Boston Globe*. The Algonquin's handsome six-story granite building was designed by Charles Follen McKim, the architect who created the nearby Boston Public Library at Copley Square. The overhead expenses of the Algonquin led the club to the brink of bankruptcy on two occasions—once during World War I, and again during the Great Depression. As recently as 1984 the Algonquin's membership was predominantly WASP, but in more recent years it has reflected a more diversified meritocracy. In the early 1980s it was the first of the private clubs to admit women, and in 1986 it admitted the club's first African American member.

The St. Botolph Club was named after the old name for Boston—St. Botolph's Town, in Lincolnshire, England. It was originally established in 1880 at 85 Boylston Street, opposite the Public Garden. It later moved to 115 Commonwealth Avenue, where it drew heavily from Boston's world of arts and letters, providing a popular meeting place for musicians, poets, artists, collectors, and authors. In 1972 the St. Botolph Club moved into the stately three-story Sprague family mansion at 199 Commonwealth Avenue, looking out onto the seated statue of the eminent Harvard historian Samuel Eliot Morison on the Mall.

The Chilton Club is one of the oldest and most prestigious clubs for Boston women. It has been described by the author Cleveland Amory as a female version of the Somerset Club—a place "where women can come and 'be women.'" There are three entrances to the Chilton Club—one for members only, off Commonwealth Avenue; one for members and their guests, off Dartmouth Street; and one for tradespeople and servants, off the alley. No member of the press is ever admitted to the club, and society editors are carefully instructed not to mention club activities in their columns. Members of the Chilton Club involve themselves in gardening, debutante teas, the Winter Ball, charity works for local hospitals, and fundraising for museums and other cultural institutions of Boston.

Cocoanut Grove Fire

During the 1930s and 1940s, Boston had a number of first-rate nightclubs, which featured dining, dancing, top-name bands, and floor shows. The center of the African American community in the South End, at the intersection of Columbus Avenue and Massachusetts Avenue, was one area where nightclubs featured the jazz bands of such well-known musicians as Duke Ellington, Fats Waller, and Count Basie. Closer to downtown, the Bay Village section of Boston had several clubs such as the Latin Quarter and the Cocoanut Grove, where groups went to celebrate anniversaries, birthdays, graduations, and other special events. During the early war years of the 1940s, families held parties at the Cocoanut Grove for young men going into the service.

November 28, 1942, was planned to be a night of celebration for members of the championship Boston College football team and their families, after an anticipated easy victory over their traditional rival, Holy Cross. When Holy Cross upset the highly rated Boston College team at Fenway Park by the embarrassing score of 55 to 12, the Eagles and their supporters had no stomach for entertainment, so they all went home to nurse their wounded pride. And it was fortunate they did. That night the Cocoanut Grove, elaborately decorated and crowded with customers, burst into an inferno of flame that trapped helpless men and women inside the building, whose doors did not open outward. The smoke, the flames, and especially the toxic fumes of plastic decorations proved fatal to 492 people, who perished in the second-worst single-building fire in American history. One benefit drawn from this tragedy was that stricter fire laws and regulations were put in place, requiring all doors in public buildings to open outward, and greater care was taken to fireproof textile materials. In caring for victims of the fire, a new drug called penicillin was discovered to be extremely beneficial in treating burns, a valuable discovery for wounded servicemen in World War II.

The Combat Zone

Almost every major city has a "red light district" where lustful pleasures of vice are available for a price. Over the years Boston has been no different. During the pre-Revolutionary period, a section of Mount Vernon, the westernmost of Boston's three hills, was often referred to as "Mount Whoredom," and identified as such on British military maps of the 1770s. According to the historian Walter Muir Whitehill, one British officer observed in his 1775 journal that while Boston might be too puritanical to construct a playhouse, no town of its size "cou'd turn out more whores than this cou'd."

By the early 1800s scandalous nighttime activities had migrated to the crowded streets of the waterfront district. Ann Street in particular became notorious for its disorderly houses, raucous singing, noisy fiddle playing, and violent street brawls. In July 1825 Mayor Josiah Quincy personally led a posse of burly truckmen to an establishment called the Beehive, to break up nightly disturbances which had gone on for a week. According to contemporary reports, "the nymphs of Ann Street" were sent scurrying into the night.

During the early part of the twentieth century, Scollay Square was the place where Harvard undergraduates and bald-headed old men could be titillated by the naughty gyrations of stripteasers, and where soldiers and sailors could enjoy the pleasures of a weekend pass. The years of World War II drew customers away from Scollay Square, however, and brought them down to the southern end of Washington Street for their weekend entertainment. The Silver Dollar Bar was just one of a number of saloons in the district between the lower parts of Tremont and Washington Streets, where prostitutes prowled the bars and cruised the alleyways. The presence of so many members of the military at this time gave the district the name of the Combat Zone.

Although a beefed-up police presence gradually reduced the number of prostitutes, by the 1960s and 1970s streets in the area extending from Chinatown to the Theater District were lined with exotic bars, strip joints, and topless dance palaces. As many of the strip joints closed down, and as some of the saloons went out of business, the Combat Zone became a center for pornographic bookstores, where people of all ages could be found browsing at all hours of the day or night.

In recent years the siting of major medical establishments to the south, the expansion of retail businesses and hotels from the north, the activities of the police, and the organized protests of Chinatown residents seem destined to squeeze the Combat Zone out of existence. If history is any guide, though, it will soon reappear in a new location.

The Common

In 1634 the early settlers of Boston purchased 45 acres of land from the Reverend William Blackstone, an eccentric Anglican clergyman whose pleasant solitude on the Shawmut Peninsula had been interrupted in the autumn of 1630, when John Winthrop and the members of the Massachusetts Bay Company arrived. The settlers set aside this parcel of land for what they called "Common use," a phrase clarified by a law of 1649 that stated: "There shall be no land granted either for house plott or garden out of ye open ground or Common field."

On this common land, against the background of the town's three towering hills (the Trimountain), the townspeople exercised their horses, pastured their cattle, and drilled their militia companies. During colonial times the Common also became a popular spot for public executions. Two Quakers, named Marmaduke Stevenson and William Robinson, were hanged on the Common on October 27, 1659, and the following year Mary Dyer, another Quaker, was hanged in the same place for defying the law and returning to Boston after her exile. The Common was also occasionally the scene of duels, some of little significance, but a few that were tragic. In 1728, for example, a young man named Henry Phillips killed a friend named Benjamin Woodbridge after a tavern argument led to a sword duel on the Common. Phillips was spirited away to France by his respected cousin, Peter Faneuil, only to die of loneliness and a broken heart in a strange and foreign land. In the same year the town fathers banned horses and carriages from the Common and turned the park into a rather fashionable setting for late-afternoon promenades, although cows were still permitted to roam freely well into the nineteenth century.

During the War of Independence, the Common was commandeered by General Thomas Gage for the construction of barracks for the British troops sent over to enforce the Coercive Acts. The winter of 1775–76 was so severely cold in British-occupied Boston that over one hundred buildings were pulled down and used for firewood. The handsome elm trees along the Common Mall were also sacrificed to the desperate need for fuel. Only when the British were forced to evacuate Boston in March 1776 was Boston Common spared such indignities and destruction.

Once the United States had achieved independence, Boston returned to peaceful pursuits and commercial enterprises. As the town's economy prospered, its population began to increase and the appearance of the town greatly improved. In 1810 a series of handsome townhouses designed by Charles Bulfinch went up along the east side of Tremont Street, opposite the Boston Common Mall. Called Colonnade Row, and extending from West Street to Mason Street, this development greatly enhanced the central area of Boston. In 1835 Mayor Theodore Lyman, Jr., had a fine alley of trees placed along the Common, from Park Street to West Street, replacing the old elms which had been cut down during the Revolution and providing a fashionable promenade. The Common now became a park everyone in the city could enjoy. Youngsters went coasting down Flagstaff Hill in the winter; during the spring, young "gallants" went strolling with their sweethearts; in the summer months entire families would spend a Sunday afternoon strolling around the Common.

For the next eighty years, the selectmen of the town stubbornly refused to allow the "advocates of trade" to make the slightest incursion into a public space that over the years had come to assume the lofty status of sacred property. Gasps of horror greeted the semi-humorous proposal made by James Michael Curley in 1915, just after his first election as mayor of Boston, that a water-pumping station be constructed under the Boston Common. Although nothing came of Curley's irreverent suggestion, the idea of finding some practical use for this valuable parcel of land in the heart of downtown Boston did not go away. During his term as governor, Maurice Tobin proposed a garage under the Common; his successor, Robert Bradford, made a similar proposal, but no action was taken.

Shortly after his fourth and final election as mayor of Boston in 1946, Curley took up the idea of an underground garage, sparking a fierce debate among the members of the state legislature. Supported by Governor Paul A. Dever and Senate President John E. Powers, however, the General Court finally approved a bill allowing a 1500-car garage to be constructed underneath Boston Common. A series of court appeals failed to prevent implementation of the bill, and in 1955 Mayor John B. Hynes set in motion the necessary funding authority. Once construction was under way, the residents of Beacon Hill and Charles Street complained continuously about the dust and the incessant banging of pile drivers from morning till night. Those "earthquake tremors" provided the background for the bitter ruminations of the poet Robert Lowell one March morning while he contemplated Augustus Saint-Gaudens's imposing tribute to Colonel Robert Gould Shaw and the gallant 54th Regiment on the edge of the Common across from the State House. As he reflected on Boston's glorious past and compromised present, he heard behind him "yellow dinosaur steam shovels" grunting away as they cropped up "tons of mush and grass to gouge their underground garage." A three-level structure underneath Boston Common was finally completed in November 1961, amid charges of widespread graft, scandal, and corruption.

USS *Constitution*

The USS *Constitution* is the oldest commissioned warship afloat in the world today. The *Constitution* was built in 1797 at Edmund Hartt's shipyard in the North End of Boston, at a cost of $302,718. It was 204 feet long, with a 43.5-foot beam, and made of white oak from Massachusetts and Maine, live oak from Georgia, and yellow pine from Georgia and South Carolina. The copper sheathing, bolts, and fittings were made by Paul Revere, using the new process of drawn copper. While excited Bostonians watched, the new vessel was launched on Columbus Day 1797. Funds for the berth at the Charlestown Navy Yard were appropriated on March 1, 1808, and in 1803 the USS *Constitution* set off across the Atlantic for the shores of Tripoli.

One of six powerful frigates commissioned by President George Washington to safeguard American merchant vessels, the *Constitution* began its celebrated career by bombarding Tripoli in 1805 to punish the Barbary pirates who were demanding tribute payments. The *Constitution*'s greatest victory came during the War of 1812, with its victory over the British warship HMS *Guerriere* in one of the great sea battles of all time. The American vessel was nicknamed "Old Ironsides" by British sailors, who watched in frustration as their cannonballs bounced off its sturdy oak hull. The *Constitution* fought forty engagements and never lost one.

After its military career the *Constitution* was saved from destruction on three occasions, each time by efforts originating in Boston. In 1830 it was rescued from the scrap heap by public indignation, aroused by Oliver Wendell Holmes's stirring poem "Old Ironsides," written while he was still a law student at Harvard. It began with the line schoolchildren all over the nation were to memorize: "Aye, tear her tattered ensign down / long has it waved on high; / And many an eye has danced to see / that banner in the sky." Nearly seventy-five years later, in 1904, when the Navy planned to use the old vessel for target practice, the Massachusetts Society of the Daughters of 1812 launched a restoration fund that saved the historic ship. And during the 1920s, when it was badly in need of restoration, the schoolchildren of Boston sent in their pennies to start a fundraising drive that spread to all the classrooms of America, producing the money that finally kept the old ship afloat.

In 1954 Congressman John W. McCormack of Boston sponsored the federal legislation that officially designated Boston as the ship's permanent home port. The USS *Constitution* is now berthed at the Charlestown Navy Yard, and at present has a crew of seventy active-duty officers and seamen. Every year, on the Fourth of July, the USS *Constitution* is towed out into Boston Harbor for its annual "turnaround" cruise that reverses its position at the berth in the Charlestown Navy Yard. In 1997, on the occasion of the ship's bicentennial, "Old Ironsides" headed out into the Atlantic Ocean—white canvas billowing from all three masts—for the first time in 116 years sailing under her own power.

John Singleton Copley

The noted Boston painter John Singleton Copley was born in Boston in 1738. He studied drawing with his stepfather, Peter Pelham, a colonial artist and engraver, and began to produce serious paintings of his own when he was only fifteen years old. At first he depicted historical subjects based on earlier engravings, but soon he was specializing in portraits of the families of Boston's growing merchant class. Largely self-taught, Copley drew his ideas and techniques from other engravers as well as from English prints. He was especially influenced by a Scots artist named John Smibert, who arrived in Boston in 1730 and who painted such prominent colonial figures as Edmund Quincy and Peter Faneuil. Copley's portraits were very realistic, with an uncanny way of revealing the distinctive character and personality of his subjects. Although he painted some full-length portraits, he appeared to favor half-length or quarter-length canvases. In time he would become famous for his portraits of such Revolutionary leaders as Samuel Adams and Paul Revere, which now hang in Boston's Museum of Fine Arts.

In 1769 Copley married Susannah Clarke, the daughter of a wealthy Boston merchant, and was able to purchase a 20-acre farm with three houses along Beacon Hill facing the Boston Common, only a short distance from John Hancock's elegant mansion. In an effort to project his talents across the Atlantic, Copley sent a painting of his half-brother, Henry Pelham, called "Boy with a Squirrel," to be exhibited by the Society of Artists in London, where it received mixed reviews. The painting drew the attention of the influential Pennsylvania painter Benjamin West, however, who urged Copley to come to London to study.

West's appeal coincided with Copley's desire to escape the growing Revolutionary crisis, especially tensions with close friends, some of whom were loyalists and others patriots. In 1774 Copley sailed to England, where he was soon joined by his wife and family. There he started a new career, continuing to paint portraits but also developing a realistic style of portraying scenes from recent history. His haunting marine painting *Watson and the Shark* (1778), depicting a sensational attack in the waters off Cuba, is an example of his flair for the dramatic. When the Revolution was over, Copley sold his Boston property to the Mount Vernon Proprietors, who were developing the south slope of Beacon Hill. Complaining that because he was far away in England the entrepreneurs had taken unfair advantage of him, Copley initiated a lawsuit in an effort to get a better price for his property. The painter's claims were denied, however, and he was forced to spend the remaining years of his life

in England, with a dwindling income. Debt-ridden, ill, and enfee-
bled, John Singleton Copley never returned to his native land. He
died of a stroke in London in 1815.

Curse of the Bambino

In 1920 Harry Frazee, owner of the Red Sox, financial entrepreneur, and self-appointed impresario, traded Babe Ruth, the famous
pitcher and home-run slugger and arguably the greatest player in
baseball, to Boston's traditional rival—the New York Yankees.

The Babe started his career with Baltimore in 1914; the following year the Boston Red Sox bought Ruth's contract from the Ori-
oles and immediately put him in the starting lineup. Although Babe
Ruth eventually became known as a home-run hitter, it was as a
pitcher that he made a name for himself with the Red Sox. When
the Sox beat the Brooklyn Dodgers four games to one in the 1916
World Series, Babe Ruth contributed to the victory by hurling a
six-hit game. Ruth's performance on the mound was also a major
factor in the Red Sox defeat of the Chicago Cubs in the World Series in 1918. After such a promising start, Boston fans could hardly
believe that Frazee could sell the Babe. But he did. The shocking
transaction brought $100,000, which Frazee used to underwrite
the New York production costs of the musical *No, No, Nanette*.
Frazee shrugged off the wave of local outrage by saying that without
Babe Ruth, known as "the Bambino," the Red Sox now could go
into the open market and buy other players who would build a
stronger and better team.

As far as many Boston sports fans were concerned, this act of vil-
lainous treachery put a curse on Boston baseball—and indeed on
Boston itself. After 1920, they pointed out, thanks to the Curse of
the Bambino, the Red Sox never again won a World Series, and
went from year to year breaking the hearts of their loyal supporters.

Many observers of the larger Boston scene feel that it is no coincidence that since 1920 more and more of Boston's other cherished
institutions have also followed the Bambino to New York. The cen-

ters of banking are now to be found on Wall Street, and the major theater productions originate both on and off Broadway. The centers of writing and publishing are all in New York, and recently the *New York Times* has taken over the *Boston Globe*. Most of Boston's retail industry has all but disappeared, and where once Jordan Marsh dominated Washington Street, the new building now bears the title of New York's famous department store, Macy's. All that started, they insist, when Boston let Babe Ruth go to New York.

Hopes that the Curse of the Bambino might finally be lifted burned brightly in the hearts of Red Sox fans during the autumn of 1999, after the Boston team overcame a two-game deficit to defeat the Cleveland Indians for the division title. Buoyed by the sparkling pitching of Pedro Martinez, the Sox then faced their archrivals, the New York Yankees, in the American League championship series. The Sox went down to defeat, and the Bronx Bombers went on to their twenty-fifth World Series title since Boston sold Babe Ruth to New York. The Curse of the Bambino is still very much alive.

❖

Frances Greely Curtis

The first woman to run for the office of mayor in Boston was Frances Greely Curtis. A member of the Women's City Club of Boston, and an elected member of the Boston School Committee for thirteen years, in 1925 Miss Curtis opened a new epoch in Boston politics by entering the mayoral race. Not only was she the first woman to aspire to the office in the city's 103-year existence, but she was also the first woman to enter such a highly disputed race. She was the lone woman in a field of some seventeen men, many of whom were veteran machine politicians.

Frances Curtis ran a simple campaign, acting as her own campaign manager and working out of her own home. She had polled 79,139 votes when she won a place on the School Committee in 1921, while James Michael Curley received only 74,261 votes that year in his campaign for mayor. She obviously hoped that those same supporters would help her achieve her goal in 1925. She said she could not understand why anyone would spend more than $40,000 (the salary for four years as mayor of Boston) on a campaign for the job, and refused to pay thousands of dollars for dazzling posters or fancy automobiles because she felt that such trappings had no place in a serious campaign. She wanted her campaign to be a contest of "character," measuring up to the high standards of political decency held by the good people of Boston.

Miss Curtis saw the job of mayor as large-scale housekeeping, in which any woman who knew the importance of managing a home on a strict budget could be successful. While men may earn the money, she noted, it was the woman's job to use the funds effectively to best advantage. She thought that as a woman she would be able to bring this idea of small-scale budget management to the large-scale needs of the city.

Unfortunately for Frances Curtis, her opponents' flashy campaigns, torchlight parades, and machine politics prevailed over her idealistic approach. She failed to get the required number of signatures to place her name on the ballot, and lost the election to Malcolm Nichols, who served as mayor of Boston from 1926 to 1930. Even though she did not become mayor, Frances Greely Curtis inspired other Boston women to hope that political opportunities were open to anyone who wanted to take a stand for democratic principles.

❖

Custom House

In 1837, when construction began on the Custom House, Boston was at the height of what has been called its granite age. Technical advances had made the cutting, hoisting, and hauling of heavy stones easier and less expensive. The new granite buildings going up all around town were a stark contrast to the red-brick federalist buildings that had come to dominate Boston in the generation following the Revolution. Granite was an ideal material for the new

Greek Revival style of architecture that became fashionable in Boston during the 1830s. Edward Everett spoke frequently of the similarities between Ancient Greece and contemporary New England, stating that they were both "iron bound, sterile, and free." And before long, the style of public buildings, private homes, banks, and museums proclaimed Boston to be the Athens of America.

Construction of the Custom House was completed in 1849. The designer of the building was Ammi B. Young, who supplied the Boston building commissioners with the original plans for a neoclassical structure. Young's plan for the Custom House was a simple cross shape, with one arm longer than the other, and crowned by a gabled roof with four pediments. The building was capped by a low, skylit Roman dome; below the pediments ran a Doric order entablature. The elegant simplicity of this structure made it one of Boston's finest neoclassical buildings, although Young's dedication to the style created some practical problems. The overhanging porticos, for example, darkened the interior, and denied the office workers much-needed light. At the time of its construction, the Custom House was one of the most expensive government buildings ever built. Each one of its massive Doric columns is a single shaft of granite weighing forty-two tons.

In 1915 a 495-foot tower was added to the original structure. Since it was authorized by the federal government, the tower was exempt from city-imposed height restrictions. As a result, the Custom House, with its new tower, remained the tallest building in Boston until the John Hancock Building was constructed in 1947 near Copley Square.

For a period of time during the 1980s, when the federal government no longer had use for the 152-year-old structure, there was some question about the future ownership and purpose of the Custom House. Eventually the Marriott Vacation Club International paid $6.1 million to the U.S. General Services Administration, and another $2.1 million to the City of Boston, for a 60-year lease on the building and an option to purchase after 60 years. After extensive renovations, Marriott created 84 time-share units in the 26-story tower, overlooking Boston Harbor, Faneuil Hall, Quincy Market, the North End, and the Financial District, that generated more than $43 million in sales revenue. Despite the construction of numerous high-rise buildings in recent years, the rather preposterous Custom House Tower, with its pointed top and garishly lighted clock, remains a distinctive part of the Boston skyline.

Mary Dyer

Durgin-Park

Announcing that it was "established before you were born," Durgin-Park Restaurant is one of Boston's most colorful eating places, a favorite of visitors and residents alike. Located in the historical surroundings of the Faneuil Hall Marketplace, Durgin-Park has become celebrated as much for its surly waitresses as for its ample servings of family-style food.

Durgin-Park was opened in 1826, when John Quincy Adams was still President of the United States, by John Durgin and a silent partner named Eldredge Park. Durgin and his family had operated restaurants in Boston since the Revolutionary War, but this new enterprise became a permanent part of Boston history. It excels at plain Yankee fare—clam chowder, cornbread, broiled scrod, venison pie, lobster, Indian pudding—served at plain prices in plain surroundings. Unshaded electric light bulbs still hang from tin ceilings over long wooden tables covered by red-checkered tablecloths. While some old customers complain that the smart-alecky, wisecracking waitresses are not as tough as they used to be, the crusty, down-to-earth atmosphere of Durgin-Park keeps the customers coming.

Mary Dyer

Mary Dyer was a good friend of Anne Hutchinson and a sympathetic supporter during Hutchinson's controversy with the Puritan town fathers. After her friend's trial and subsequent exile, in 1638 Mary Dyer and her husband moved south to Rhode Island. When she became a Quaker, Dyer found herself a member of a religion outlawed in the Massachusetts Bay Colony. Puritans especially detested members of the Society of Friends (also known as Quakers), those "Children of the Light" who followed the ministry of George Fox in seventeenth-century England. They declined to pay tithes to the established church, refused to take off their hats, and repudiated the leadership of those they called a "hireling ministry." Puritans looked upon Quakers as both religious heretics and political subversives.

Mary Dyer first felt the weight of Puritan oppression when she was arrested while traveling through Boston in 1657. After her release, she returned to Rhode Island, but two years later she was once again taken into custody in the Puritan capital when she returned to visit other Quakers who were imprisoned and awaiting execution. William Robinson and Marmaduke Stevenson, along with Mary Dyer, were led from their cells to the Common with a 200-man guard. Anytime one of the Quakers tried to harangue the crowd, the drummers drowned them out. Following the execution of the two men, Mary Dyer was led to the gallows, blindfolded, and a noose was placed around her neck. At the last minute, her son interceded on her behalf. The authorities relented, and ordered her transported out of the colony—with a warning not to return. When Mary Dyer returned the following year to spread the doctrines of Quakerism, she was promptly taken into custody, sentenced to death, and hanged on Boston Common on June 1, 1660. The death of Mary Dyer eventually prompted King Charles II to order the anti-Quaker statutes to be overturned.

In 1959 a seated bronze statue of Mary Dyer was placed in front of the east wing of the Massachusetts State House. The work of Sylvia Shaw Judson, the statue was erected by the Commonwealth with a legacy from Zenas Ellis of Fair Haven, Vermont. Seated modestly, her eyes lowered and her hands folded on her lap, Mary Dyer faces the Boston Common, the scene of her brutal execution.

Emerald Necklace

Emerald Necklace

After the Civil War, Boston's downtown was becoming congested, and the multiplication of both public buildings and commercial structures was fast eliminating green space. Prompted by the growing interest in good health, exercise, outdoor living, and the conservation of natural resources, many prominent civic leaders decided it was time to create a series of playgrounds, scenic parks, and recreational areas in the city.

In 1878 city authorities brought to Boston the famous landscape architect Frederick Law Olmsted, a native of Hartford, Connecticut, and the designer of New York's Central Park, to create an attractive sweep of parkways that would serve to define the boundaries of the city as well as to provide places of natural beauty for the enjoyment and edification of all its citizens. Constructed between 1878 and 1895, Olmsted's park system in Boston was one of the most massive public projects ever undertaken by the city. Encompassing over two thousand acres of open land, Olmsted's plan for a string of sparkling ponds and sylvan parks—eventually called the Emerald Necklace—ran west from the Public Garden down Commonwealth Avenue to the Fenway; across the Back Bay Fens; south along the Jamaicaway to Franklin Park; then east down Columbia Road and along the South Boston strandway to Marine Park at City Point.

To persuade practical-minded city administrators, Olmsted tactfully camouflaged his aesthetic visions by emphasizing that his plans would provide a better drainage system and more effective flood control. In April 1886 Olmsted explained to the Boston Society of Architects how the Fens, where the Muddy River meets the Charles, was crucial to his overall plan. He worked with the superintendent of sewers and the city engineer, Joseph Phineas Davis, in constructing a series of conduits, channels, and causeways that stretched for some five miles, from the Fens to Franklin Park. Olmsted regarded the short Boylston Street bridge over the Fens as "the most conspicuous object in all the scheme," and asked his friend Henry Hobson Richardson, the noted architect of Trinity Church, to design the handsome archway.

Beyond the mundane if important goal of flood control, Olmsted's Emerald Necklace scheme had a more idealistic purpose. According to the landscape historian Cynthia Zaitzevsky, Olmsted felt that the kind of civilized city life he had experienced growing up in Hartford, Connecticut, was under threat in the nation's larger cities. He planned his parks, therefore, as neighborhood "breathing spaces," designed to provide fresh air and healthy exercise for the people living in tenement districts. The urban biographer Witold Rybczynski agrees that Olmsted intended his parks to have a "social role," offering a meeting place that reinforced "social discourse." Olmsted believed that well-designed parks, by improving the landscape, would have a civilizing effect on the people who used them.

Unfortunately, a land development boom in late nineteenth-century Dorchester did away with visions of a rustic, tree-lined Columbia Road. In 1897 plans calling for the widening of streets along the boulevard, accompanied by the installation of telephone wires, electrical cable, and street lights, caused Boston's street commissioners to give up hope for the completion of Olmsted's original design. Plans for the boulevard remain unfinished to this day. The Metropolitan District Commission has never taken responsibility for the management of Columbia Road, and most residents today are unaware that is was supposed to have been the final link in the Emerald Necklace.

Although Olmsted died in 1903, his influence on the Boston landscape continued. In 1900 his son, Frederick Law Olmsted, Jr., had created at Harvard the first formal training program in landscape architecture; he also became a major influence in establishing the National Park Service. The Olmsted family business continued to operate in the town of Brookline until 1979, when the Park Service took over custody of its documents, plans, and photographs. The Park Service has turned the Olmsted Historic Site on Warren Street into an educational and research institution that maintains archives and offers courses in landscape history and design.

❖

Leif Ericsson

Although Christopher Columbus is widely regarded as the man who discovered America in 1492, many Americans propose other candidates. The Irish argue that St. Brendan arrived as early as the sixth century; the Welsh insist that Prince Madoc made the voyage in 1170; the Portuguese claim João Corte Real was the true discoverer of the New World.

Those of Scandinavian heritage are certain that the Norsemen—the Vikings—were the first to arrive in North America, and claim that archeological remains of Norse explorers can be found in Newfoundland, dating back 500 years before Columbus landed in the Bahamas. Drawing upon traditions handed down in the Norse sagas, many suggest that the Vikings sailed south from Newfoundland and entered New England waters. Residents of Newport, Rhode Island, point to a round stone tower as evidence of a Viking landing; citizens of Dighton, Massachusetts, argue that markings on a large rock near the Taunton River are actually Norse carvings.

During the nineteenth century a number of Bostonians were convinced that the Norse sagas provided evidence of the Viking presence in the Boston area. Eben Norton Horsford, a professor of chemistry at Harvard College, maintained that Leif Ericsson and his Vikings sailed their longboats into Boston Harbor in the year 1000. He also claimed that Leif's brother Thorwald took the boats up the Charles River as far as a site called Norumbega—which Horsford said was a corruption of the word Norway.

As a permanent reminder to his fellow Bostonians of their Viking roots, on October 29, 1887, Horsford unveiled a bronze statue of Leif Ericsson standing in the bow of a Viking longboat. Fashioned by the well-known sculptor Anne Whitney, the figure stands at the corner of Commonwealth Avenue and Bay State Road, near Kenmore Square. Not long after providing the statue of Leif, Horsford purchased a piece of land along the Charles River, where he erected a large stone tower, similar to the one at Newport, Rhode Island, with a metal plate commemorating what he was convinced had been a Viking settlement. The tower still stands behind a small picnic area off Norumbega Road, not far from the intersection of Route 128 and the Massachusetts Turnpike.

Evacuation Day

Evacuation Day is a holiday in Suffolk County that commemorates the evacuation in March 1776 of the British occupation forces from the town of Boston during the Revolutionary War. Additional British military forces had been brought to the Boston area during the early 1770s as tensions increased between the Boston patriots and the mother country. The Boston Tea Party in December 1773 had led Parliament to close the Port of Boston, to place Boston under martial law, and to replace the civil governor with a military governor-general. Additional reinforcements of British troops turned Boston into a virtual armed camp, with a force of some 9,000 British regulars—in a town whose civilian population had already dropped below 10,000—serving as a veritable occupation force at their base on the Shawmut peninsula.

Soon after General George Washington came to Cambridge in July 1775 to take over command of the Continental Army, he set his mind on driving the British forces out of Boston. His determination to force an evacuation was strengthened when Colonel Henry Knox, a former Boston bookseller, arrived with a large number of heavy cannon he had dragged through deep snowdrifts all the way from Fort Ticonderoga in upstate New York. With the arrival of these guns in Cambridge on January 24, 1776, Washington began to make plans for moving his men into the nearby peninsula called Dorchester Neck and mounting his guns on a series of hills called Dorchester Heights.

On the night of March 4, under cover of diversionary bombardments at other locations, a long train of some 2,000 American soldiers made their way secretly and silently through Roxbury and Dorchester, and then onto the peninsula of Dorchester Neck (the present South Boston). Working swiftly through the night, the rebels constructed fortifications and gun emplacements along the heights that overlooked the town of Boston and Boston Harbor. When the British awoke the next morning, they discovered American guns menacing not only their forces in the town but also their ships, riding helplessly at anchor in the harbor.

Although Sir William Howe considered a military response, he decided that evacuation was the only sensible alternative. In return for a British promise not to burn the town, Washington agreed not to fire upon the British vessels as they departed. The transports, carrying the 9,000-man British military garrison, along with nearly 1,100 American loyalists, sailed into Boston Harbor on their way to Nova Scotia. On March 17, 1776, General Washington's troops marched into the liberated town of Boston, to find it a tragic shambles. Trees had been cut down, barns and warehouses razed, and fences ripped down for firewood. Churches and meetinghouses had been used as stables, private homes had been used as hospitals, monuments and public buildings had been defaced and mutilated. Much work had to be done to restore the old colonial town to its former condition.

That the liberation of the town took place on March 17—the feast day of St. Patrick—did not go unnoticed among the later Irish Catholic population of Boston. Indeed, one of the enduring legends among the Boston Irish was that in consideration of the date, and because one of his military aides, Brigadier General John Sullivan, was an Irishman, General Washington had proclaimed the password for that day to be "Saint Patrick." For many years the Irish of the city held parades on March 17 in honor of St. Patrick, and during the 1880s the city fathers authorized the closing of the Boston Public Library on that day, much to the disgust of local Yankees. In 1901 the City of Boston authorized a St. Patrick's Day parade in South Boston on March 17 under the guise of a public commemoration of the British evacuation of Boston in 1776. Since that time, Boston has had an official holiday on Evacuation Day, which fortuitously (and incidentally, of course) happens to fall on St. Patrick's Day—thus neatly avoiding a conflict between church and state.

54th Regiment

Famine Memorial

In a small, tree-shaded triangular plot at the intersection of Washington and School Streets in downtown Boston, along the Freedom Trail, stands a memorial commemorating the 150th anniversary of the Great Famine that between 1845 and 1850 caused so many immigrants from Ireland to come to Boston. The idea for such a memorial in Boston was first suggested in 1991 by then-mayor Raymond L. Flynn. In April 1996 the idea was renewed by Mayor Thomas M. Menino, who asked the developer Thomas J. Flatley, an Irish immigrant from Mayo, to head the Boston Memorial Project. Flatley called upon representatives of Boston's business, civic, religious, and academic communities to form a 52-member committee to study the project.

In the course of two years the Boston community, from large corporations to individual donors, raised one million dollars to construct a 6,000-square-foot Famine Memorial Park in the heart of downtown Boston, not far from the waterfront where the immigrants came ashore and only a block away from Franklin Street, where the first Catholic church was located. Working closely with the Boston Art Commission, as well as with a variety of citizen groups and neighboring businesses, the committee selected a landscape-design team to create the park. It then chose Robert Shure of Woburn, a nationally known artist, as the sculptor for the memorial.

Unveiled on June 28, 1998, the Irish Famine Memorial consists of two life-size groups: one depicts a family back in Ireland, impoverished and desperate; the other depicts a family arriving in Boston, filled with hope and determination. Around this central monument have been placed a series of eight granite pedestals on which brief narratives provide visitors with moving episodes related to "An Gorta Mor"—the Great Famine. Over one million Irish people died of starvation when a fungus destroyed the country's potato crop, and another two million people left the Old Country forever, great numbers of them coming to America.

In addition to commemorating the Great Famine, the Irish Famine Memorial is also a tribute to all other immigrant groups who have come to Boston, seeking hope and refuge in the New World. The Famine Institute of Boston was designed as a living memorial, which draws upon the historical experience of the nineteenth-century famine to provide education and assistance for people suffering famine throughout the world today.

Faneuil Hall

In 1742 a two-story brick building was constructed near Boston's Town Dock at "the cost and charge" of Peter Faneuil, the son of a French Huguenot (Protestant) merchant from La Rochelle, who had settled in Boston in 1691. In 1749 young Faneuil announced that he wanted to express his appreciation to the town by offering to "erect a noble and complete structure . . . for the sole use and benefit and advantage of the town." Because a number of local businessmen feared the competition posed by a large central market, the town council almost did not accept the generous offer, but finally voted to do so by the slim margin of 367 to 360. In the Puritan tradition, Faneuil Hall was designed to be a multipurpose building. On the ground floor was a public market where citizens could purchase their meat, fruits and vegetables, and fish. The second floor contained rooms for town officials, as well as a sizable hall for town meetings and civic gatherings. A fire in 1761 consumed everything except the brick exterior, but the structure was soon rebuilt in its original form.

In 1805 Charles Bulfinch enlarged Faneuil Hall to its present form by doubling the width of the building and adding a third story, which eventually became the headquarters of the Ancient and Honorable Artillery Company. Even after Boston became a city in 1822, Faneuil Hall continued to be used for civic functions and political gatherings, soon held against the background of George Healy's impressive painting of Massachusetts Senator Daniel Webster staunchly defending the Union in his second reply to Senator Robert Y. Hayne of South Carolina.

Access and control of Faneuil Hall during the early nineteenth century was generally a prerogative of the city government. A resident had to petition to use Faneuil Hall, present at least fifty signatures, and obtain approval, usually from the Board of Aldermen, although members of the Common Council often insisted on exercising their powers. Petitioners had to pay the city a rental fee of $20 for day use, $25 for evening use, and $50 for a dinner. They were also required to absorb the costs of any police protection, as well as of any damages incurred. Use of the Hall was denied a number of times before 1860, either because of the views of city leaders or as a result of mob action. In 1847, for example, a temperance meeting was broken up by an angry mob; in 1850 a Free-Soil meeting suffered the same fate; and that same year Daniel Webster was refused use of the Hall because he had supported the Compromise of 1850. Throughout the antebellum years, Abolitionist groups were often turned down, usually because city authorities feared the outbreak of mob violence.

After the Civil War, Faneuil Hall continued as the site for appearances of such old-time political figures as the Massachusetts Senator Charles Sumner, the abolitionist orator Wendell Phillips, the African American spokesman Frederick Douglass, and the noted physician and writer Oliver Wendell Holmes. By the 1870s and 1880s, however, the rules governing the use of the Hall began to change, and so did the nature of the speakers. Free use of the Hall was first proposed in the Common Council in 1878, and in 1879 the rental fees were lowered to $10 a day and $15 for an evening event. In 1888 the practice of waiving fees was introduced, first for veterans' groups, and then for charitable associations. By 1895 the rules were changed to allow fees to be waived for any group that formally requested it, and petitions with fewer than fifty signatures were also accepted.

Because of these modifications in the rules, the use of Faneuil Hall increased markedly during the late nineteenth century, and the issues debated there reflected the anxieties and concerns of more working-class members of the community. During the 1870s, for example, groups of teachers and members of the fire department used the Hall to voice their opinions; during the 1880s newsboys, garment workers, and railroad conductors rallied for higher pay and better working conditions; and during the 1890s local charitable groups, fraternal organizations, and patriotic societies used the Hall's facilities to publicize their activities.

The new city charter in 1910 made granting permission for the use of Faneuil Hall a prerogative of the mayor or his designate. At the present time, Faneuil Hall is still a busy place. The first floor, still a marketplace, has been substantially expanded and modernized, but merchants and salespeople operate their shops and services in ways of which Peter Faneuil would have approved. An information desk staffed by personnel from the National Park Service is also located on the first floor for the benefit of tourists and visitors. On the third floor, above the Great Hall, which is still used for political and civic functions, is the home of the Ancient and Honorable Artillery Company of Massachusetts, with a meeting hall, a library, and a museum of military history.

Since 1741 the cupola of Faneuil Hall has been surmounted by a huge copper weathervane, originally designed by Deacon Shem Drowne in the form of a gilded grasshopper. According to many authorities, the figure was modeled on a similar grasshopper weathervane atop the Royal Exchange in London, placed there by the British financier and founder of the Exchange, Sir Thomas Gresham. On January 4, 1973, the caretaker of Faneuil Hall found that the grasshopper weathervane was missing. No one could understand how a large metal ornament four feet high and weighing nearly forty pounds could be taken from the roof without anyone seeing it happen. State police and city detectives launched an all-points search for the priceless relic, with no results—until they received a tip. They discovered the weathervane hidden away in the belfry of Faneuil Hall itself, tucked under a pile of old flags. The grasshopper was promptly restored to its rightful place atop the cupola, and Bostonians could go back about their business.

Fannie Farmer

Fannie Merritt Farmer, born in 1857, was the eldest daughter of a father who was an editor and printer, and a mother who was described as a "notable housewife." While a junior at Medford High School, near Boston, Fannie suffered the first of a series of attacks of ill health that left her permanently disabled. Confined to her home, where she helped her mother, Fannie took an interest in cooking. She soon turned their home into a boarding house whose excellent food attracted well-paying customers. At the age of 30, she enrolled in the Boston Cooking School; after graduation she was kept on as assistant to the director, and when the director died two years later, Fannie Farmer was elected director of the school.

Fannie was struck by the lack of a scientific cookbook—instead, collections of simple home recipes called for a "pinch" of this and a "dash" of that. In 1896, at the age of 39, Fannie Farmer put together a cookbook of her own, introducing the idea of level spoon and cup measurements, and persuaded a dubious Boston publishing house to print three thousand copies at her own expense. The enterprise proved to be an astounding success, and in future years millions of copies of *The Boston Cooking School Cook Book* were sold to a receptive public.

In addition to being a successful author, Fannie Farmer was also a popular public speaker whose lectures on cooking drew audiences of hundreds of cooks, chefs, and homemakers. Her lectures were reprinted in the *Boston Evening Transcript* and appeared in other newspapers all over the country. Undoubtedly because of her own disability, Fannie paid particular attention to the preparation of food for sick persons, hospital patients, and invalids. She often lectured to nurses and dietitians, and one year gave a course on dietary preparations at Harvard Medical School. Fannie Farmer spent the last seven years of her life in a wheelchair, from which she gave her last lecture, just ten days before she died in 1915 at the age of 58.

Fenway Park

Fenway Park, the home of the Boston Red Sox, opened on April 20, 1912, with a game pitting the local favorites against the New York Highlanders—soon to become the traditional rival Yankees. Fenway Park is the oldest major league baseball stadium in the country. (Until recently it shared that distinction with Navin Field in Detroit, later named Tiger Stadium, which opened on the same day and closed in 1999.)

The Red Sox team went through a series of names, going back to a club called the Red Stockings which had played in the 1870s. At various times they called themselves the Pilgrims, the Puritans, and even the Plymouth Rocks, before settling on the Red Sox in 1907. For several years the Red Sox played on the old Huntington Avenue Grounds (now part of Northeastern University) until John J. Taylor, son of the *Boston Globe* publisher General Charles H. Taylor, decided to build a new ballpark. Located in the Fenway area of the city, Fenway Park opened officially the same week in 1912 that the *Titanic* sank. Taylor sold the club later that same year, and without adequate direction the organization fell into disarray. Although the Red Sox managed to win the World Series in 1912, 1915, 1916, and 1918, after owner Harry Frazee traded Babe Ruth to the New York Yankees in 1919 the team has never again won a Series. In 1926 the wooden left-field bleachers went up in flames, and not long after that the Great Depression cut into the club's profits.

In 1933 the Sox's fortunes took a turn for the better when the young millionaire Tom Yawkey bought the ball club, and within a year put some $2 million into refurbishing Fenway Park. Concrete bleachers replaced the old wooden ones, the size of the grandstand was increased, a larger scoreboard was installed, and a new left-field wall was built that soon became known as the "Green Monster." Thirty-seven feet high and 240 feet long, the Wall is capped by a 23-foot screen that keeps baseballs from bouncing off pedestrians on the bordering Lansdowne Street. "No one knows when the left-field wall was first called the Green Monster," writes the Boston sportswriter Dan Shaughnessy, "but it stands as the signature feature of this singular baseball park." Yawkey officially reopened his "new" Fenway Park on April 17, 1934, and now that Prohibition was over the park began serving beer for the first time. Various changes have taken place in Fenway Park over the years. During the 1950s, for example, Ted Williams, a powerful left-handed batter, was said to be responsible for moving the bullpen from the right-field corner to the front of the right-field bleachers so that he could have a clearer shot for his home-run hits. In 1946 skyview boxes were added on either side of the press box, and during 1988–89 the press box itself was replaced by a plush, glass-enclosed section called the 600 Club.

After Tom Yawkey died in 1976, his widow, Jean Yawkey, remained an active general partner and president of the Red Sox until her death in 1992, when John Harrington became the chief executive officer of the organization. Because of a growing number of structural problems, water leakage, rotting wood, and uneven concrete slabs on the lower concourse, there has been growing pressure for the construction of an entirely new Fenway Park in a different location, or a substantially upgraded Fenway Park at its present site. One consideration in any new construction is the desire for a substantial increase in the number of luxury boxes for influential corporations, institutions, and individuals, in order to generate additional revenue for the ball club. In any case, according to an analysis conducted by the mayor's office, to renovate the 87-year-old Fenway Park would cost almost as much as Harrington's proposal to build a new $545 million ballpark adjacent to the old field. The size of the park itself is another consideration; Harrington wants to replace the 33,871-seat ball park with a new facility that will seat up to 45,000 fans. The various interests of nearby residents, stockholders, politicians, and baseball fans will all play a part in the fate of old Fenway Park.

Fidelity Investments

Massachusetts Investors Trust claims to have invented the modern mutual fund process in 1924, an investment method quickly picked up by several other Boston investment companies, initiating an industry that eventually became a significant part of the Massachusetts economy. At the present time, almost one-quarter of all mutual-fund dollars are managed by such Boston-based companies as Putnam, John Hancock, and Fidelity Investments.

Fidelity Investments' Magellan Fund, created by Edward C. Johnson in 1963, began quietly under another name, and for many years served mainly as a vehicle for the investment of Fidelity's own funds. When Peter Lynch took over the fund's management in 1977, he sparked a new era in the financial-services industry. With his professional knack for making money multiply, and his personal ability to dramatize the process in an understandable manner, Lynch was able to convince ordinary working people that Magellan was not just for the wealthy individual and institutional investors. Now retired from his active management position in the company, although he frequently appears in its television commercials, Lynch helped establish Fidelity as the world's largest mutual-fund company, managing some $450 billion in mutual funds, and contributed to putting Boston on the map as a center for the booming money-management business.

The 54th Regiment

The Emancipation Proclamation that went into effect in January 1863 not only freed the slaves, but also made it possible for African Americans to serve in the armed forces of the United States. Governor John Andrew received authorization to recruit the nation's first all-black regiment—the 54th Massachusetts Infantry

Regiment—under the command of Colonel Robert Gould Shaw, scion of an old Boston Brahmin family.

The gallantry of the 54th Regiment during the Civil War, and especially the great losses the unit suffered in its brave but futile assault on Fort Wagner in Charleston, South Carolina, on July 19, 1863, moved Bostonians to engage the sculptor Augustus Saint-Gaudens to create an appropriate memorial to the young officer, who was buried in a common battlefield grave with his valiant black soldiers. The high-relief bronze stands atop Beacon Hill, directly across from the Massachusetts State House, showing Colonel Shaw on horseback leading his proud men into battle. When it was originally dedicated in 1897, the monument bore only the names of the white officers; in 1984, the names of the sixty-two black infantrymen who died in the assault at Fort Wagner were also added. Sergeant William Carney of the 54th Regiment was wounded three times saving the American flag from capture by the Confederates, and was the first African American to win the Congressional Medal of Honor. The story of the 54th Regiment and its heroic assault on Fort Wagner was told graphically in director Edward Zwick's Academy Award–winning 1989 film *Glory*.

But the heroism of the gallant 54th Regiment did not end at Fort Wagner. During 1864 the African American unit from Boston took an active part in the fighting around Charleston, South Carolina, and watched as the forces of General William Tecumseh Sherman came sweeping up from Savannah through the Carolinas early in 1865. Once he had taken the city of Columbia on February 20, 1865, Sherman battered his way to Charleston, which was hastily evacuated and set afire. Two companies of the 54th Massachusetts Regiment were among the first Union soldiers to march into the stricken city, with smoke and flames still rising from its skeletal ruins—the city where the first shots of the Civil War had been fired. Confident and disciplined, the black soldiers trooped into the city in close-order formation, stacked their rifles, and set to work putting out the fires and saving whatever property they could. "On this ever memorable day," wrote one Northern reporter, "they made manifest to the world their superiority in honor and humility."

Three days later, troops from the 55th Massachusetts Regiment, the second all-black unit recruited by Governor Andrew, also entered Charleston. With Lt. George Thompson Garrison, son of the famed Boston abolitionist, at the head of one of the companies, the African American troops marched into the Confederate city singing "John Brown's Body." The irony of the situation was not lost on the Boston abolitionist orator Wendell Phillips, who was beside himself with joy. "Can you conceive a bitterer drop that God's chemistry could mix for a Son of the Palmetto State," he asked, "than that a Massachusetts flag and a colored regiment should take possession of Charleston?"

When he first established the 54th Regiment, Governor Andrew expressed his awareness that the success or the failure of this first all-black regiment would do much "to elevate or depress the estimation in which the character of the Colored American will be held throughout the World." The heroism of African Americans soldiers and sailors in the Civil War more than justified the governor's confidence in their ability as fighting men, as well as in their devotion to the Union.

For three decades, the ceremonial sword of Colonel Robert Gould Shaw, given to him by his uncle in June 1863 to commemorate his promotion to the rank of colonel, was housed in the museum of Boston's Old North Church. On September 24, 1999, the sword was presented to the Museum of Afro-American History at a ceremony at the African Meeting House on Beacon Hill as one more tribute to a gallant regiment.

Filene's Basement

A trip to Filene's Basement has become as much a part of visiting Boston as touring the city's numerous historical attractions, marking this particular department store as a unique part of the city's history. The Great Fire of 1872, a catastrophic event that wiped out Boston's entire business district, provided an opportunity for the city to rebuild and redesign its downtown. Summer, Washington, Federal, Congress, Milk, and Hawley streets, for example, were substantially widened; Franklin, Pearl, Oliver, and Arch streets were extended. The city was able to make its business center more accessible, increase tax values, and create space for competitive retail enterprises like Filene's Department Store.

The opening of the Park Street Subway in 1897 further stimulated commercial activity in this downtown area. It provided easy access for thousands of people from the surrounding neighborhoods to the downtown shopping district, and made it possible to remove streetcar tracks from Tremont Street, north of Boylston Street. In 1923, surface streetcars were also taken off Washington and Summer streets, as well as the eastern end of Boylston Street, further improving pedestrian traffic. The increase in the number of automobiles and trucks, however, together with the absence of parking spaces, would continue to create serious traffic problems which would not be addressed until well into the twentieth century.

Filene's Department Store had been founded by Edward A. Filene, and was originally located on the south corner of Washington Street, before moving in 1912 to its present location on the opposite corner. The new store, with its greater space and improved facilities, was able to expand its operations and enlarge its distribution. It was also able to gradually increase its size by absorbing a number of adjoining buildings until it covered the entire block bounded by Washington, Summer, Franklin, and Hawley streets. In 1929, Filene's absorbed the R. H. White Company, one of Boston's oldest department stores, and a short time later Filene's itself became affiliated with the Federated Department Stores, Inc. Throughout his life and career, the founder of the store, Edward A. Filene, was active in Boston's civic and financial affairs. He was the author of a project called "Boston 1915," designed to bring members of the Boston community together to develop a five-year plan for the city's growth and development. When the outbreak of World War I forced an end to that project, in 1919 he established the Twentieth Century Fund to fund organizations to come up with plans to improve economic conditions in the city.

Filene's Department Store can also claim credit in 1908 for pioneering one of the most successful basement departments in the country. At first, Edward Filene used the basement store to dump leftover inventory from his own store at markdown prices, but before long the Basement was buying leftover merchandise from other department stores as well. The Basement would go almost anywhere for a bargain: in 1940, for example, just before France was invaded by the Germans during World War II, the Basement cornered the market on French fashions, and Boston shoppers had a field day.

Filene's Basement store tags each sale item with the original date of arrival and a sale price. After two weeks, its "automatic discount" starts at 25 percent; after three weeks it goes up to 50 percent; after four weeks it reaches 75 percent. After five weeks, remaining goods are donated to charity. Residents of Boston, eager for sales, move in human waves through tables loaded with newly arrived closeout articles from other stores, frequently trying on clothing right in the aisles rather than using the dressing rooms. Perhaps the wildest scenes in the Basement take place during its annual sale of expensive wedding gowns at bargain prices. Thousands of customers (often aided by mothers, sisters, and aunts) burst through the doors as soon as they are opened, run through the aisles, and grab dresses off the racks, either to try on themselves or to swap with other customers.

Filene's Basement opened its first branch in 1978, and expanded during the 1980s, when it became a separate division of Federated Department Stores, Inc., which now operates Macy's. In 1991, purchased by an investment group, the company went public, but soon ran into increasing competition. New shopping trends, the popularity of suburban malls, the multiplication of discount outlets, and the increase in consolidations and mergers have created challenges that Filene's Basement will have to meet in order to survive. After losing millions of dollars and the support of its vendors, who refused to ship merchandise any longer, in August 1999 Filene's Basement Corporation was finally forced to file for bankruptcy in federal court. The 91-year-old company announced plans to close seventeen underperforming stores, including four stores in Massachusetts. Filene's Basement, the famous flagship store in Boston's Downtown Crossing, however, was not affected by the announcement.

Floating Hospital

The Boston Floating Hospital is today located near Boston's Chinatown area as part of Tufts–New England Medical Center. At one time, however, the Floating Hospital was, in fact, a ship that actually went to sea.

In 1894 the original vessel, painted white and christened the *Clifford*, was also known as the "white ship of mercy." Its primary objective was to provide care and treatment for children under the age of six who had serious intestinal problems. The vessel was designed to give sick children the healthful benefits of fresh sea air, as well as to prevent the spread of infectious diarrhea. Nurses and other health care providers were on board to treat diseases that were especially prevalent during the summer months. From its permanent berth at Boston's North Pier, the *Clifford* made trips up and down Boston Harbor every day during the months of June, July, and August. Postgraduate courses on ward care and dietetics were regularly offered to nurses in a ten-week program aboard the Floating Hospital.

In 1927 disaster struck when the *Clifford* was destroyed by fire. To replace the ship, in 1931 Henry Clay Jackson and Paul Wilde Jackson generously supplied funds to build the Jackson Memorial Building at 20 Ash Street, adjacent to the Boston Dispensary. Inside the doors of the Jackson Memorial Building is a brass sculpture of Dr. Henry Ingersoll Bowditch, from 1909 to 1923 physician-in-chief of the Boston Floating Hospital.

Freedom Trail

Early in March 1951 William Schofield, the chief editorial writer for the *Boston Herald Traveler,* published an article about the difficulties confronting visitors who came from all over the world to see Boston's historical shrines. In trying to navigate the complex maze of Boston's streets, they usually managed to see one or two sites, but never got a chance to appreciate the total historical picture. What the city needed, wrote Schofield, was some kind of well-marked footpath through the city—a "Puritan Path," a "Liberty Loop," a "Freedom's Way"—to lead visitors to a comprehensive view of Boston's historical treasures.

Boston's new mayor, John B. Hynes, who was enjoying his first year in office after defeating James Michael Curley in 1949, was intrigued by Schofield's proposal. Eager to attract more visitors to Boston and to build good relations with the local business community, Hynes turned the project over to Paul Hines, his director of celebrations, for implementation. Local business and civic leaders, seeing obvious commercial advantages, let it be known that they would cooperate with the mayor's office.

In June, it was agreed that the project would be called the Freedom Trail, and Senator Leverett Saltonstall was named the first president of the Freedom Trail Foundation. At first, a series of simple plywood markers were used to identify sites along the route which led to the State House, the Old Granary Burying Ground, King's Chapel, the Old South Meeting House, the Old State House, Faneuil Hall, the Paul Revere House, the Old North Church, the Copp's Hill Burying Ground, and then across the bridge to Charlestown to the USS *Constitution* and Bunker Hill.

By 1953 the wooden markers had been replaced by sturdier metal signs, and local businesses were well aware of the commercial results of some forty thousand visitors and tourists walking the Freedom Trail each year. In 1958 the Advertising Club adopted the Freedom Trail as a permanent community project, as did the Greater Boston Chamber of Commerce. The John Hancock Company defrayed the costs of the first brochures; businessmen and bankers made charitable contributions; the city paid for the creation of the now familiar red paint and brick line that leads visitors to some of the most important historic sites in Boston.

The Freedom Trail Foundation was incorporated as a nonprofit agency in 1964, and since that time has been supported by a strong public and private coalition. The National Park Service—which, since 1976, has disbursed over $50 million in capital improvements for historic sites along the trail—has also provided trained person-nel for interpretive services, educational programs, and guided tours. The Foundation has also worked closely with the City of Boston, and in 1997 Mayor Thomas Menino appropriated over $1 million for additional capital improvements along the Freedom Trail's 2.5-mile route through the city. The Freedom Trail is part of the Boston National Historical Park, which maintains a visitor cen-ter at 15 State Street, directly across from the Old State House.

In anticipation of the millennium, a group called the Boston His-tory Collaborative has expanded the Freedom Trail concept. The Collaborative is made up of more than thirty organizations, includ-ing the New England Historic and Genealogical Society, the Boston Public Library, the International Institute of Boston, the Mayor's Office, and the Massachusetts Office of Tourism. The Collaborative has created a literary trail as well as a maritime trail, and has com-pleted a series of immigration trails linked with local ethnic associa-tions and neighborhood historic societies. Starting at the Shaw Me-morial across from the State House, the Black Heritage Trail identifies such sites as the African Meeting House and the Smith School, which trace the history of Boston's nineteenth-century Af-rican American community. The Collaborative has also launched a Web site that provides research assistance for those researching their family histories. This Web site emphasizes the history of the various ethnic and racial communities of Boston.

Fugitive Slaves

Because of its reputation as the "cradle of liberty," Boston was an at-tractive haven for African Americans fleeing the bonds of slavery in the antebellum South. Despite a series of fugitive slave laws passed by the U.S. Congress since the 1790s, governors of the northern states made little effort to enforce these laws or respond to requests for the return of runaway slaves. Once a fugitive slave made it to a northern state, it was generally assumed that he or she was free.

A major change in the status of runaway slaves occurred in 1850.

In an effort to break the legislative logjam over whether to admit slavery into the southwest territories acquired as a result of the Mexican War, Congress agreed to a series of compromises: California would come into the Union as a free state; popular sovereignty would prevail in the New Mexico Territory, allowing the settlers themselves to determine whether they wanted slavery; traffic in slavery would be prohibited in the District of Columbia; and a new Fugitive Slave Act would go into effect. Unlike previous laws, the Fugitive Slave Act of 1850 empowered Federal Marshals to apprehend fugitive slaves in any state of the Union, without going through the state authorities. No trial would be conducted, and no testimony would be taken from an alleged fugitive; all that was needed was proper identification by the owner.

In an effort to preserve the Union, Senator Daniel Webster of Massachusetts gave his famous "Second of March" address calling for the passage of the Compromise proposals—a speech for which he was later excoriated by prominent Boston abolitionists. The belief of Webster and many other Northern congressmen that the new law would never be implemented was sadly mistaken. During the early 1850s a number of northern cities saw the Federal Marshals at work, and witnessed at firsthand the capture of alleged fugitives and their return to slavery. In February 1851 a black man named Shadrach Minkins was apprehended, but he was spirited away from the authorities by a group of local black residents. Two months later Thomas Sims was taken into custody and placed under heavy guard until he could be returned to the South.

Conservative Bostonians joined with radical Abolitionists to frustrate the intention of the law. They formed a Vigilance Committee, and distributed placards warning black residents whenever "slave-catchers" were in town. They also provided funds for the legal defense of those who were apprehended. So intense was the outrage of the entire city that when a black man named Anthony Burns was seized as a fugitive slave in May 1854, authorities were forced to post 200 policemen and some 2,000 uniformed soldiers along both sides of State Street so that Burns could be marched safely to the ship that would take him back to Virginia.

The fugitive slave cases in Boston during the early 1850s

brought about an important change in the attitude of conservative elements of the city, which had stood aloof from the unsavory slavery controversy. On May 30, 1854, the *Boston Times* reported that because of the Anthony Burns case a number of prominent Boston businessmen "who have never before given their influence on the anti-slavery side" had taken a new position on "the great question of the day."

G

Boston Garden

❖

"Gangplank Bill"

"Gangplank Bill" was the highly irreverent but commonly accepted term used by many Boston Catholics to identify His Eminence, William Henry Cardinal O'Connell, the impressive churchman who ruled over Boston's Roman Catholic population during the first half of the twentieth century. A portly and lordly prelate who lived in princely style, his annual return from vacation in Nassau in the Bahamas was covered by reporters who photographed the archbishop as he strode down the gangplank at Boston Harbor—hence the popular nickname.

Born December 5, 1859, to working-class Irish parents in the mill town of Lowell, Massachusetts, young O'Connell graduated from Boston College, entered the priesthood, and studied at the North American College in Rome. There he excelled in his studies, expanded his love of music, and made the acquaintance of prominent Church officials. After his ordination in June 1884 O'Connell served as a curate in Medford, and was later transferred to St. Joseph's Church in Boston's crowded West End, where he spent the next nine years. In 1895 Father O'Connell was brought to Rome to serve as rector of the North American College, which deepened his appreciation of the Roman scene and further enhanced his political future in the Church. In 1901 the Holy See named O'Connell bishop of Portland, Maine, where he remained until 1907, when he assumed office as Archbishop of Boston after the death of Archbishop John Williams.

Taking over his responsibilities with vigor and determination, the 48-year-old O'Connell set out to achieve several objectives. The first was to modernize the operations of the archdiocese, which was a rather loose confederation of relatively independent parishes under the direction of strong pastors. O'Connell insisted on a much more centralized administrative structure. From now on, no local decisions about budgets, construction, management, or appointments were to be made without notifying the Archbishop and getting his express approval—in writing. Needless to say, it was not an approach that won the new Archbishop many friends among those who had been accustomed to making their own decisions and running their own domains.

The second area of concern for O'Connell was to forge a powerful and unified Catholic community by encouraging religious organizations and associations. With an ample supply of priests and nuns, and with the seminary fairly bursting with bright replacements, Cardinal O'Connell (he was elevated to the rank of Cardinal in 1911) presided over an era of almost unparalleled zeal and devotion. On Sundays and Holy Days of Obligation, Catholic churches were filled to overflowing, and weekday Masses in the early hours of the morning were regularly attended by members of the faithful before their workdays began. In the ethnic neighborhoods of Boston, Catholics participated in a perpetual calendar of religious devotions that not only bound them together as a parish but also manifested their membership in a universal church. Week in and week out, they attended holy hours, rosaries, stations of the cross, novenas, triduums, missions, retreats, and various other pious services. The Holy Name Society became the leading religious organization for laymen, while women in great numbers joined the Legion of Mary as well as numerous leagues and sodalities.

Another initiative that O'Connell undertook to build a more powerful and committed Church was to encourage local Catholics to discover their own Catholic and Celtic roots, rather than striving to emulate Anglo-Saxon models. He worked to create a sharp distinction between the members of the Catholic community and their non-Catholic neighbors. Catholics were not to enter a Protestant church or attend non-Catholic religious ceremonies; they were not to join such organizations as the Boy Scouts, the Girl Scouts, the YMCA, or the YWCA. Instead, young people were encouraged to join the Catholic Youth Organization (CYO), where they could join other young Catholics in marching bands, baseball teams, public-speaking programs, and similar activities. Catholics were to attend Catholic schools and colleges whenever possible, and the Cardinal personally persuaded Mayor John F. Fitzgerald of Boston to have his daughter Rose give up plans to attend Wellesley College in favor of instruction at the Academy of the Sacred Heart.

During the first half of the twentieth century, "the Cardinal" meant only one person in Boston. Members of the state legislature spoke respectfully of "Number One"; city councilors waited to hear about "Lake Street's" position on public issues; newspaper reporters referred to "Number Eight"—the prelate's license plate number. Until his death in 1944 at the age of 85, William Henry Cardinal O'Connell was one of the most powerful figures in Boston. There were those who strongly opposed Cardinal O'Connell's personal style as autocratic and his ecclesiastical policies as divisive. Others, however, staunchly supported his determined and successful efforts to transform what had been an insecure and deferential Catholic population into a strong, unified, and self-assured community in a city whose Puritan traditions had once held immigrant Catholics in such low regard that jobs were openly advertised with the stipulation "No Irish Need Apply." He could now proudly proclaim that the old tide of Protestantism was receding and that a new wave of Irish Catholicism was sweeping over the region. "The Puritan has passed; the Catholic remains," he announced, and did his best to make sure his pronouncement came true.

The Garden

In 1921 a former cowboy named Tex Rickard constructed a 90,000-seat wooden stadium in New Jersey to stage the championship fight between Jack Dempsey and Georges Carpentier. Using all sorts of publicity to promote what he billed as "the fight of the century," Rickard was convinced by the million-dollar gate from the fight that championship boxing was a lucrative form of entertainment that would attract thousands of spectators.

Rickard went on to build Madison Square Garden in New York City as a major venue for boxing and other sporting events, and its success prompted Rickard to add a sports center in Boston as another link in his ambitious chain of entertainment empires. For a full year, Causeway Street, in Boston's North End, literally shook as some 1,500 cement pillars were driven 50 feet into the ground to provide a solid basis for what would become the Boston Garden. At a cost of $4 million, Tex Rickard built a structure that seated 14,000 spectators, and that would go on to become one of the longest-lived indoor sports arenas in the country.

Saturday, November 17, 1928, was opening night for the newly constructed Boston Garden, located next to North Station. Thousands of Bostonians paid anywhere from 50 cents to 5 dollars a ticket to attend the opening-night festivities, which started with an Army private demonstrating that he could assemble a machine gun blindfolded in only 40 seconds. The main event, however, was a boxing match in which the local favorite, Dick "Honey Boy" Finnegan of Dorchester, defeated challenger Andre Routis for the featherweight title.

During the dangerous decade of the 1930s, which saw the stock market collapse, the Depression, and the uncertainties of Hoover economics, the manager Walter Brown used great ingenuity in booking the Garden with events that would attract paying customers. Rodeos, horse shows, three-ring circuses, and even indoor ski-jumping kept the Garden operating during the difficult years. But it was boxing for which the Garden was originally built, and perhaps its most famous fighting event was when the local North End favorite Tony De Marco won the welterweight championship of the world in 1955.

During the late 1930s and into the early 1940s, however, it was hockey that took over Boston Garden, when the hard-hitting, fast-checking Boston Bruins filled every seat in the house with screaming fans. For nearly a decade, players like Milt Schmidt, Eddie Shore, and other members of the famous "Kraut Line" dominated the National Hockey League, winning the Stanley Cup three years in a row from 1939 to 1941 and keeping the Garden filled to capacity.

After 1946, when a new so-called parquet floor, constructed of some 247 pieces of wood paneling, was designed to be laid down to cover the Garden ice, basketball caught on as a major attraction in Boston. Soon the Boston Celtics were bringing overflow crowds into Boston Garden. As the years went on, despite obstructed views, occasional blackouts when the electricity failed, and soaring temperatures because no air conditioning was available, die-hard Celtic fans loved "the Garden" as a place to watch their favorite team.

After nearly seventy years of active service, however, it was felt that the Boston Garden had served its purposes and should be replaced by a more up-to-date sports center with more comfortable seats, unobstructed views, and a proper climate-control system. A new, $160 million, state-of-the-art Fleet Center was constructed, built only 9 inches away from the outside wall of the old Boston Garden, which remained in operation until the construction was completed. The old Garden was then carefully dismantled from the inside out. Despite the Fleet Center's bright lights, fancy video scoreboard, and shiny surfaces, many old-time Bostonians still feel that the old Boston Garden, with its distinctive parquet floor, can never be replaced.

William Lloyd Garrison

On the Commonwealth Avenue Mall, just off Dartmouth Street, there is a seated statue of William Lloyd Garrison. Sculpted by Olin Levi Warren and unveiled in 1886, the seated figure's relaxed pose and placid features give little indication of the violent passions this man unleashed in nineteenth-century Boston as the leader of the Abolition movement.

William Lloyd Garrison was born in the North Shore seaport town of Newburyport, Massachusetts. Deserted by his father and abandoned by his mother by the time he was 12, young Garrison worked at various jobs before becoming an apprentice in the printing trade. In 1829 he was editing a small newspaper in Vermont when he was visited by an antislavery editor from Baltimore named Benjamin Lundy, who asked Garrison to become co-editor of his weekly publication *Genius of Universal Emancipation.* Garrison later moved to Boston, where he became active in working for the antislavery cause, denouncing the American Colonization Society's proposal to send slaves back to Africa as "White-Manism."

On January 1, 1831, William Lloyd Garrison published the first issue of his own newspaper, *The Liberator*, which denounced slavery as a moral evil and demanded the total and immediate uncompensated emancipation of slaves. The stirring words he used to describe his determination in this effort are inscribed on the base of his Boston statue: "I am in earnest. I will not equivocate. I will not excuse. I will not retreat a single inch. And I will be heard." A short time later, in the basement of the African Meeting House on Beacon Hill, Garrison helped found the New England Anti-Slavery Society as the vehicle for achieving his goal of emancipation.

At the start, Garrison and his followers were regarded by most Bostonians as members of a small lunatic fringe who were perverting the natural law, defying Biblical tradition, and endangering good financial relations with the slaveholders of the South. Members of the Abolition movement were subject to personal ridicule, social ostracism, and occasional violence. In 1835 Garrison himself was attacked and almost lynched on Boston Common when an angry mob burst into a meeting of the Boston Female Anti-Slavery Society and dragged him off to Boston Common at the end of a rope. Only the fortuitous appearance of city constables saved him from further harm.

Garrison, however, was never deterred from his moral purpose by threats or by force. Even when some of his friends and supporters suggested more moderate tactics or political adjustments, he would never agree to the slightest compromise. He steadfastly refused to cooperate with political parties as long as they continued to function under a Constitution that sanctioned slavery. "The Constitution," as he viewed it, "was a covenant with death and an agreement with hell."

Despite his strict insistence on pacifism and nonviolence, after the 1861 attack on Fort Sumter, Garrison came out in support of President Lincoln's carefully worded decision to use force to suppress a rebellion—not to fight a war. Seeing the Civil War as a heaven-sent opportunity that would inevitably lead to the emancipation of the slaves, he continued to support Lincoln patiently and loyally, even when some of his more radical colleagues, like Wendell Phillips, became critical of the president's intentions.

With the defeat of the Confederacy in 1865 and the passage of the Thirteenth Amendment, the freedom of slaves had finally become the law of the land. Now that his goal had finally been achieved, in May 1865 Garrison resigned as president of the American Anti-Slavery Society, and in December 1865 he published the last issue of *The Liberator*. In spite of declining health, Garrison continued to work until his death in 1879 on behalf of the newly freed African Americans, fighting for greater equality between the races.

❖

The Great Fire

Throughout its long history, Boston had always been haunted by the specter of fire. As early as March 1631, Deputy Governor Thomas Dudley put out an order that "no man shall build his chimney with wood, nor cover his house with thatch." Despite such precautions, conflagration was always a present danger. After a particularly disastrous fire in 1711, Boston was divided into several fire districts, administered by officers called "Firewards," who were issued a special badge and a 5-foot-long red staff topped with a brass spire. These men headed up companies of young volunteers who elected their own officers, designed their own uniforms, held an annual supper, and together developed considerable political influence in the town. In March 1760 another terrible fire swept from Cornhill through Dock Square to the waterfront, burning down more than three hundred buildings and leaving more than a thousand people homeless out of a total population of around fifteen thousand.

After Boston became a city in 1822, Mayor Josiah Quincy reorganized and modernized the fire department, replacing the colorful but often ineffectual volunteer companies with salaried and uniformed professionals. After the Civil War, the commercial district in downtown Boston, in the area of Summer and Washington Streets, went through a period of redevelopment and expansion. A series of large granite buildings, five and seven stories high, replaced lower-rise buildings. Lined up side by side, these new buildings formed solid blocks of granite along both sides of very narrow streets. Despite periodic warnings by Fire Chief John S. Damrell, no action was taken to guard against a serious fire. The city's water supply was known to be inadequate, water pipes were old and rusted, and many fire hydrants were seriously defective; there were not enough fire engines, or healthy horses to draw the heavy equipment.

On the evening of November 9, 1872, fire broke out in a building on the corner of Summer and Kingston Streets, not far from where South Station is located today. In a matter of minutes both sides of Summer Street were ablaze, as the fire roared northward through the granite tunnel and then swung east down Arch and Devonshire Streets, shooting flaming sparks and hot cinders in all directions. While one part of the conflagration fanned northeast up Milk Street toward Washington Street, another raced south down Federal and High Streets toward the waterfront.

By the time the catastrophe had burned itself out on the following day, the Great Fire had gutted some 65 acres of Boston's central commercial and business district, destroying property valued at $75 million. Some 776 buildings had to be demolished, and insurance companies went bankrupt paying claims. Most of the downtown area had to be completely rebuilt and modernized, while the city's fire department was reorganized and made more professional. Hydrants were improved, water pipes were replaced, new steam-powered engines were substituted for horse-drawn wagons, and a uniform building code was established to protect the city from future fires.

On a larger scale, the Great Fire of 1872 caused a major shift in the city's center. A number of churches, public institutions, and commercial establishments took the occasion to move out of the old part of town and take up residence in the new Back Bay and Copley Square area. Henry Hobson Richardson built the First Baptist Church on the corner of Clarendon Street and Commonwealth Avenue in 1873, the year after the fire. In 1874 Trinity Church began construction of a new church in Copley Square to replace the old one in downtown Boston; the Old South Church was almost immediately replaced by the New Old South Church in the Back Bay in

1877. The Boston Public Library also moved from its downtown location to a permanent site in Copley Square.

Greater Boston Chamber of Commerce

During the early 1800s, while Boston was still a small town, a group of about a thousand grain merchants and shippers formed the Grain Exchange, which served for many years as a central meeting place for those engaged in the grain trade. Much later, in 1885, a 500-member Boston Produce Exchange and a 300-member Boston Commercial Exchange were consolidated with the original Grain Exchange to form a new Chamber that would represent the businessmen of Boston who made their living from trade on the sea.

To house this new organization, on January 21, 1892, a seven-story Grain Exchange Building was dedicated at India and Milk Streets in downtown Boston, not far from the waterfront. Constructed of pink granite and designed in the French Romanesque style, the handsome landmark has survived and is at present owned and managed by the Beal Company.

On June 15, 1909, the Massachusetts legislature gave a charter to a new organization called the Boston Chamber of Commerce. This body was formed by merging the elements of the old Chamber with a new group called the Boston Merchants' Association, intended to give business leaders a more effective voice in such public policy issues as government regulation, municipal fiscal policy, transportation services, and public health issues. In 1952, with the movement of many of Boston's city-owned businesses out to the suburbs, the organization changed its name to the Greater Boston Chamber of Commerce in order to extend its area of corporate representation. From its headquarters at 125 High Street, officers and members of the Chamber of Commerce continue to serve as catalysts and coordinators of the transformation of Boston, as the extensive operations of the Big Dig, together with ambitious developments along the South Boston waterfront, promise to bring remarkable economic and demographic changes to Boston in the twenty-first century.

H

"Honey Fitz"

Sarah Hale

Present-day publications such as *Vogue, Harper's Bazaar,* and *Good Housekeeping,* magazines written primarily by women for women, can trace their origins back to early nineteenth-century Boston, and to a woman named Sarah Hale.

Born in 1788, Sarah Buell grew up on a New Hampshire farm, and in 1811 married a promising lawyer named David Hale. Between 1815 and 1822, the couple had five children; just a few days after the birth of the last child David Hale died. For the next few years the young widow eked out an existence making women's hats and doing millinery work, while developing her writing skills. She sent articles to magazines, mailed poems to journals, entered literary contests, and in 1827 published a novel called *Northwood.* On the strength of this book, a Boston minister invited her to become editor of a new monthly magazine for women called the *Ladies' Magazine.* Hale readily accepted, and threw herself into the enterprise with such enthusiasm that within a year the publication was already a success.

A magazine for women was not a new idea—there were several published in Boston during the 1820s. Most, however, were edited and published by men. They were filled with fashion plates, sentimental stories, and news items clipped from other publications. *Ladies' Magazine* was the first of its kind to be edited by a woman; it was also the first to publish its own original material. Moreover, Sarah Hale had no intention of fostering either fashion or frivolity. She was about the more serious business of "female improvement," encouraging women to develop their powers and abilities to become moral and spiritual exemplars within that "woman's sphere" that was uniquely their own. Hale reassured any male readers that if women read her magazine they would become better wives, mothers, daughters, and housekeepers, thus promoting "domestic felicity."

Her role as editor of such a well-known journal led Sarah Hale far beyond her own "sphere" to become a notable public figure.

Whether in articles extolling motherhood, essays denouncing violence, poems lamenting the loss of a loved one, editorials promoting patriotism, or tracts decrying materialism, Sarah Hale continually emphasized the importance of women's education. She came out in support of schools, academies, and seminaries for women, although not necessarily to train them for public careers. Rather, she saw the educated woman working out of her home as a subtle force for culture and progress, who exerted her effect not by engaging in political action or public demonstrations, but by the power of female "influence." What becomes of the world and what becomes of mankind, Hale told her readers in 1832, depends on "the secret, silent, influence of women."

Hard hit by an economic depression, by 1836 the *Ladies' Magazine* was in such serious financial trouble that Sarah Hale consolidated with a Philadelphia rival, *Godey's Lady's Book.* Hale remained in Boston for a few years after the merger, but in 1841 she moved to Philadelphia. *Godey's* continued to be an influential fashion magazine, expanding its illustrations of bonnets, crinolines, bustles, and hoops by using color plates, woodcuts, and copper plates. But largely through Sarah Hale's influence, it also began to assume the characteristics of a literary periodical with original essays, poems, and stories that attracted a large audience. In addition to her work on the magazine, during the 1840s and 1850s Hale also wrote and edited a number of popular books for women on such subjects as etiquette, childrearing, and housekeeping, becoming a nationally known figure to an expanding market of female readers.

Harvard University

Harvard University is the oldest institution of higher learning in the United States. Although most of the university is located in the city of Cambridge, many people regard Harvard as a uniquely Boston institution. Its historical origins, educational philosophy, and social mission relate it to John Winthrop's ideal of creating a "city upon a hill" for all to see, admire, and emulate.

One year after the establishment of the Boston Latin School in 1635, the Great and General Court of the Massachusetts Bay Colony voted funds to establish a college across the Charles River in a town then called Newetowne. Thus was Harvard College born in 1636, receiving its name a few years later in honor of the Reverend John Harvard, a Presbyterian minister who had come to the colony in 1637, and upon his death the following year willed to the college 780 pounds sterling, as well as his 400-volume library. Newetowne was also renamed Cambridge, after the university John Harvard had attended in England.

Although one of the purposes of Harvard College was to train ministers and provide the Bay Colony with a steady supply of Puritan clergymen when the present ones "shall lie in the dust," the founders of Boston also wanted to "advance learning and perpetuate it to posterity." They were determined that the future teachers, jurists, writers, doctors, statesmen, and other professional leaders of the colony should have available to them the classical education provided by such English universities as Cambridge. In 1655 tuition at Harvard was two pounds. If they lacked cash, students could come up with the equivalent in items such as wheat, beef, furs, firewood, turnips, apples, butter, and rum. Those who entered Harvard in colonial days faced a mandatory curriculum with required study of grammar, logic, rhetoric, religion, arithmetic, geometry, astronomy, metaphysics, ethics, natural science, Greek, Hebrew, and ancient history. In those days, interestingly enough, nobody studied Latin at Harvard. It was assumed that all students entering Harvard had already acquired proficiency in Latin at grammar school; they were expected to speak it freely in all their Harvard classes.

Dr. Oliver Wendell Holmes pointed out that students at Harvard were assigned their individual ranks in the college catalogue in accordance with "their parents' condition." This ranking determined the order of their seating in chapel, their location when they marched in college processions, their precedence for classroom recitations, and the sequence in which they served themselves at table. The ranking of students corresponding to their family's social and financial position continued throughout the nineteenth century. Josiah Quincy, the former mayor of Boston and president of Harvard from 1829 to 1845, once remarked as he pointed to the Harvard catalogue: "If a man's there, that's who he is. If he isn't, who is he?"

Harvard Yard, just off Harvard Square, is the heart of the university. It is in this 300-year-old enclosure of colonial buildings, green grass, and towering trees that all first-year students at Harvard College are housed. Entering the Yard from the gate off Massachusetts Avenue, opposite Dunster Street, one finds the old yellow Wadsworth House (1727) on the right and the red-brick Massachusetts Hall (1720) on the left; directly ahead is Harvard Hall, a classroom building on the site of the original Harvard Hall that was destroyed by fire in 1764. Nearby is Hollis Hall (1763), a dormitory where Ralph Waldo Emerson and his friend Henry David Thoreau lived as Harvard students. Separating the "old" Yard from the "new" Yard beyond is University Hall, a handsome gray granite structure designed by Charles Bulfinch. Outside, facing the "old" Yard, is a seated statue of John Harvard, a fictional likeness executed by the well-known sculptor Daniel Chester French.

On the opposite side of University Hall, with Henry Hobson Richardson's Romanesque-style Sever Hall in the background, is the "new" Yard, where commencement exercises are held each June—on a day when tradition has it that it never rains. On the right-hand side is Widener Library, the third-largest library in the United States, with a collection of more than 5.5 million books. The massive Classical structure was the result of a gift from the mother of the Harvard graduate Harry Elkins Widener, class of 1907, who went down with the *Titanic* in 1912. Facing Widener Library across the grassy expanse is the stately Memorial Church, dedicated to the Harvard men killed in both World Wars, and a reminder of Harvard's religious origins.

Outside the immediate confines of the Yard are many other buildings that contribute to Harvard's academic and cultural preeminence. To the north is the modernistic Science Center with the imaginative Tanner Fountain in the foreground. To the right is Memorial Hall, a massive red-brick structure done in the Ruskin-Gothic style so popular in the Victorian era. It is a monument to the 136 Harvard men who died for the Union in the Civil

War (the 64 graduates who fought for the Confederacy are not included), and in recent years it has been renovated and restored to its original function as a dining hall. In 1999 its ornate tower, destroyed in a fire in 1956, was restored to the Cambridge skyline. The apse of Memorial Hall contains the 1200-seat Sanders Theater, a favorite site for concerts, lectures, performances, and poetry readings.

In the immediate vicinity are several of Harvard's best-known art museums. On the corner of Quincy Street and Broadway is the new Arthur M. Sackler Museum, which houses collections of Asian art; farther along Quincy Street, across from Sever Hall, is the Fogg Art Museum, done in conservative neo-Georgian style. Next to the Fogg is the Carpenter Center for the Visual Arts, whose massive curves and open spaces are the creation of Le Corbusier. These are only a sampling of the numerous museums that display Harvard's expertise in such subjects as archaeology, botany, ethnology, geology, mineralogy, natural history, zoology, Germanic studies, and Semitic studies.

On the south side of the Yard is located Holyoke Center, on the corner of Massachusetts Avenue and what is now JFK Street (formerly Boylston Street). From this location down to the banks of the Charles River can be found many of Harvard's undergraduate dormitories. Adams House is prominent with its shining golden dome, and across the way the flatiron-shaped Lampoon Building (the Castle) is the home of the famous college humor magazine. Moving down JFK Street toward the Charles River are Kirkland House and Eliot House, while Dunster House and Mather House are farther along on Memorial Drive.

For generations after its founding, there were few changes in traditional forms, social customs, and academic procedures at Harvard. Until well into the nineteenth century, daily attendance at chapel was required; the small number of students came from the same socioeconomic backgrounds and followed a heavy regimen of rigidly prescribed studies that emphasized the classics, philosophy, and mathematics, taught by a small number of faculty members who were undifferentiated by formal departments.

Things changed dramatically in 1869, when Charles William

Eliot became president. Over the forty years of his tenure, he transformed Harvard from a small college into a modern university. Concentrating all undergraduates in the College, he instituted what at the time was considered a radical reform called the "elective system," which allowed students to choose a greater diversity of courses. Eliot also enlarged and upgraded the faculty and encouraged the recruitment of students from all over the country. At the same time, while strengthening the undergraduate college, President Eliot also stimulated the development of professional schools and research centers at Harvard by placing greater authority in the hands of their respective deans and faculties. In 1872 the Master of Arts, the Doctorate in Science, and the Doctor of Philosophy degrees were established, and in 1890 the Graduate School of Arts and Sciences was formally organized. In addition to making the Divinity School nondenominational, Eliot effected substantial reforms in both the Law School and the School of Medicine, establishing more rigorous standards for admission, insisting on the "case method" for law and internships for medicine, and demanding written examinations as a prerequisite for graduation.

When A. Lawrence Lowell was named president of Harvard in 1909, he not only continued the academic expansion begun by Eliot, but also pressed for greater diversity in the makeup of the Harvard student body. In his inaugural address, Lowell argued that for Harvard to base the social life of its students upon divisions of wealth and family was to fail in fulfilling its natural mission of bringing together young men of promise from every level of society and from every part of the country. At the very same time that Woodrow Wilson, the young president of Princeton University, was fighting to break up the elite fraternities at his institution, Lowell was trying to do away with the invidious distinctions between the "gold coasters" who lived in the more posh residences along Mount Auburn Street and the students who lived in the campus dormitories, in order to make Harvard a more democratic and "progressive" institution.

Today, although based in Cambridge, Harvard University owns some 456 acres of land in Boston—twice the area it occupies in Cambridge. The Boston holdings include the Arnold Arboretum; the medical, dental, and public health schools; and a large business school and athletic complex. Harvard accounts for a population of some 18,000 students scattered among its two colleges and ten graduate and professional schools. To administrate this academic complex, Harvard has two governing bodies: The smaller and more powerful body is called the Corporation, composed of the president, the treasurer, and five fellows. A self-perpetuating body, the Corporation holds legal title to all the university's property and exercises managerial control over its operations. The second body is the thirty-member Board of Overseers, which gives advice to the Corporation. The members of the Board are elected by the alumni for six-year overlapping terms. The consent of the Overseers is required for such major decisions of the Corporation as faculty and administrative appointments, although this consent is rarely withheld.

Despite the remarkable growth of Harvard University, the expansion of its programs, the diversity of its specialties, and the extraordinary contributions its graduate and professional schools have made to both the academic world and to public life, most Harvard graduates still regard the College as the heart and soul of the institution. The old grads continue to view the Yard as the center of academic life, and they continue to participate actively in the affairs of the college. During Saturday afternoons in the fall, they travel to Harvard Stadium to root for the Crimson eleven, or they take the train to New Haven to watch "the Game" at the Yale Bowl. They often visit the Cambridge campus, watch baseball games or track and field events, attend concerts or lectures at Sanders Theater, participate in Harvard committee meetings. Every June, bankers, financiers, scientists, novelists, and public officials from all over the country clear their calendars so that they can meet their classmates and take part in the week-long schedule of events connected with the annual Harvard Commencement and their class reunions. For these graduates, Harvard is not merely a college, it is a way of life.

In 1879 a group of women led by Elizabeth Cary Agassiz created the "Harvard Annex" so that women could receive instruction by members of the Harvard faculty. In 1894 this association of women became Radcliffe College. In 1943 women students were allowed in Harvard classrooms for the first time, but it was not until 1963 that

Radcliffe students received Harvard diplomas signed by both presidents, leading to the first joint Harvard-Radcliffe commencement in 1970. Radcliffe's Schlesinger Library has become the foremost library of the history of women in the United States, while the Bunting Institute, named after the former president Mary Ingraham Bunting, has established a distinguished community of women scholars, scientists, and artists. On October 1, 1999, Radcliffe College officially merged with Harvard University, becoming one of Harvard's schools, the Radcliffe Institute for Advanced Study.

Hatch Shell

The Hatch Memorial Shell is an outdoor concert stage on the east bank of the Charles River, where it stretches along a series of islands and lagoons running perpendicular to the Back Bay streets from Arlington west to Fairfield. This section of Boston's Back Bay is known as the Esplanade.

The Hatch Shell is the result of a gift from Maria E. Hatch. Upon her death in 1926, her will left $300,000 to the City of Boston to be used in creating a park, a playground, or some other form of public enterprise that would serve as an appropriate memorial to her brother, Edward Hatch. The money was put to use in 1940 for the construction of the Hatch Shell on the Charles River Esplanade. The shell, with its seven concentric circles of concrete and granite, was designed by Richard Shaw, and the structure stands just across the 1953 Arthur Fiedler Footbridge near the junction of Arlington and Beacon Streets.

The most well-known concerts at the Hatch Shell are performances by the Boston Pops, the Boston Symphony Orchestra's sister organization, which has been presenting concerts of light classical music since 1885. The outdoor concerts were originally the dream of Arthur Fiedler, conductor of the Pops for half a century, who in 1929 chose the Esplanade as the site for his pioneering concerts to bring orchestral music to the people during the warm summer months. Fiedler conducted free concerts on the Esplanade until his retirement in 1979, and then ceded the orchestra to John Williams, who in turn handed the baton over to young Keith Lockhart in 1995. Every year on the Fourth of July, hundreds of thousands of spectators fill the riverbanks and the hundreds of boats floating in the Charles River Basin to listen to the concert, cheering lustily at its rousing conclusion with the 1812 Overture accompanied by a finale of fireworks that explode into the summer skies. It is a uniquely Bostonian way to celebrate the Declaration of Independence and the birth of American freedom.

❖

The Hi-Hat

During the 1930s and 1940s, Boston's African American South End community, east of Symphony Hall, was the exciting center of Boston's "Harlem," where some of the nation's leading jazz musicians could be found.

The Hi-Hat, located at the intersection of Massachusetts and Columbus avenues, was a well-known nightclub, where mixed audiences of blacks and whites gathered to enjoy such celebrated black jazz artists as Fats Waller, Lionel Hampton, Count Basie, and Duke Ellington as they pounded out famous numbers like "One O'Clock Jump" and "Take the A Train." Just up the street on Massachusetts Avenue were smaller clubs like the Rainbow Room and the Savoy Cafe, where more sophisticated jazz enthusiasts gathered to hear Lester ("Prez") Young, Buck Clayton, and Cootie Williams play, and where jazz musicians from the other nightspots gathered after their regular gigs were over to jam together well into the early hours of the morning.

Along Huntington Avenue, the Roseland Ballroom and the Raymor-Playmor Ballroom were large dancehalls that featured the music of many of the large white bands of the era, such as those of Benny Goodman, Jimmy Lunceford, Charles Barnett, and Woody Herman, which played for all-night dancing. "The sounds were heard for miles around," recalled Reginald Weems, who grew up in the South End, reveled in the music, and frequented Estelle's,

Jobil's, and the other barbecued-chicken restaurants in the area. "It was a bright, lively, active community," he recalled, where "the streets were jammed, and so were the clubs."

By the 1960s, however, Boston's brief "Harlem Renaissance" had passed. The era of the big bands was clearly over, and the advent of rock music left little room for traditional jazz. More to the point, perhaps, race relations in Boston had deteriorated and mixed audiences were no longer welcomed in each other's neighborhoods. The rapid and remarkable growth of the city's African American population after World War II transformed the South End from what had been essentially a multicultural neighborhood into an almost all-black community. With the resistance of Boston's white establishment to growing demands of African American leaders for better housing, more job opportunities, and improved education, the stage was set for a racial crisis that would divide the city and poison race relations for many years to come. The Hi-Hat scene of people of all races united by music unfortunately became a distant memory.

Holocaust Memorial

On October 22, 1995, political officials, civic leaders, representatives of the Jewish community, and residents of Boston attended the initial lighting of the New England Holocaust Memorial in Boston. Six glass towers, etched with the identification numbers of the Holocaust victims, vividly and painfully recall the six main death camps and the grim smokestacks where six million Jews died horrible deaths during World War II at the hands of the Nazis. Located between Government Center Plaza and the historic Blackstone Block on Union Street, the Memorial's proximity to the Freedom Trail provides it high visibility and reminds visitors to the city of the history of one of the many communities who are a part of Boston.

"Honey Fitz"

John Francis Fitzgerald was born February 12, 1863, in a small wooden tenement in Boston's North End. His father was an immigrant from Ireland who owned a small grocery and package-goods store, where he sold food products by day and operated a popular saloon by night. Young John was bright and competitive; he graduated from Boston Latin School, and was admitted to Harvard Medical School without examination because of his excellent academic record. The sudden death of his father in 1885, however, forced the young man to leave school and go to work to help his mother keep the family together.

The North End's ward boss, Matthew Keany, took a liking to young Fitzgerald, made him his assistant, and trained him in the ways of local politics. A seat on the city's Common Council gave him additional political experience, so that when Keany died suddenly in 1892, the 29-year-old Fitzgerald was able to take over as the new boss of Ward Six. He immediately used his new power base to win a seat in the state Senate, where he became one of the youngest senators on Beacon Hill. Two years later, in November 1894, "the boy candidate," as he was called, ran a successful campaign for the United States House of Representatives from the Ninth Congressional District.

On September 14, 1905, the popular Irish-born mayor of Boston, Patrick Collins, died suddenly while on vacation, and the entire city was thrown into public mourning. Hardly were the eulogies over when Fitzgerald announced himself a candidate for the vacant position. Despite angry protests from many of the other ward bosses, Fitzgerald barnstormed the city in a motorcade that allowed him to make speeches in every one of the city's twenty-five wards. He adopted the habit of ending his talks with a mellifluous rendition of "Sweet Adeline," which eventually earned him the title of "Honey Fitz."

John F. Fitzgerald, the first Boston-born Irish Catholic mayor of Boston, was sworn into office on January 1, 1906, promising to create "a bigger, better, busier Boston." Despite his assurances of a "businesslike" administration, his City Hall office on School Street was thronged with cronies, lobbyists, pensioners, contractors, and office-seekers of all kinds. In a very short time, Republican critics and members of a reformist Good Government Association were accusing the Fitzgerald administration of widespread graft and corruption. Denouncing the "evils of Fitzgeraldism," in November 1908, the Republicans succeeded in electing George Albee Hubbard as mayor of Boston.

Having removed Fitzgerald from office, the reformists changed the City Charter to make sure he would not return. They abolished the eight-person Board of Aldermen; they reduced the forty-eight-member Common Council to a nine-member City Council; and they increased the power of the mayor by extending his term to four years. To implement these changes, they chose as their candidate James Jackson Storrow, a successful banker and impeccable public servant, to be the first in a new line of modern executives. Fitzgerald, however, upset all the predictions. Calling for "Manhood against Money," and launching a whirlwind campaign that brought him into every ward of the city, Fitzgerald defeated Storrow in the 1910 campaign and became the first mayor to hold a four-year term—much to the chagrin of the Good Government Association.

The only hope the Yankees had left was that when Fitzgerald finally completed his four-year term in 1914 he would depart public life and retire to the suburbs, leaving the mayor's office to some deserving Republican. It came as a surprise to them when 39-year-old James Michael Curley, another Boston-born Irish politician, announced that he planned to succeed Fitzgerald in 1914. When Fitzgerald showed signs of changing his mind and running for another term, Curley cleverly let it be known that he was planning to give a series of public lectures. One of these, titled "Great Lovers, from Cleopatra to Toodles," was a very thinly veiled reference to Fitzgerald's well-known dalliance with a 23-year-old cigarette girl known as "Toodles." Deciding that discretion was the better part of valor, Fitzgerald pleaded ill health and quietly withdrew from the campaign.

After his withdrawal from the 1914 race, Fitzgerald seems to have lost his political self-confidence, and although he made several attempts at a comeback during the 1920s and 1930s, he never won an election again. Until his death on October 3, 1950, at the age of 87, however, Fitzgerald continued to be a beloved elder statesman in the Boston political community, and was destined to have an influence on American politics that went far beyond his own limited achievements. As the result of the marriage of his favorite daughter, Rose, to Joseph P. Kennedy, the son of his political counterpart in East Boston, Patrick J. Kennedy, "Honey Fitz" became grandfather to a President of the United States (John F. Kennedy), an Attorney General and U.S. Senator from New York (Robert F. Kennedy), and a U.S. Senator from Massachusetts (Edward M. Kennedy), as well as great-grandfather to U.S. Representatives and other political figures from the Kennedy clan.

Julia Ward Howe

Born in 1818 to a banker's family in New York City, after the death of her mother Julia Ward was raised by a strict and demanding father. The young girl had formal schooling until she was 16, after which she had tutors in German, Greek, French, and other academic subjects. At an early age Julia showed a special aptitude for composition, and looked forward to writing "the novel or play for the age."

While visiting a friend in Boston, 22-year-old Julia met 40-year-old Dr. Samuel Gridley Howe, the director of the Perkins Institution for the Blind. Despite the disparity in their ages, the two were married in 1843 and made their home in an old colonial house in a bucolic location in South Boston, not far from the Perkins Institution. It was a happy home called Green Peace, with a staff that included a gardener, a cook, a governess, a nurse, and several servants. Julia played the piano, taught songs to her five children, supervised family plays, and greeted the procession of important visitors from all over the world who came to visit the celebrated Dr. Samuel Gridley Howe.

Despite her husband's disapproval, Julia Ward Howe continued to pursue her literary ambitions, writing stories and children's plays, and in 1854 publishing a book of poems anonymously with Ticknor and Fields. When the Civil War broke out in 1861 Dr. Howe was named to the United States Sanitary Commission, and in November 1861 Julia accompanied her husband to Washington, D.C. While sitting in a carriage, Julia and her companions heard a unit of Union soldiers marching by singing a rowdy version of "John Brown's Body." A friend leaned over and suggested that she should write "some good words for that stirring tune." Later that night, according to her own testimony, Julia awoke from her sleep and "the long lines of the desired poem began to twine themselves in my mind." She submitted her poem "The Battle Hymn" to the *Atlantic Monthly,* which published it in its February 1862 issue. The stirring poem, with its famous opening words "Mine eyes have seen the Glory of the coming of the Lord," proved to be an immediate success, not only among Union troops but also among the entire Northern population. By viewing the tragic conflict in Biblical terms as a fulfillment of God's destiny for mankind, Mrs. Howe's inspirational vision associated the Union cause with the most sublime ideals.

After the war Julia Ward Howe continued to pursue a literary career, while becoming increasingly active in the movement for woman's suffrage. She was elected president of the New England's Woman's Club, and in 1868 became president of the New England Woman Suffrage Association. When her husband died in 1876, however, Julia was faced with serious financial worries, and in order to raise money set off on a series of lecture tours that took her not only to all parts of the United States, but also to England, Europe, and the Middle East. Although lecturing had brought her national prominence, Julia was content to spend her later years quietly ensconced in her home on Beacon Hill, reading and writing. Julia Ward Howe died on October 5, 1910, at the age of 91, and was buried at Mount Auburn Cemetery in Cambridge, as a group of children from the Perkins School for the Blind sang a final tribute to her memory.

The Hub

In the middle of a lecture on early nineteenth-century Boston at a prominent local educational institution, a student with a puzzled look raised her hand and asked the instructor: "What is this 'Hub' you keep talking about?" In response to the audible gasps and startled looks of her fellow students, she explained meekly: "I'm from Oregon."

The term "Hub" is a popular reference to a description of Boston in the 1850s by Dr. Oliver Wendell Holmes in his famous series of essays, *The Autocrat of the Breakfast Table.* Actually, Holmes asserted that the Massachusetts State House in Boston was "the hub of the solar system."

There was no particular outcry in response to Holmes's characterization—either one way or the other. Most Bostonians of that period seemed to quietly accept the view that such an exalted position of their city was simply a fact of life that needed no further explanation. It was quite obvious that John Winthrop's original vision of a "City upon a Hill" had come to fruition in the mid-nineteenth century, in a city whose political, cultural, and economic superiority was a beacon for the entire world—indeed, the whole solar system.

Today, on the sidewalk just outside the main entrance of Filene's Department Store at the intersection of Washington and Summer Streets, passersby can see a bronze marker set into the concrete with Holmes's words altered to read: "Hub of the Universe." Just to let visitors know!

Anne Hutchinson

Daughter of a prominent clergyman, Francis Marbury, of Lincolnshire, England, Anne Hutchinson received an early education in her home that laid the foundation for her widely recognized intellectual brilliance, spiritual knowledge, and religious devotion. In September 1634 Hutchinson arrived in Boston with her husband and children, devotedly following her favorite preacher, John Cotton, a dominant force in both religion and government in the early days of the Bay Colony.

The Hutchinsons and their children—eventually numbering fifteen—lived on a piece of land in the Shawmut Peninsula that is to-day the site of the Old Corner Book Store, on Washington Street. Anne Hutchinson became well known in the Boston community for her skills as a midwife, but she acquired even greater notoriety for her outspoken views on Biblical and theological matters, which she put forth at popular weekly meetings in her home. At these meet-ings, she and other women of the town would discuss the sermons of the previous Sunday, going so far as to analyze them for errors, omissions, and examples of hypocrisy. Hutchinson and her follow-ers concluded that the orthodox clergymen of the town were unfit to preach, and at one point walked out of a service en masse when a particular clergyman rose to preach. Hutchinson was soon arguing a doctrine called Antinomianism, which held that the Holy Spirit dwells in every person. According to Hutchinson, a Christian needed to provide evidence of good works or sanctification in order to achieve salvation, beyond the realization of Christ in oneself.

Hutchinson's outspoken ideas were regarded as a dangerous as-sault on the traditions of the Puritan congregation and the authority of the Puritan magistrates. John Winthrop moved to put an end to her influence, and in November 1636 she was brought before the magistrates, charged with the civil offense of acting in disruptive ways inappropriate for a woman. Winthrop had no doubt that this woman of "haughty and fierce carriage, of nimble wit and active spirit, and a very voluble tongue" was the ringleader of all "these distempers." But thanks to the Lord, he concluded, the spell had been broken, and the woman who was the "root of all these trou-bles" was now brought before the seat of justice.

Questions and accusations were flung angrily against Hutchin-son, who defended herself with remarkable skill and Biblical knowl-edge until, in an unguarded moment, she blurted out that God would punish her accusers. Asked how she knew this, she snapped: "By my own immediate revelation." Announcing that this was her-esy, the magistrates ordered her banished from the colony. A few months later this civil punishment was followed by formal excommunication from the church.

Hutchinson left Boston, and with a few others founded a settlement in Newport, Rhode Island, where they lived until 1642. Fearing that Massachusetts authorities were preparing to send a military expedition against the settlement, she fled to Long Island, where in August 1643 she and five of her children were killed by Indians. Boston clergymen rejoiced when they heard the news, declaring that the "American Jezebel" had finally been destroyed by God.

A figure of Anne Hutchinson, her face uplifted, her small daughter by her right side, her left arm clasping a Bible to her breast, stands outside the west wing of the Massachusetts State House on Beacon Hill. Created by the sculptor Cyrus E. Dallin, the bronze statue was given to the Commonwealth in 1922 by the Anne Hutchinson Memorial Association and the State Federation of Women's Clubs.

Ice

"The Ice King"

Frederick Tudor was the son of a prominent Boston judge. His brother William, who was interested in literature, helped found the Boston Athenaeum in 1808 and then in 1811 started *The North American Review*. Frederick, however, was an enterprising young man who was much more interested in making money than in writing articles. At the age of 22, Frederick came up with the idea of shipping blocks of ice from his father's pond in Saugus to the West Indies. Most people thought he was either completely mad or impossibly stupid to think that a cargo of ice could withstand a voyage through tropical waters—a view that seemed confirmed when a shipment of 130 tons of ice Tudor sent to Martinique in 1805 failed to survive the journey.

Frederick Tudor did not give up, however. For years he sought new ways of using doubled-sheathed vessels and sealed-off cargo holds to preserve his product. After experimenting with all sorts of fillers in which to pack the ice, he finally settled on pine sawdust as the most efficient insulation. All the while, he slowly expanded his business to such American ports as Charleston, Savannah, and New Orleans.

In addition to dealing with the technical problems of shipment, young Tudor also had to create a profitable market for his new product. As a salesman he had to persuade potential customers of the pleasures of drinking cold beverages, and as a distributor he had to instruct purchasers how to store the ice properly in hot weather. His entrepreneurial effort proved highly successful, and in May 1833 Tudor made his first venture to India, arriving in Calcutta with almost two-thirds of his cargo of 180 tons of ice safely intact.

Between 1836 and 1850, according to Samuel Eliot Morison's *Maritime History of Massachusetts*, the lucrative Boston ice trade was extended to every large port in South America and to the Far East. For several generations after the Civil War, until cheap artificial ice was invented, the export of ice taken out of North Shore ponds continued to be a mainstay of the New England economy, and Frederick Tudor was memorialized in Boston lore as "The Ice King."

Influenza Epidemic

As the military operations of World War I began to move into the final phases in Europe, Americans became aware of the eruption of a strange malady that was taking on the signs of a serious epidemic. Bostonians first learned about the disease in August 1918, when the *Boston Herald* reported that thirty sailors had been taken off their training ships at Commonwealth Pier suffering from what was called Spanish influenza, because it was believed that the unknown virus had originated in Spain. By early September, the number of cases had gone up to 119, and subsequent reports told of thousands of young soldiers stricken with the ailment at Camp Devens.

Influenza went on to take a terrible toll in major cities throughout the United States. Health officials could only recommend getting fresh air and exercise, and avoiding crowds. Bostonians, however, went ahead with mass rallies in support of the Liberty Loan drive to help the war effort, and on September 11, 1918, also jammed into Fenway Park to watch the Red Sox defeat the Chicago Cubs in the World Series. By the end of the month, when the influenza epidemic reached its frightening peak, the *Boston Globe* reported the death of 206 people. The Boston Stock Exchange closed; theaters, clubs, lodges, and other gathering places were shut down; at the end of the first week in October Boston schools were ordered closed until further notice. Doctors and nurses worked overtime during the crisis, while sisters of the Daughters of Charity visited homes and dispensed medicine, and priests made their somber rounds giving the Last Rites and burying the dead. Deaths were occurring so fast, and gravediggers were so scarce, that secondhand circus tents were used to cover stacks of coffins in local graveyards until proper arrangements could be made. "In the last week of October 1918," wrote one historian, "2,700 Americans died 'over there' in the battle against the Kaiser's army. The same week, twenty-one thousand Americans died of influenza in the United States."

Although the suffering continued for months, by November 1918 the worst effects began to diminish. Schools reopened on October 21, boxing matches started up again at various clubs, schoolboy football games resumed, and saloons, billiard parlors, and soda fountains were allowed to open their doors to customers. And when whistles shrieked and church bells pealed on November 11, 1918, people felt free to go out into the streets and celebrate the news of the Armistice that marked the end of the war. Hundreds of Boston Catholics flocked to the Cathedral of the Holy Cross in the South End to attend a special Mass of Thanksgiving celebrated by Cardinal O'Connell, and the following evening hundreds more crowded into Symphony Hall to enjoy a gala celebration organized by city officials. The great influenza epidemic had finally passed, although many families' lives and fortunes were changed forever.

Jordan Marsh

"Mrs. Jack"

Often referred to as "Mrs. Jack"—although never to her face—Isabella Stewart Gardner was one of Boston's most energetic, unpredictable, and flamboyant citizens. The daughter of a prosperous New York dry-goods merchant named David Stewart, in 1860 she married John Lowell Gardner, son of the last of the East India merchants, and moved to the Gardner family home at 152 Beacon Street as a permanent resident of Boston. With all the money she needed (her father left her $3 million), Mrs. Gardner could do whatever she pleased and, indeed, was often heard to say, with a wave of her hand, *"C'est mon plaisir."* This phrase was engraved over the main entrance to her later residence at Fenway Court.

Isabella Stewart Gardner made her mark on late nineteenth-century Boston society in three ways: as a colorful and capricious women who bedazzled staid Boston society with her eccentricities; as a patron of the arts who discovered unusual talent and encouraged it; and as a connoisseur and collector of fine art in her own right who left to Boston the results of her extraordinary good taste.

At a time when most Proper Bostonians were either Unitarian or Episcopalian, Mrs. Gardner became a Buddhist for a while, before becoming an active and devoted High-Church Episcopalian. She rode around the city in an elaborate carriage, complete with two liveried footmen as well as a coachman. She was reported to drink beer, and on one occasion strolled down Tremont Street with a lion named Rex on a leash. Although she was said to be "plain of face," she was proud of her attractive figure and in 1888 chose John Singer Sargent to paint a controversial portrait of her in a black low-cut gown with a rope of pearls around her narrow waist—the first of several paintings by Sargent. This particular portrait was considered so daring when it was unveiled, however, that it was withdrawn from public view until after her death.

When her 2-year-old son died in 1865, Mrs. Gardner fell into such a deep depression that her husband took her on an extended trip abroad to assuage her grief. Her exposure to foreign cultures and new artistic experiences stimulated her interest in the fine arts, and when she returned to Boston she became friends with members of Boston's artistic and cultural community. She supported or associated with painters like John Singer Sargent and James McNeil Whistler, writers like Henry James and Henry Adams, and local academic figures like the Harvard art historian Charles Eliot Norton. Isabella Stewart Gardner also demonstrated an active interest in the music of late nineteenth-century Boston. William Gerricke, conductor of the Boston Symphony, was a constant friend and visitor, as was Tymoteusz Adamowski, first violinist of the symphony, and his colleague Charles Martin Loeffler, co-first violinist and a distinguished composer in his own right. Mrs. Gardner also was a patron of the Italian composer and pianist Ferruccio Busoni, as well as of Pier Adolfo Tirandelli, director of the Venetian Symphony, whom she later helped secure a post with the Cincinnati Symphony Orchestra. Mrs. Gardner was perhaps most conspicuous, however, as a patron of women artists and musicians. She encouraged the work of Ruth St. Denis, a major influence in modern American dance; she supported the performances of the Australian soprano Nellie Melba; and she was influential in helping Margaret Ruthven Lang become the first woman to have her compositions performed by the Boston Symphony Orchestra.

When her husband Jack died in 1898, Mrs. Gardner once again went into a deep depression, and was advised by her physician to take up a hobby that would distract her from her grief. With typical energy and enthusiasm, she immediately threw herself into the acquisition of great works of art. She availed herself of the counsel and assistance of the young art critic and dealer Bernard Berenson, who traveled throughout Europe and purchased on her behalf, among other important works, several Rembrandts, two Botticellis, two Raphaels, a Rubens, a Degas, and a Titian—all of which would later be displayed at her museum. While on a visit to Italy herself, Mrs. Gardner purchased a complete Venetian palazzo, much of which she had dismantled and shipped back to Boston. Already in her sixties, in the following years she worked closely with the architect Willard T. Sears to reconstruct the palazzo, showing up daily to supervise the project according to her personal specifications. Mrs.

Gardner built her "palace" not merely as a beautiful Renaissance structure, but also as a place to house her famous art collection.

Work on the palazzo was completed in 1901, and for the next two years Mrs. Gardner arranged her collections on three floors, which surround a central garden courtyard filled with flowery plants and trees. She opened Fenway Court on New Year's night, 1903, serving champagne and doughnuts to a select group of invited guests. Thereafter, Isabella Stewart Gardner used Fenway Court as her home during her lifetime, opening the galleries to public view twenty days a year. After her death in 1924, Fenway Court (or "Mrs. Jack's Palace," as some called it) was opened as a public museum. One stipulation was that the arrangement of the collection, including priceless works like Titian's *Rape of Europa,* Vermeer's *The Concert,* and Sargent's *El Jaleo,* never be changed, and that no works be added or sold. The Isabella Stewart Gardner Museum became a permanent tribute to "the greatest of grandes dames," as Cleveland Amory described her in his *Proper Bostonians,* a woman who "persisted in regarding herself as a sort of dedicated spirit to wake up Boston."

A sad epilogue to the story of Mrs. Jack's Palace took place on March 18, 1990, when thieves made their way into the building and walked off with thirteen works of art valued at an estimated $200 million, including Vermeer's *The Concert,* two major Rembrandts, a fine work by Degas, and an oil painting by Manet. Since Mrs. Gardner's will forbade any changes in the permanent location of artworks in the museum, now empty spaces denote the absence of these priceless works of art.

❖

Jimmy's Harborside

Jimmy's Harborside is a landmark Boston seafood restaurant, located for over 40 years on Northern Avenue alongside the city's bustling Fish Pier, where rusty trawlers bring in their catch while screeching seagulls swoop low across the waters. Jimmy's is as much a tribute to the hard work and perseverance of Boston's immigrant population as it is to the standards of good cooking and friendly service.

Early in the twentieth century, when a new wave of immigrants was coming into America from the nations of southern and eastern Europe, 15-year-old Demetrios Efstratios Christodoulos arrived in Boston from the Aegean island of Mytilene. He had nothing more than $13 in his pocket, but visions of opportunity in his mind. As Jimmy Doulos, his adopted American name, the young man served his apprenticeship as a chef at the Bromfield Street Café until 1924, when he established his own small restaurant, a nine-stool café called the Liberty at a location close to the Boston Fish Pier. In those days, the Boston waterfront was an unlighted, desolate area, but Jimmy's Liberty Café was able to attract many customers. Every morning Jimmy would go to the Fish Pier and personally select all his fish for his customers, and then return to the kitchen to prepare his "catch of the day" and put his chowders on the stove. The word spread, and soon the small café had a regular clientele of dockworkers, stevedores, and fishermen whose jobs brought them to the waterfront every day.

In 1955 Jimmy Doulos enlarged his operations, opening a new restaurant on the original site of his Liberty Café. The first restaurant in the nation to offer profit-sharing to its employees, Jimmy's Harborside was a family establishment where Jimmy himself was on hand for the next 26 years to extend a personal welcome to customers. At his death in 1981 his son James Doulos, otherwise known as Charlie or "Jimmy Jr.," took over the business. Since he was eight years old, young Jimmy had worked seven days a week, learning every facet of the business from the ground up in the hardworking family tradition. In 1956, after graduating from Harvard College, Jimmy Jr. became president of the Harborside, as well as its chief executive officer.

Except for a neon sign over the entrance, the restaurant's plain and unadorned exterior blends inconspicuously into the ordinary work-a-day surroundings of the waterfront; inside, the décor features a "Jimmy Jr." boat bar and banks of windows looking out into Boston Harbor. Friendly waiters and waitresses, many of whom have been with Jimmy's for years, attend to large family gatherings,

visiting couples, groups of clergymen, and clusters of well-known
political figures. The menu, specializing in seafood, has been bringing customers back to the waterfront location for over forty years.

In 1980 Charlie Doulos opened a satellite restaurant called
Jimbo's Fish Shanty directly across the street, and a few years later
opened another Jimbo's in the South Shore town of Braintree. Both
seafood restaurants feature model locomotives traveling along
tracks suspended from the ceiling, to dramatize the hobo theme.
The Doulos family waits to see what changes the Big Dig and the
expansive new developments on the South Boston waterfront will
bring to one of the oldest and most colorful parts of the city.

❖

Jordan Marsh

In 1841, an enterprising 19-year-old named Eben Dyer Jordan began a small dry-goods business at 168 Hanover Street in Boston's
crowded North End. Ten years later, Jordan went into partnership
with Benjamin L. Marsh, launching an enterprise that would make
Jordan Marsh a household name in Boston. As business expanded
and new properties were acquired to accommodate the merchandise that came from all over the world, Jordan Marsh changed locations several times before it finally settled permanently at 450 Washington Street.

Upon Eben Jordan's death in 1895, his son Eben Jordan Jr., together with Edward J. Mitton, took over direction of the company.
They modernized by installing telephones, electric lights, and ele-
vators, and startled the retail world by selling to customers on
credit. After the deaths of Jordan and Mitton in the early 1900s, the
business was taken over in succession by George W. Mitton, by his
brother Richard in 1930, and then in 1937 by his son Edward R.
Mitton. By this time Jordan Marsh was a full-line department store
that attracted customers from all over Boston and its neighborhoods. During Christmastime, the brilliantly lighted display windows of Jordan Marsh drew children and their families to see the famous "Enchanted Village," featuring tableaus portraying the story

of Bethlehem, Santa Claus, scenes from Dickens's *Christmas Carol*, and other familiar images of the season.

With the demographic changes of the postwar 1950s and 1960s, Jordan Marsh expanded into suburban shopping centers throughout the Northeast, where customers could take advantage of free parking, air conditioning, and numerous stores under a single roof. During this same period, Jordan Marsh also undertook an ambitious reconstruction of its downtown Boston store at the corner of Washington and Summer Streets. Customers' changes in shopping habits and patterns of residence, combined with corporate mergers and financial difficulties, cut deeply into Jordan Marsh's operations. During 1989 Jordan's became enmeshed in the troubles of its Toronto-based owner, Campeau Corp., which was forced to file for bankruptcy, and the following year, Jordan's closed several of its stores in the Greater Boston area. During 1994–1995, Federated Department Stores merged its Abraham & Straus/Jordan Marsh unit into Macy's East as part of its planned merger with R. H. Macy & Co. and began laying off workers. Finally, on January 11, 1996, the announcement came that Jordan Marsh stores would officially change their name to Macy's and operate under the Macy's East division of Federated Department Stores Inc. One more time-honored, Boston-owned business had lost its local identity, although Mayor Thomas Menino has seen to it that the Enchanted Village survived for Boston children to visit on City Hall Plaza at Christmastime.

K

The Steaming Kettle

The Steaming Kettle

When the Oriental Tea Company opened its establishment on Court Street in 1874, in Boston's Scollay Square area, it commissioned the coppersmiths Hicks and Badger to fashion a massive copper teakettle to hang outside the building as a sign of its specialty. To advertise its grand opening, the company offered a prize of a chest of 40 pounds of tea to the customer who could make the nearest guess as to the capacity of the large kettle—one guess per purchase.

When the contest was over, on January 2, 1875, a crowd the *Boston Post* estimated at fifteen thousand people gathered to view the official measurement. A platform had been built around the kettle, where a Boston court judge and the city's Sealer of Weights and Measures presided over the ceremony. When the lid was removed, a small boy popped up out of the kettle. After he was lifted out, he was followed by another—and then another—until eight boys and a man wearing a tall silk hat had emerged. Then the announcement of the prize took place. Out of the thirteen thousand guesses handed in, eight persons had guessed the correct amount: 227 gallons, 2 quarts, 1 pint, and 3 gills. The prize of tea was shared among the eight winners.

Over the years, the copper kettle, with a steady stream of steam coming out of its spout, became a landmark in the city, even as it was moved to different locations when the buildings to which it was attached were replaced by new buildings or, during the 1960s, torn down to make way for the new Government Center that eliminated most of old Scollay Square. Fortunately the old kettle was preserved and was eventually suspended above a first-floor door in the curved red-brick building known as the Sears Crescent. There, on the south side of the new City Hall Plaza, visitors can still see the gleaming kettle spouting its steam into the air, a delightful remnant of old Boston, not too far from its original location in a Scollay Square that no longer exists.

❖

King Philip's War

When the English Puritans first settled on the Shawmut Peninsula in 1630, they had few serious problems with the native peoples in the area. A series of plagues and epidemics during the early 1600s, including smallpox, chicken pox, measles, and other so-called childhood diseases brought in by Europeans, to which the natives had no immunity, had whittled down the Indian population along the Massachusetts seacoast from about 3,000 to a mere 500. In 1633, three years after the establishment of the Puritan colony, a smallpox epidemic reduced the ranks of the local Indians even further.

As the number of white settlers in the Massachusetts Bay Colony doubled between 1650 and 1675, and as new arrivals moved westward and southward, their desire to acquire more land collided with the determination of native groups like the Naragansetts and the Wampanoags to keep what had always been theirs. Metacom, the sachem of the Wampanoags, or King Philip, as the English called him, was forced to accept one humiliation after another at the hands of the settlers, until Indian resentment against them began to build. The explosion came in Plymouth in June 1675, when an English jury hanged three natives for killing a Harvard-educated Christian Indian named John Sassamon. There were immediate outbreaks of burning, looting, and violence, as King Philip's warriors attacked a number of English settlements.

Meeting in Boston, local colonial leaders formed the New England Confederation, which created a large military force out of the militia companies of Boston and surrounding New England towns. Despite their numbers, however, the Confederation was unable to capture King Philip or pin down his highly mobile warriors, who frustrated them with hit-and-run tactics. By November 1675 English settlements in the upper Connecticut Valley had been laid waste by Indian attacks, and by the following spring Philip's warriors were attacking the towns of Lancaster, Medfield, and Weymouth, less than 20 miles from Boston.

By the late spring of 1676, however, the Indian offensive began to peter out. The difficulty of obtaining food and weapons for the warriors, combined with the effects of exposure and starvation on their families, caused some groups to return to their villages and others to surrender. Indians identified as ringleaders of the native uprising were shot or hanged, while some 450 captives were imprisoned on Deer Island in Boston Harbor and later sold into slavery. On August 12, 1676, the Boston-led military forces attacked a Wampanoag village near Bridgewater, and afterward discovered that one of the Indians they had killed was King Philip. After his body had been decapitated and quartered, the troops proudly displayed the chief's head on their triumphal march back to Boston.

The costs of the war for the white settlers had been enormous. Two-thirds of New England's towns had been attacked, many of them burned to the ground. Crops were ruined, trade was impaired, and one white man out of ten in Massachusetts had been lost in the fighting. The costs for the natives were even greater. Several thousand Indians had been killed in the course of King Philip's War, and many of their native villages had been completely devastated. For the native peoples of New England, it was the last serious attempt to halt the loss of their lands and the destruction of their culture as white settlements moved inexorably into the wilderness.

King's Chapel

King's Chapel was the first major stone building in the country. It replaced a smaller wooden chapel on the same site, which continued to function as a church even as the new building was being built around it. Designed in 1749 by Peter Harrison of Newport, Rhode Island, regarded as the most notable architect of colonial America, it was the first large building in the colonies to be built of quarried stone. The Georgian interior was modeled on the church of St. Martin-in-the-Fields in London; the double Corinthian columns in the interior of the church were rare in English churches of the period, and are unique among American colonial churches. A planned steeple and spire were never finished, and in an effort to save money the columns were built of wood and made to look like stone. Before the Revolutionary War, King's Chapel served as the headquarters of all colonial Anglican churches in America.

After the War for Independence, in 1787 King's Chapel became the first Unitarian Church in America under its first post-Revolutionary minister, the Reverend James Freeman. The pulpit is the oldest in continuous use in the United States.

❖

"Know-Nothings"

The influx of Irish Catholics into Boston during the early nineteenth century caused increasing fear and anxiety among the Protestants of Anglo-Saxon heritage who composed a great part of the city's population. Contemptuous of the Irish Catholic immigrants' national origin as well as their Papist religious beliefs, native Bostonians feared their effect on social norms, cultural standards, and democratic political traditions.

As the number of Irish immigrants increased during the 1820s and 1830s, driven by English land policies, episodes of bigotry and violence began to erupt in Boston. In 1834 an angry nativist mob burned down an Ursuline convent of Irish Catholic nuns in nearby Charlestown; in 1837 a street riot broke out in the Irish section of town between a company of Yankee firemen returning from a fire and a group of Irish mourners conducting a funeral procession. The resultant "Broad Street Riot," reportedly involving some fifteen thousand persons at the height of the clash, was symptomatic of rising tensions between the Yankees and the Celts.

But if native Bostonians were alarmed at this first wave of Irish Catholics, they were astounded at the flood of new immigrants who sought shelter in America when the catastrophic potato blight in 1846 brought death, starvation, and disease to the poor people of Ireland. In just one year, 1847, the city of Boston, which had been taking in Irish immigrants at the rate of about four or five thousand a year, was inundated by over 37,000 arrivals, most of whom were listed simply as "labourers." They came to Boston sick, penniless, and exhausted, settling where they came ashore. Living in filth and squalor in the congested streets of the North End or in dilapidated shacks and makeshift cellars along the waterfront, they struggled to survive in their new and hostile environment.

In the face of this newly enlarged "Catholic menace," many native-born Americans felt that the massive immigration produced by the Great Famine had transformed what had been essentially a local problem into a national catastrophe that called for a national response. During 1852–53 a number of local patriotic organizations combined to form the "American Party," a national political party designed to protect the United States from the "insidious wiles of foreigners." The organization was highly secret, complete with handshakes and passwords, and became popularly known as the "Know-Nothing Party" because its members were pledged to absolute secrecy regarding the organization, its activities, and its membership. Their standard response to any question about it was: "I know nothing." The object of the new third party was to keep newly arrived immigrants in a subservient position while it developed legislation to put much stricter controls on further Catholic immigration.

In an amazingly short period of time, political power in such East Coast cities as Boston, New York, Philadelphia, and Baltimore swung to the new party. In Massachusetts, the American Party succeeded in electing the governor, all the state officers, the entire state Senate, and all but one member of the House; Jerome Van Crowninshield Smith, a longtime nativist, became mayor of Boston. Once its members took office, the Know-Nothing legislature announced itself ready to eliminate "Rome, Rum, and Robbery," and lost little time in pushing forward a program of "Temperance, Liberty, and Protestantism." In addition to proposing a so-called Twenty-One-Year Law that would prevent any immigrant from voting until he had been a Massachusetts resident for twenty-one years, the legislature dissolved all Irish militia companies and confiscated all their military equipment. The reading of the Protestant version of the Bible (the King James version) was made compulsory in all public schools, and in February 1855 a joint committee was formed to inquire into "certain practices" alleged to be taking place in nunneries and Catholic schools. The members of the so-called Nunnery Committee undertook inspections of local Catholic schools with such heavy-footed insensitivity that it lost credibility and was quickly dissolved.

As the presidential election of 1856 approached the American Party made plans to organize a national convention and put a Know-Nothing president in the White House. In the spring of 1856, however, startling reports from the Kansas Territory, where the issue of slavery was being hotly contested, changed the balance of political power throughout the nation. On May 21 proslavery forces sacked the "Boston abolition town" of Lawrence, Kansas, and carried off a number of Free-Soil leaders. Three days later, a Free-Soil defender named John Brown and several of his followers hacked to death five proslavery settlers in bloody retaliation for the attack on the Free-Soilers. And then came the news from the nation's capital that Massachusetts Senator Charles Sumner had been severely beaten on the floor of the Senate chamber by an enraged Southern congressman named Preston Brooks. By the summer of 1856 it was clear that the issue of slavery was the immediate and all-consuming preoccupation of voters in all parts of the country. There was little chance that something as nebulous and contrived as the "Catholic menace" would be able to distract the nation's attention from the problem of slavery, which might well bring about the destruction of the Union.

The triumph of the American Party, although swift and spectacular, was remarkably short-lived. When its presidential nominee, the former president Millard Fillmore, received the electoral votes of only a single state (eight votes from Maryland), it was evident that its moment of glory had passed. Despite its pitiful collapse, however, the Know-Nothing movement was a dramatic and frightening example of the fear with which white nativists, in Boston and in other parts of the country, regarded the influx of Catholic immigrants, and the lengths to which they would go to keep the outsiders in their place.

Louisburg Square

The Last Hurrah

The distinctive nature of Irish politics in Boston is best revealed in Edwin O'Connor's classic political novel *The Last Hurrah* (1956). O'Connor draws heavily upon the uproarious career of Boston's perennial mayor, James Michael Curley, dubbed by his biographer Jack Beatty "The Rascal King," to create the fictitious character of Mayor Frank Skeffington. The novel revolves around the 72-year-old Skeffington's last political campaign for reelection as mayor of Boston. The story is set against the background of the conflicts between the Irish and the Yankees, the differences between the Catholics and the Protestants, the feuds between the loyal old hangers-on with their roots in the neighborhoods and the ambitious young newcomers with ties to federal power. O'Connor paints a colorful portrait of Skeffington, seen through the eyes of a curious and affectionate young nephew, as the corrupt and powerful head of a ruthless political machine, and yet a man whose keen sense of compassion and human understanding make it possible for him to maintain the loyalty and devotion of his political followers.

The nephew is amazed at his uncle's skill at manipulating people's foibles, taking advantage of human weaknesses, and exploiting the emotions of crowds, whether at political rallies, strategy sessions, or Irish wakes. But it is all in vain. O'Connor skillfully presents Skeffington's ultimate defeat, his "last hurrah," as a foreshadowing of the demise of a whole generation of old-fashioned Irish ward bosses all over the country when the federal government became a major force in providing the social and economic benefits that used to be distributed as patronage by the ward bosses at the local level. To one observer, the reason for Skeffington's defeat was simple: "He played the old game too long, and the Irish have changed too much."

The Late George Apley

Written by John P. Marquand, a Harvard graduate who worked for the *Boston Transcript* for a time, *The Late George Apley* (1937) is a brilliant satire cleverly constructed as the personal memoir of a fictitious character. It is a fascinating, warm, and witty portrayal of a Proper Bostonian who supposedly lived from 1866 to 1933, etched against the tradition-bound history of three generations of Apley men who had done much to shape the social, economic, and cultural history of the Boston in which they lived.

As George Apley comes of age during the latter part of the nineteenth century, he is acutely conscious of the responsibilities his distinguished ancestry has imposed upon him to maintain the high moral and ethical standards of the past. Although he considers himself a compassionate and tolerant man, he unconsciously reflects the values of his own class in the decisions he makes in the face of new ethnic forces which are threatening to change the city. George Apley is not at all opposed to change and modernization—he simply wants to control them in the best interest of those values and principles he has always subscribed to. His views become especially poignant as he instructs his son in the traditions and responsibilities of the members of the Apley family, preparing him to act with others of his class as the self-appointed guardians of a Boston whose rapid changes have already made them relics of an earlier time.

The Liberty Tree

On the exterior of a building at 630 Washington Street, on the corner of Essex Street at the northern edge of what was previously known as Boston's Combat Zone, is a plaque marking the site of the original Liberty Tree. Underneath a depiction of the tree itself are the words SONS OF LIBERTY 1766 / INDEPENDENCE OF THE COUNTRY 1776.

The tradition of the Liberty Tree had its origins on the morning of August 14, 1765. Enraged by the passage of the Stamp Act, colonial patriots hung two effigies on one of the great elm trees located on the corner of the present Washington and Essex streets. One was a dummy representing the local tax official, Andrew Oliver; the other was a gigantic boot with a figure of the Devil peeping out—a reference to Lord Butte ("Boot"), who was reported to have instigated the disgraceful act that colonials believed violated their right to have taxes passed only by bodies in which they were represented.

On that same morning, the Sons of Liberty and other patriot groups selected one of the largest elms to serve as their "Liberty Tree," a symbol of their united opposition to the British tax. The area around this stand of old elm trees provided ample room for thousands of Bostonians to gather, to demonstrate, and to vent their anger in what became known as "Liberty Hall." So-called liberty trees soon made their appearance in almost every town and village along the coast. "No tree in English history—not Jack Code's Oak, not the 'Royal Oak' that sheltered Charles the Second," writes Esther Forbes in *Paul Revere and the World He Lived In*, "caused more trouble than this Boston tree."

The British were eventually to have their revenge, however. During the military occupation of Boston, firewood was so scarce during the freezing cold winter of 1775–76 that almost everything made of wood was used for fuel. "The British simply hacked buildings like forests, ships and trees like logs," writes Jane Holtz Kay in *Lost Boston*. "With glee, they downed the Liberty Tree." The old elm was unceremoniously chopped down by a group of Tories and turned into fourteen cords of firewood. After the war was over and independence secured, a Liberty Pole was set up in the spot where the Liberty Tree had once stood, now opposite a shop that Paul Revere opened to sell English goods to local Boston customers.

In 1824, when General Lafayette came to visit Boston for the first time in the forty years since the Revolutionary War, Bostonians came from near and far to pay their respects to the aged hero at the site on Washington Street where they had earlier agitated for independence. They gathered beneath a 25-foot gold-lettered arch that had been erected for the occasion on the site of the old Liberty Tree stump. Lafayette was reported to have been "much affected" by this patriotic display, appreciating that he was upon "the stamping ground of the Revolution and in front of the old Liberty Tree."

During the nineteenth century the David Sears commercial building was constructed on the old historical site, and was appropriately named the Liberty Tree Building. It had a series of elegant stores on the ground level and magnificent ballrooms on the second and third floors. The Sears building later fell into disrepair, until in recent years it was completely restored as part of an economic revival of lower Washington Street. The Liberty Tree Building, designated as a historic site by the Boston Landmark Commission, at present houses the Boston office of the Massachusetts Registry of Motor Vehicles.

Locke-Ober's

In 1880 Frank Locke and Louis F. Ober opened a fashionable European-style restaurant in the heart of Boston. Tucked quietly away just off the intersection of Washington and Summer Streets, at the end of a small alleyway called Winter Place, it was known at various times as the Dutchman's, the Winter Place Restaurant, Locke's, and finally Locke-Ober's. For over a century it has been known for its superb cuisine, fine service, and touch of Old World elegance. For nearly a century, too, it was patronized principally by important members of Boston's legal, financial, and political establishment.

Until recent years the dining room on the ground floor of Locke-Ober's, with its plush Victorian decor, leather-upholstered chairs, long bar, and large nude painting was restricted to men only. Women were permitted to dine only in the private rooms upstairs, with heavy draperies and dark mahogany furniture, although by custom the ladies were allowed in the first-floor dining room on New Year's Eve, or when the Harvard-Yale game was held in

Cambridge—and even then, only when the Crimson eleven triumphed.

In recent years, as the climate of downtown Boston has changed, Locke-Ober's has changed as well. "The regulars aren't as regular anymore," observed one frequent diner, commenting on the declining number of prominent lawyers, politicians, and businessmen who come to lunch regularly at their favorite haunt, seated at their special tables. Nowadays the upstairs dining rooms sit mostly empty, the tables decked out with fine silverware, elegant china, and stiff linen napkins. Rumors have been circulating that a well-known woman restaurateur is interested in purchasing and renovating the 124-year-old institution. A woman taking charge of "one of the last bastions of Boston Brahmin's male guard" would indeed be a fascinating turn of events in a city that does not take to change easily.

Logan International Airport

What is now known as Logan International Airport had its beginnings as a small landing field for biplanes at Jeffries Point in East Boston, a narrow spit of windswept land jutting out into Boston Harbor. The field officially opened in 1923 as the East Boston Airport, with festivities that included an air meet. Three years later, in 1926, the first passenger–air mail flight arrived from New York, and a short time later a propeller-driven plane left for Hartford and New York City with some 337 pounds of mail.

In 1927 Charles Lindbergh and his "Spirit of St. Louis" were welcomed to the East Boston Airport on the way back from his historic solo flight across the Atlantic. During World War II the airport became an active center for transatlantic flights, and in 1947 the airport became "international" with the inauguration of regular overseas flights to Canada, Bermuda, Lisbon, and London.

In 1943 the state legislature named the airport in honor of Major General Edward L. Logan, a native of South Boston who commanded the Yankee Division during World War I. A man who reputedly never flew in an airplane in his life, his statue stands at the airport's entrance. The following year, Logan Airport entered the jet age with the start of prop-jet service to Philadelphia and Miami. In 1959 the Massachusetts Port Authority (Massport) took over operation of Logan Airport.

In 1973 Massport dedicated the world's tallest airport control tower at Logan International Airport. The 22-story tower, 285 feet tall, gives FAA controllers a full view of all air operations areas. Logan handles more than 26 million passengers a year, with daily flights to Europe, Asia, and Africa. In order to accommodate the great increase in air traffic for both domestic and overseas flights, the land area of Logan Airport has expanded enormously over the course of a quarter of a century, mostly through landfill, to 2,400 acres. The increased number of large jet planes taking off and making landings at Logan, combined with the expansion that brought landing strips much closer to surrounding residential neighborhoods, has created serious problems of noise, air pollution, and environmental hazards, as well as controversies over real estate values. To offset some of these problems, Massport has insulated more than 4,600 dwellings in neighborhoods close to the airport to provide soundproofing against plane noise, and has also undertaken the construction of a system of buffer zones to improve the quality of life for local residents.

Recent proposals to construct an additional landing strip at Logan Airport have caused longstanding differences between Massport officials and residents of the surrounding neighborhoods to flare up anew. Massport authorities insist that for the responsible handling of greatly increased air traffic at Logan Airport, in a safe and efficient manner, the addition of another landing strip is absolutely essential. They point out that there has been no substantial expansion since 1977, and that Logan is now the sixth-worst airport in the country for flight delays. Local residents, however, have raised objections to the increased noise and air pollution that will result from additional flights, as well as the negative effect increased air traffic will have on housing prices and real estate values in the area. These residents are asking Massport to make more use of regional airports at such locations as Worcester, Massachusetts; Manchester, New Hampshire; and Providence, Rhode Island.

Louisburg Square

Perhaps one of the most distinctive sites in the Beacon Hill area is a small, privately owned plot of green grass and elm trees, closed off by a black iron fence and surrounded by a private way paved with cobblestones. This commonly owned park is the property of the Louisburg Square Proprietors, which is regarded as America's first homeowners' association. The tree-shaded oval is highlighted by two statues—Christopher Columbus standing at one end and the Greek statesman Aristides at the other. The park runs between Pinckney and Mount Vernon streets, and along with the houses bordering it is known as Louisburg Square, the residential heart of the fashionable Beacon Hill district.

It is assumed to have taken its name from the victory of the English over the French at Louisbourg, Nova Scotia, in 1748, an engagement in which many Bostonians were involved; visitors are cautioned that the preferred local pronunciation is the English form, "Looisburg," and not the French form, "Looieburg." Surrounded by bowfront townhouses dating from the 1830s and 1840s, the area is reminiscent of the small residential squares Charles Bulfinch must have seen during his travels in London. (One writer has suggested that the plan for the square may have been based on a design by Bulfinch.) In recent years, the custom of lighting the windows of the charming dwellings around Louisburg Square with candles on Christmas Eve, with the old inside shutters left open, while communal groups sing Christmas carols, is even more reminiscent of old London in the days of Charles Dickens.

Over the generations, Louisburg Square has been home to a fascinating and eclectic group of people. During the nineteenth century, such prominent writers and intellectuals as Louisa May Alcott, author of *Little Women;* her father, Bronson Alcott; and John Gorham Palfrey, the historian and editor of the *North American Review,* made their home there. William Dean Howells lived in that section of Beacon Hill, as did the novelist Henry James and Samuel Gray Ward, a prominent banker and philanthropist. For more than a century, the social-service-oriented sisters of the Anglican convent of the Society of St. Margaret maintained a residence in Louisburg Square, leaving for Roxbury in 1990. And in recent years such well-known figures as the playwright Archibald MacLeish, the physician and best-selling author Robin Cook, United States Senator John Kerry and his wife Teresa Heinz, and the Boston Celtics owner Don Gaston have made Louisburg Square their Boston address.

Lowell Institute

During the 1830s and 1840s Boston was the center of a remarkable outburst of creative literary activity. Noted poets, writers, and essayists such as Ralph Waldo Emerson, Henry David Thoreau, Henry Wadsworth Longfellow, and Oliver Wendell Holmes, together with historians such as Jared Sparks, William Hickling Prescott, John Lothrop Motley, and Francis Parkman, formed the basis of a glittering literati that became world famous.

Raised to believe in "the infinite capacity of human nature," Boston's intellectual leaders felt an obligation to extend the benefits of this cultural renaissance to every citizen of Boston, regardless of class or station. At a time when the so-called Lyceum lecture system was gaining ground in many parts of the United States, the Boston literati worked with a number of local organizations to establish lecture programs throughout the city. Edward Everett and Daniel Webster led the way by creating the Useful Knowledge Society; in a short period of time other groups followed. The Boston Lyceum, the Mercantile Library Association, and the Mechanics Association were among the best-known groups that helped make the "lecture habit" a distinctive Boston phenomenon.

Upon his unexpected death in 1836, John Lowell, eldest son of the textile entrepreneur Francis Cabot Lowell, left half of his estate ($250,000) for a fund to underwrite in perpetuity free public lectures for adult audiences. The Lowell Lectures proved to be extremely popular in their day, with as many as eight to ten thousand people applying for tickets to a particular course of lectures by nationally known scholars like Benjamin Silliman in chemistry or James Russell Lowell in poetry, or by Ralph Waldo Emerson, Edward Everett, or Oliver Wendell Holmes speaking on their own choice of subjects.

Over the years, although its free public lectures remained popular, the Lowell Institute shifted the focus of its activities. In 1862 the first trustee, John Amory Lowell, placed some funds into a series of free, college-level courses at the new Massachusetts Institute of Technology. In 1903 the third trustee, A. Lawrence Lowell, directed other sums into supporting a two-year mechanical and electrical engineering course. He also set up the University Extension Program at Harvard, where students could attend evening courses in the liberal arts taught by Harvard faculty members.

In the early 1940s the position of Trustee of the Lowell Institute passed to Ralph Lowell, who in 1946 persuaded several neighboring colleges and universities to join in a venture in educational broadcasting called the Lowell Institute Cooperative Broadcasting Council. In order to obtain an FM license from the FCC, the Lowell Institute formed the WGBH Educational Foundation, Inc. (the initials stood for Great Blue Hills, although some local wags said they really indicated "God Bless Harvard").

Seven years later, generous funding from the Edward and Lincoln Filene Fund, as well as support from the Fund for Adult Education, encouraged the WGBH Foundation to apply to the FCC for a television license to produce educational programs, which it received on July 16, 1953. Thus the century-old Lowell Institute moved into the educational television business. WGBH is now one of the country's leading producers of public television programming, and the Lowell Institute's teaching program has become part of the Harvard Extension School, which offers part-time study in the evenings to some 13,000 students each year.

M

The Boston Massacre

"The Mahatma"

Born in Boston on December 3, 1859, of immigrant parents from County Cork, Martin Lomasney was forced to leave grammar school at the age of 11 when both his father and his mother died within a year. He earned money by selling newspapers, shining shoes, and running errands, until a local politician provided him with a series of city jobs as a laborer, a lamplighter, and a health inspector.

Lomasney grew up to be a thickset man, with a massive dome, gold-rimmed spectacles, a small moustache, and a prominent jaw that jutted out in an aggressive fashion. He could be easily identified at a distance by the battered old straw hat he wore rain or shine throughout the year. A perennial bachelor, he lived a simple life in a modest rooming house, attended church regularly, neither drank nor smoked, and avoided public functions whenever possible.

In 1885 Martin Lomasney, his brother Joseph, and a group of close friends founded the Hendricks Club, named after Grover Cleveland's first vice-president, who was regarded as a friend of the Irish. At the Hendricks Club the men of the West End's Ward 8 could meet, gossip, exchange information, play cards (dice and liquor were not allowed), and engage in political discussions. Lomasney kept a permanent office on the second floor of the Hendricks Club, which was originally located in a building near the North Station and later moved to Bowdoin Square. From this office, the "Mahatma," as he came to be known because of his exalted rank in the community, worked day and night to provide for the needs of his people and to protect them from what he called "the inquisitorial terrors of organized charity." Lomasney knew full well that the humiliating experience of poor Irish immigrants suffering rude interrogations by insensitive and often hostile city welfare officials in order to receive public assistance brought back painful memories of the treatment of the Irish by their English overlords.

Lomasney and his associates served not only as an employment agency and a charitable bureau, but also as a center for political planning and strategy, turning the Hendricks Club into what he called "a machine for getting votes." The needs of the poor, uneducated, often unemployed immigrant people of the district were basic but largely unattainable: food and clothing, dentures and eyeglasses, jobs and pardons, medical care and legal advice. The reward for political support was the assurance by the ward boss that he would fill these basic needs. As Lomasney once philosophized: "The great mass of people are interested in only three things—food, clothing, and shelter. A politician in a district like mine sees to it that his people get these things. If he does, then he doesn't have to worry about their loyalty and support." It was as simple as that. Power and patronage went hand in hand in the Irish neighborhoods.

In addition to establishing himself as the undisputed ward boss of the West End's Ward 8, Lomasney also decided which candidates for city office would, and would not, receive the backing of his powerful political organization. Lomasney also participated actively himself in public affairs at both the city and the state levels. Starting in 1896, he ran successfully for two terms in the state Senate; served another year in the House of Representatives; and then sat on the Board of Aldermen, where he became a powerful influence on citywide affairs. Later Martin Lomasney returned to Beacon Hill to resume his House seat in the state legislature, where the "Mahatma" would remain for the greater part of the next twenty years.

Today, one of the few lasting commemorations of the "Mahatma" is a small street called Lomasney Way that runs beside the Fleet Center. Ironically, the street looks out onto the fashionable townhouses of the Charles River Park project, constructed during the 1960s on the rubble of the old West End where Martin Lomasney once exercised his influence as one of the city's most powerful ward bosses.

Make Way for Ducklings

In 1941 Robert McCloskey wrote and illustrated a book for children called *Make Way for Ducklings,* which almost immediately became a popular classic, not only for children but for grownups as well. The story tells of Mr. and Mrs. Mallard, who flew into Boston looking for a place to live and found a likely little island in the pond in the Public Garden. Frightened away by a boy on his bicycle, they flew over Boston to find a more peaceful spot. Louisburg Square looked pleasant, but there was no water; so they continued on to the Charles River, where they nestled in the bushes along the bank. Here Mrs. Mallard laid eight eggs, while Mr. Mallard flew off to find a permanent home in the Public Garden.

Mrs. Mallard taught her eight fledglings how to swim, how to dive, and how to walk in a straight line. When she thought they were ready, she headed across the busy streets of Boston toward the Public Garden. Officer Michael stopped the traffic so that Mrs. Mallard and her ducklings could cross Charles Street safely and parade into the Public Garden. When nightfall came, they all swam to their little island and went happily to sleep.

In 1987, in commemoration of the 150th anniversary of the Public Garden, the Newton artist Nancy Shon created a bronze sculpture, *Mrs. Mallard and Her Eight Ducklings.* With Mrs. Mallard in the lead, the eight ducklings—Jack, Kack, Lack, Mack, Nack, Ouack, Pack, and Quack—parade in single file across the Garden's grounds. The figures of the ducklings have become a major attraction for thousands of visiting children who hug them, kiss them, or ride proudly on their backs.

Massachusetts General Hospital

In 1810, according to the account in Robert Dalzell's *Enterprising Elite,* two of Boston's leading physicians, James Jackson and John C. Warren, circulated a letter among the town's wealthy residents outlining the need for a hospital to care for "lunatics and other sick persons." The following year the state legislature voted to incorporate such an undertaking, but only on condition that the supporters raise $100,000 of private money within a five-year period. Prominent Bostonians made substantial individual contributions and also organized vigorous door-to-door campaigns in all parts of the community to raise the necessary funds. On July 4, 1818, the governor and his council joined with "a great concourse of citizens" to witness the laying of the cornerstone of the Massachusetts General Hospital, the "general" in its name signifying its intention to serve "the whole family of man."

After the selection of Prince's Pasture on the banks of the Charles River in Boston's West End as the site, Charles Bulfinch was chosen to design the main building of the new hospital on Allen Street. This was Bulfinch's last architectural commission in Boston; his friend Alexander Parris took over supervision of the building when Bulfinch moved to Washington, D.C., at the request of President James Madison to rebuild the nation's Capitol and restore other buildings the British had burned in 1814. The handsome hospital of Chelmsford granite, designed in the Greek Revival style with a pedimented portico of massive Ionic columns, is topped by a shallow, saucer-like dome.

For many years, wealthy members of the Boston Associates, a group connected through business, family, and investments, took a strong personal interest in the MGH. Dr. Jackson was the brother of Patrick Tracy Jackson, a well-known merchant and financier; Francis Cabot Lowell, the textile manufacturer, was elected to the hospital's first board of trustees. Twenty-seven members of the Boston Associates served as hospital trustees, while many more made substantial contributions on a regular basis. In January 1844 the trustees voted to add two new wings to the Allen Street building in response to the demands of a growing urban population. Once again the general public responded generously to a fund drive that was directed by such well-known figures as Thomas Handasyd Perkins and Abbott Lawrence.

On October 16, 1846, one of the great discoveries in medical history was demonstrated in the hospital's operating theater. On that day, the Boston dentist William T. G. Morton demonstrated the use of anesthesia to eliminate pain during surgery. Using a glass inhaler, Morton administered ether to a patient with a tumor on his jaw; when the patient awoke he informed the audience that he had felt no pain during the operation to remove the tumor. Known since that time as the Ether Dome, the operating theater, originally designed by Charles Bulfinch, has been carefully restored to commemorate the historic medical event.

With the advent of ether, the number of surgeries being performed in America increased enormously—but so did the danger of infection. During the Civil War, more men died from infection in the field hospitals than on the battlefield. In 1864 the Scottish surgeon Joseph Lister demonstrated that carbolic acid was an effective antiseptic in the operating room. Five years later, while studying abroad, Boston's Dr. J. Collins Warren visited Dr. Lister in Glasgow. He brought the idea of the antiseptic technique back to the MGH, and subsequently promoted it at every opportunity, eventually revolutionizing the care of surgical patients. Another MGH physician, Dr. Reginald H. Fitz, in 1866 identified an inflamed appendix as the cause of a mysterious and often fatal abdominal infection, which he labeled "appendicitis." The new surgical procedure to treat it gained immediate international acceptance and further enhanced the growing reputation of the MGH.

While the MGH was making advances in medical and surgical care, it was also concerning itself with mental illness. In 1816 it purchased an 18-acre estate in Charlestown (now Somerville) and established a hospital for the mentally ill that offered facilities for sixty patients. Under the direction of Dr. Rufus Wyman, it was the first institution of its kind to administer humane and effective treatment instead of merely providing custodial care. Designed as a separate department of the MGH, it generally provided discreet and understanding care for members of Boston's more prominent families who suffered from mental illness. By the 1840s, however, with the influx of foreign immigrants contributing to the increase in the city's population, the demands on the hospital's services grew steadily. In 1892 the institution was named McLean Hospital in honor of a local merchant, John McLean, who made generous bequests from his estate.

Because of the increasing noise created by the nearby railroad in the Charlestown area, the trustees of McLean worked with Frederick Law Olmsted to select a more remote and tranquil site for the hospital, settling on 114 acres of land in the suburban town of Belmont. By 1895 all operations had been transferred to the new location, where a cluster of buildings were arranged in an arc around the main yellow-brick Administration Building. In time other structures, including a Rehabilitation Center and a highly recognized Research Center, expanded the operations as well as the size of the institution. Today, McLean Hospital, affiliated with Harvard Medical School as well as MGH, ranks as one of the most respected psychiatric research and treatment facilities in the nation.

In the meantime, Massachusetts General Hospital continued to contribute advances to medicine. In 1925 it was the first hospital to establish a tumor clinic for the study of cancer; the following year it provided the first description of the cause and treatment of lead poisoning. In 1929 the first successful operation for hyperparathyroidism took place at the MGH, and in 1927 the hospital made a pioneer effort in nuclear medicine with the first use of radioactive iodine in thyroid studies. The first successful reattachment of a completely severed human arm was conducted at the MGH in 1962, and in 1964 it demonstrated the first practical method of freezing blood for storage.

With the increase in staff, the growing number of patients, the expansion of programs, and the multiplication of departments, the MGH rapidly outgrew the original Bulfinch building, and new construction continued well into the twentieth century. The Baker Memorial Hospital, designed for patients of moderate means, opened in 1930, the result of a million-dollar grant from Richard and Ellen Baker. In memory of his philanthropic brother, Bradbury White gave $2.5 million to establish the George Robert White Memorial Building, dedicated on October 16, 1939. The Gray Building was constructed in 1968, and the Cox Building for Cancer Research and Treatment went up in 1974. Over the course of nearly two hundred years, the Massachusetts General Hospital has grown from a modest nineteenth-century general hospital to one of the most highly recognized medical institutions in the United States.

❖

Massachusetts Historical Society

The Massachusetts Historical Society (MHS) is the oldest historical society in the United States and the first in the Western Hemisphere devoted primarily to collecting Americana and publishing in American history.

The MHS was founded in 1791. According to Jeremy Belknap, its first corresponding secretary, its purpose was "to *seek* and *find,* to *preserve* and *communicate,* literary intelligence, especially in the historical way." At the time of its founding, the Society was lodged in the northwest corner of the attic of Faneuil Hall. Several years later it was more than happy to accept the offer of rooms above the central arch in the graceful curve of buildings that formed Charles Bulfinch's Tontine Crescent in Franklin Street. The Society remained in that location until 1831, when it moved to 30 Tremont Street, on a site adjoining King's Chapel Burying Ground, where it remained for nearly seventy years. Belknap began to build the holdings of the Society's collection almost immediately, and under his vigorous leadership the MHS grew extensively, issuing its first publication within a year of its founding.

In an age before advanced degrees and academic specialization, educated gentlemen involved themselves in all kinds of scientific research and historical investigations. The original members of the MHS, mostly graduates of Harvard College, were largely educated and cultured amateurs who devoted themselves to gathering manuscripts and artifacts pertaining to the history of Massachusetts. Many saw the Massachusetts Historical Society as a sort of Royal Academy, a select institution where distinguished men were honored for their remarkable achievements and their civic service.

In 1899 the Massachusetts Historical Society moved to a handsome new Georgian Revival building at 1154 Boylston Street, at the corner of the Fenway, where it remains today. The Society's primary interest is the curation of more than 3,000 separate manuscript collections of personal papers and institutional records. The papers of John Adams, second president of the United States, and the papers of his son, John Quincy Adams, sixth president of the United States, are said by some members to constitute the equivalent of two presidential libraries at a single location. Items including the diary of Samuel Sewall, judge at the famous Salem witchcraft trials; the papers of Paul Revere; and even the private writings of Thomas Jefferson have attracted scholars and writers from all over the world. Holdings in American colonial history, the Revolutionary period, and the Civil War era provide valuable sources for researchers, as do materials in such subjects as religion, law, medicine, women's history, and international commerce. In addition to manuscripts, the Society has collections of rare books, monographs (some 200,000), historical maps (over 5,000), and broadsides (more than 20,000), as well as an impressive collection of portraits, busts, engravings, early daguerreotypes, and modern photographs.

During the course of the twentieth century, the Massachusetts Historical Society saw two significant changes. First, although members still must go through an elective process, the membership has increasingly come to reflect the diversity of the general community. Second, although academic credentials are not a requirement for membership, the MHS has become more professional in its procedures and in its relationship with a broader public. To encourage the use of its holdings and to stimulate the advancement of learning the MHS, through its Center for the Study of New England History, regularly sponsors research projects, scholarly conferences, and academic seminars involving faculty members and graduate students from all over the country. In addition to lectures and speaking programs for its own membership, the MHS also sponsors lectures for the general public at such neighboring institutions as the Boston Public Library. During 1999 some 8,300 square feet of interior space in the century-old home of the Massachusetts Historical Society on Boylston Street were renovated to create new offices as well as more extensive archive space. A new administration area was created, and a number of the various building systems were substantially upgraded, preparing the oldest historical society in America to serve the needs of future historians and a broader public.

Mechanics Hall

In the days before Boston had any large structure designed to accommodate professional conventions, trade meetings, or commercial conferences, a large, sprawling auditorium was erected in 1881 along Huntington Avenue, only a short distance west of Copley Square. Called Mechanics Hall, the structure was designed by the architect William Gibbons Preston and erected by the Massachusetts Charitable Mechanic Association, a fraternal organization founded in 1795 with the silversmith Paul Revere as its first president.

Mechanics Hall had a red-brick facade, decorated with medallions and ornaments of terra cotta. For generations, its vast, cavernous interior housed not only trade conferences and commercial gatherings but also musical productions, track meets, and midweek wrestling matches during the 1930s featuring such local favorites as Nick Lutz, Ernie Dusek, Danno O'Mahony, The Angel, The Shadow, and El Diablo. At ringside, Harry "Whitey" Kaunfer would open the first match of the night with "Hello, hello, hello!" and the crowd would respond with "Hello, hello, hello!" Mechanics Hall also hosted an annual succession of boat shows, automobile shows, dog shows, flower shows, sportsmen's shows, and fishing shows at which celebrities such as Red Sox hitter Ted Williams would put on public displays of fly-casting for thousands of fans.

On January 9, 1959, a two-ton wrecking ball, swinging from a 90-foot boom, pulverized the walls of Boston's 78-year-old Mechanics Hall to make way for a $12 million convention center that would be part of the new Prudential Insurance Company project that was under way in Boston's Back Bay.

❖

"Mister Boston"

A man who could have stepped right out of the pages of John P. Marquand's classic novel *The Late George Apley,* Ralph Lowell so remarkably personified the spirit of the Beacon Hill Brahmin that in his later years he was almost universally known as "Mister Boston."

Born in July 1890, Ralph Lowell was a member of a distinguished Boston family that included two notable poets, four federal judges, a famous college president, a pioneering industrialist, and an eminent astronomer. Ralph graduated from Harvard in 1912, and after a world tour took a position in the First National Bank of Boston. He saw service in the United States Army during World War I, was mustered out with the rank of major, and began working for the investment banking house of Lee, Higginson & Company, where he was made partner in 1929. At that point he began assuming the kind of social responsibilities he felt were commensurate with his family's name and his own good fortune. He joined the boards of the Massachusetts Society for the Prevention of Cruelty to Children, for example, as well as the North Bennett Street Industrial School, which taught manual skills to immigrant youths in the North End.

After suffering personal losses when Lee, Higginson was forced to liquidate in 1929, he persuaded the New York firm of Clark, Dodge & Company to take over Lee, Higginson's stock department and put him in charge of the Boston office, where he became a partner in 1937. He survived the Great Depression, continued to admire Herbert Hoover, and professed to despise Franklin D. Roosevelt and his "crackpot schemes."

In 1942 the chairman of the Boston Safe Deposit & Trust Company died, and Ralph Lowell was invited to accept the chairmanship of a company that specialized in the administration of trusts. At about the same time, he became Trustee of the Lowell Institute, and began looking for new ways to expand his family's commitment to adult education. In 1947 he persuaded neighboring colleges and universities to join Harvard University in forming the Lowell Institute Broadcasting Council for educational radio. In 1951 they formed the WGBH Educational Foundation Inc. in order to secure a television license, which the FCC granted in 1953. By 1960 Ralph Lowell had become popularly known as "Mister Boston"—one of the city's busiest corporate executives. Bank president, Trustee of the Lowell Institute, member of Harvard's Board of Overseers, president of the Museum of Fine Arts, life member of the MIT Corporation, he was also on the board of sixty-five other institutions, including six hospitals and twelve welfare organizations.

Although he remained thoroughly committed to old Boston ways and old Harvard traditions, Ralph Lowell also saw that Boston was changing and made an effort to change with it. He highly respected Boston's dignified Catholic archbishop, William Henry Cardinal O'Connell, and later enjoyed a warm personal relationship with the prelate's more informal successor, Richard Cardinal Cushing. In 1960 Lowell agreed to serve on Boston College's Board of Regents and two years later accepted an honorary degree from the Jesuit university. At the same time, he expanded his associations with members of Boston's Jewish community, attended the 70th anniversary dinner of the Combined Jewish Philanthropies, and joined the executive board of the Massachusetts Committee of Catholics, Protestants, and Jews.

After he had stepped down as president of the Boston Safe Deposit & Trust Company, in December 1959 Ralph Lowell agreed to accept the chairmanship of a coordinating committee of leading Boston businessmen to work with the newly elected mayor of Boston, John F. Collins, in planning the future of the "New Boston." Because it held most of its meetings in a basement conference room adjacent to the Boston Safe's giant vault, the group was quickly dubbed "The Vault," and under Lowell's seven-year chairmanship became a critical force in changing the face of the old city.

In 1973, on the occasion of the 150th anniversary of Boston's city charter, the 83-year-old Ralph Lowell was among seven persons awarded the title "Grand Bostonian," an appropriate tribute to his lifelong service and dedication to Boston. On May 15, 1978,

Ralph Lowell died. His funeral service was held at a crowded Memorial Church in Harvard Yard—something of which the Late George Apley would have heartily approved.

❖

The Molasses Explosion

Since colonial days, molasses has been a distinctive part of the Boston economy and a staple of the local diet. Continued demand for Boston baked beans, cornmeal and molasses, brown bread, Indian pudding, and the ever-popular candy "kisses" caused large amounts of molasses to be stored along Boston's busy waterfront.

Shortly after noon on January 15, 1919, the North End of Boston was rocked by a gigantic explosion. A huge molasses storage tank belonging to the Purity Distilling Company on Commercial Street, opposite Copp's Hill, suddenly exploded, firing metal rivets in all directions and sending some 14,000 tons of liquid molasses cascading like molten lava down the streets of the North End. Altogether 21 people lost their lives in the flood, and more than 150 were injured by a tidal wave of molasses that crested at more than 30 feet. Horses were swallowed up, houses were destroyed, and warehouses were smashed to pieces before the heavy liquid finally settled, spread out, and congealed into an almost solid mass. Although the sticky mess was finally cleaned away with fire hoses, salt water, and sand, local residents of Boston claimed for many years to come that, especially on hot summer days, they could smell the sweet odor of molasses wafting through the air.

❖

Museum of Fine Arts

Among American art museums, Boston's Museum of Fine Arts is second only to New York City's Metropolitan Museum of Art in the size and quality of its collections. During the early nineteenth century, most of the finest works of art in the old city were housed at the

Boston Athenaeum. By the 1860s, however, the top floor of the Athenaeum's home on Beacon Street was so filled to overflowing that its Fine Arts Committee explored other sites. In February 1870 the state legislature established the Trustees of the Museum of Fine Arts and awarded the group a 91,000-square-foot lot in Copley Square. Here was erected the first museum building to house and exhibit important collections, many of which were loans or gifts from prominent Boston families. Designed by Sturgis and Brigham and opened to the public on July 4, 1876, the nation's centennial, the building stood on the present site of the Copley Square Hotel. A large gabled brick edifice, with Gothic-style arches and polished marble columns topped with red- and buff-colored terra-cotta capitals, the first museum struck many Bostonians as a rather bizarre structure.

By the 1890s it was agreed that the Copley Square building had become inadequate for the needs of the organization. The risk of fire, the shortage of natural light, and the lack of space for expansion were among the reasons cited for a change of site. In 1899 the trustees approved the purchase of 12 acres of land on Huntington Avenue in the Fenway section of the city. The Fenway, only recently revived by the landscaping work of Frederick Law Olmsted, was being developed as an elegant haven for the arts. The presence nearby of Symphony Hall, the Massachusetts Horticultural Society, the Boston Opera House, and Isabella Stewart Gardner's grand residence made the Fenway seem a natural location for the museum.

The first phase of moving to Huntington Avenue was the construction of a special gallery to experiment with different types of lighting for art exhibits. In the meantime, members of the building committee traveled to Europe for three months, visiting the Louvre and more than a hundred other structures to find models for their Boston museum. The resulting plans called for a structure seven times larger than the old museum in Copley Square. The architect R. Clipston Sturgis was engaged to draw up the preliminary plans, while Guy Lowell, a graduate of Harvard, a student of MIT's program in architecture, and a product of the Ecole des Beaux Arts in Paris, was brought in to supervise the completion of the project.

Noting the essentially conservative taste of Boston, the committee suggested an overall Neoclassical design for the new building, in keeping with the styles of such nearby structures as Symphony Hall, Horticultural Hall, and the Harvard Medical School. The entrance to the building on the Huntington Avenue side has a four-column portico, set back between the encircling wings, and is reached by a semicircular driveway. The forecourt, with its projecting wings, was designed to provide a commanding presence on Huntington Avenue. The approach is made less impersonal by Cyrus Dallin's sculpture *Appeal to the Great Spirit,* placed on the lawn of the forecourt.

Once inside, there is a large rotunda and a grand staircase illuminated by colorful murals painted by John Singer Sargent depicting figures from Greek mythology. The dome of the rotunda actually had to be rebuilt in order to create enough surface space for Sargent's murals. When the rotunda was unveiled to the public on October 20, 1921, it was such a success that Sargent was asked to continue his decorations over the main staircase. Once again, major alterations had to be made in the building to meet Sargent's needs, including the elimination of walls in favor of six columns that admitted more light and allowed visitors to look through into the galleries. On November 3, 1925, the main staircase was opened, and the public was able to view Sargent's spectacular work for the first time.

The new Museum of Fine Arts at its new Huntington Avenue location was formally opened on November 9, 1909, and was made available to the general public on November 15. During the first week, when admission was waived, the museum welcomed 37,500 people through its doors. Almost immediately, the 1909 building had to be expanded to house additional collections, and between 1911 and 1915 the Evans Wing, the result of a single gift from Mrs. Robert Dawson Evans in memory of her husband, was added in order to increase the exhibit space. Between 1928 and 1988 additional wings provided more room for acquisitions: the Decorative Arts Wing; the George Robert White Wing; and the West Wing, designed in a modernistic style by the architect I. M. Pei. Most recently, the Remis Auditorium helped to expand the scope of the museum's offerings and to provide more facilities for the general public, offering lectures, films, and concerts.

Thanks to the generosity of such nineteenth-century Bostonians as the zoologist Edward Sylvester Morse and the Brahmin physician William Sturgis Bigelow, the Museum of Fine Arts has built up the finest and largest collection of Japanese art outside Japan. During the recession of 1991, facing shrinking attendance and a $3 million deficit, the Museum used its preeminence in Japanese art to persuade the Chamber of Commerce of Nagoya, Japan, to invest $50 million to establish a branch of the MFA in Japan itself. It was agreed that the MFA would supply the art, Nagoya business leaders would supply the money, and the city of Nagoya would supply the location. The newest "wing" of Boston's Museum of Fine Arts, therefore, is located in Nagoya, Japan.

Besides its internationally known collection of paintings and sculpture, the holdings of Boston's Museum of Fine Arts number more than a million objects, ranging from Egyptian mummies to Greek vases, from Peruvian tapestries to Japanese gardens, from Paul Revere silver bowls to elegantly furnished European drawing rooms. The MFA has also been host to a number of the most important traveling exhibits of recent years. In 1999 the museum's director, Malcolm Rogers, instituted a sweeping and controversial reorganization of the museum's curatorial structure, grouping departments by geography rather than medium, to encourage collaboration within the museum and improve its outreach to the Boston community.

The "New Boston"

The "New Boston"

By the time John B. Hynes defeated James Michael Curley in the 1949 mayoral race, many observers felt that Boston's best days were over. For half a century, the city had been irreparably divided: In the downtown area lived the Yankees, the Protestants, the Republicans, and the businessmen; in the surrounding neighborhoods lived the Irish, the Catholics, the Democrats, and the laborers. By the first quarter of the twentieth century, the Yankees controlled the finances of Boston; the Irish controlled the city's politics. The reciprocal hatred of the two groups made it practically impossible to muster a united front against the deterioration of the city.

Changes in the American economy had dealt Boston a series of heavy blows. During the 1930s and 1940s, in order to take advantage of natural resources and lower labor costs, the textile mills and the shoemaking industry moved south, out of New England. The increase in overland truck traffic and the coming of the airplane brought overseas shipping to a halt. By the time World War II broke out, the city's extensive railroad terminals were filled with empty railroad cars rusting on their tracks. The coffee houses, the wool houses, and the leather houses along Summer Street gradually closed their doors, as other cities came to dominate trade in these products from Central and South America.

The decline in Boston's economy was mirrored in the steady deterioration of the city's infrastructure. Years of neglect, a decade of Depression, and a generation of bitter political feuding between Irish politicians and Yankee financiers had taken their toll. By the end of World War II the city was in terrible condition. City income was going down; city taxes were going up; established businesses were moving out of town. Private homes and public buildings continued to decline at a frightening rate, and many of the old Back Bay mansions were being transformed into rooming houses or college dormitories. It was obvious that drastic changes would have to be made if the inner city were to be saved from the ravages of urban blight and the neighborhoods rescued from municipal neglect.

After his victory over Curley, Mayor Hynes set out to change the direction of the city by creating a "New Boston." Conveying an air of quiet confidence and personal integrity, Hynes began to pull together a working coalition of Irish political leaders and Yankee business spokesmen. For the first time, the city solicited the expertise of several colleges and universities in the area. Specialists from Harvard furnished valuable economic studies; planners from MIT produced architectural designs; Boston College initiated a series of Citizen Seminars that provided a forum for public discussion of urban issues. Hynes himself offered his own vision of a modernized Boston. He established an Auditorium Commission to design a multipurpose hall to host meetings and conferences. He created a Government Center Commission to develop an area for city, state, and federal office buildings. He spoke about plans for a World Trade Center to restore Boston's place as a center of international commerce. And he elaborated on a proposal to use the old Boston & Albany railroad yards in the Back Bay area, between Boylston Street and Huntington Avenue, as the site for a regional headquarters for the Prudential Insurance Company.

Slowly Hynes restored outsiders' confidence in the city, which began receiving funds from the federal government as well as investments from private corporations. He launched a program of slum clearance in many parts of Boston, and in 1947 authorized the Boston Housing Authority (BHA) to begin the demolition of a small area in the South End, the New York Streets area, to make way for profitable industrial development. The following year the BHA turned its attention to the West End, one of the city's most congested neighborhoods, which was totally demolished in favor of a complex of high-rise luxury apartments, modern shopping centers, and sprawling parking lots.

Choosing not to run for another term, Hynes left office in January 1960 and was succeeded by Mayor John F. Collins, who had defeated State Senator John E. Powers the previous November in a stunning political upset. Because of adverse public reaction to the ruthless manner in which the West End demolition had turned poor people out of their homes without adequate provisions for relocation, there was every reason to believe that urban renewal in Boston would be stopped dead in its tracks. John F. Collins was strongly committed to the idea of the "New Boston," however, and within months had brought in Edward J. Logue, an experienced city planner from New Haven, to become director of the newly created Boston Redevelopment Authority (BRA). At the same time he appointed the highly respected Monsignor Francis J. Lally, editor of *The Pilot,* chairman of the BRA board. These two appointments helped Collins reassure the public that urban renewal would be directed in both a professional and a compassionate manner. Collins also reactivated the coalition of city business leaders initiated by his predecessor, establishing regular advisory meetings with a group of downtown bankers, financiers, and executives known as "The Vault."

With enthusiastic support from Boston's downtown financial community, aided by increased federal funding during the mid-1960s from the Democratic administrations of John F. Kennedy and Lyndon B. Johnson, urban renewal literally transformed the face of the old city. The $200-million Prudential Center complex that rose on the site of the old railroad yards in the Back Bay revitalized the entire area from Copley Square to Massachusetts Avenue. A massive conference building called the War Memorial Auditorium (later named the John B. Hynes Auditorium) added further to the district by attracting tourists, visitors, and conventioneers. The construction of the Prudential tower stimulated the construction of a major hotel, a complex of business offices, and several shopping centers. Closer to the center of town, the multi-million-dollar Government Center Project took over some 60 acres previously occupied by Scollay Square, Haymarket Square, and Bowdoin Square. There now arose a modernistic new City Hall and an expansive red-brick plaza, surrounded by impressive new state and federal office buildings.

The spirit of urban renewal proved contagious, and public efforts were supplemented by private efforts in many parts of the city. The Christian Science Church, for example, launched an ambitious construction program that included new administration buildings, apartment complexes, merchandise marts, and a lovely 700-foot-long reflecting pool that lighted up the previously dull approaches to Symphony Hall. In the old South Cove area below Chinatown, the Tufts–New England Medical Center transformed a rundown retail zone into a major center for medical and dental research. In Copley Square, the John Hancock Insurance Company erected a glass-clad, 60-story office building directly across from Trinity Church, while across the way the Boston Public Library authorized the construction of an ingeniously modernistic addition to its original Florentine structure.

Although by the late 1960s federal funding had begun to dry up as a result of the skyrocketing financial demands of the Vietnam War, Collins's successor as mayor of Boston, Kevin H. White, continued the momentum of urban renewal after he took office in 1968. Not only did White use his energy and charisma to dramatize the "New Boston" and publicize the numerous advantages of Boston as a "World Class City," but he also continued the transformation of the city. The old Quincy Market district, directly behind Faneuil Hall, had become so badly dilapidated that in 1956 city planners called for its wholesale demolition. In 1963, however, BRA administrator Edward Logue decided to completely renovate the historic market buildings—a task whose completion carried over to the White administration after 1967. Despite predictions that it would be impossible to attract people back to the city, Kevin White worked with James Rouse of Maryland to develop a lively market complex. The plan worked; the Faneuil Hall Marketplace was an immediate success. After it opened in August 1976, it attracted some 10 million visitors during its first year of operation.

Plans were also put forward for the reconstruction and modernization of Boston's old and rundown waterfront district along Atlantic Avenue. A new and popular aquarium was constructed at the end of Central Wharf, high-rise residential towers arose looking out on Boston Harbor, and a series of restaurants, shops, and imaginatively designed recreational areas replaced stretches of muddy walkways, rotting wharves, and broken pilings.

In the course of some twenty years—from about 1950 to 1970—the city of Boston had been transformed from a poor,

broken-down, old town of red-brick tenements and wooden houses
into a successful, modern metropolis of soaring skyscrapers of shining glass and gleaming steel. Not everyone was happy with the
changes; many complained that Boston was losing its unique appearance and its Old World charm, and the architecture of the new
City Hall and Government Center in particular has found few advocates. But the alternative—allowing Boston to slip into financial
bankruptcy and structural decay—would have risked losing its
standing as one of America's great cities.

❖

Newspaper Row

During the first half of the twentieth century, a stretch of Washington Street in downtown Boston, between State Street and School
Street, was known as Newspaper Row. This area was the center of
most of the publicity houses, journals, and newspapers in the city.
At one point it was the home of the *Post,* the *Globe,* the *Herald,* the
Traveler, and the *Daily Advertiser,* all of which competed for the
readership of the city's public. Day and night, this section of town
pulsated to the rhythm of the presses and the rush of deadlines, creating around-the-clock excitement.

In an era before radio and television, everybody in Boston knew
that you could get the latest news on Newspaper Row, even before
the newspapers went to press. Workers chalked the major headlines
of the moment—election returns, baseball scores, prizefight knock-
outs, gruesome murders, disastrous explosions—on large outdoor
blackboards for passersby to read, or for crowds that gathered at the
time of major events.

By the 1950s, however, economic shifts and demographic
changes spelled the doom of Newspaper Row. Rising financial
costs, national competition, and the expansion of radio and television news programs forced a drastic reduction in the number of
newspapers serving America's major cities. In Boston, only the
Globe and the *Herald* managed to sustain themselves in a diminishing market, and then only by associating with national publication

syndicates. Urban renewal, increased automation of the printing process, and the need for greater space made the old Newspaper Row location obsolete.

The *Boston Globe* moved out of downtown to a more accessible location in the Columbia Point section of the city and in 1990 was taken over by the *New York Times*. The *Boston Herald* moved to more spacious quarters in the South End, where it became part of Rupert Murdoch's chain of publications until it returned to local ownership under Patrick Purcell. The colorful days of Newspaper Row, reminiscent of the old "Front Page" movies of the 1930s, with their hard-bitten, cigar-chomping reporters and "sob-sister" female columnists, simply faded into the past.

North End

On the northern side of the jagged coastline of the old Shawmut Peninsula, overlooking the waters of Boston Harbor, is a protuberance of land that became known as the North End. In colonial days, English immigrants dominated the district, primarily merchants who built commercial property along the shoreline and constructed their personal residences a few blocks away. By the time of the American Revolution, the North End had become home to a number of Boston's wealthiest citizens, including Thomas Hutchinson, the royal governor, who sailed away from the North End to the safety of England on the eve of the Revolution.

During the colonial era, the North End was also home to the town's first small African American community, located on the west side of the Copp's Hill Burying Ground. Some were slaves, purchased to serve as butlers, drivers, and household servants; some were free residents who worked aboard ships or maintained small shops and businesses around the docks. Eventually, as the number of white immigrants grew, the black residents moved away from the wharves and established a more permanent black neighborhood farther inland, on the north side of Beacon Hill.

The influx of immigrants from Ireland during the 1820s and 1830s began to change the demographics of the North End, and after the terrible potato famine of the 1840s waves of desperately poor Irish immigrants packed into the district, settling a few painful steps from the docks where they had come ashore. By the 1860s and 1870s the North End had become a stronghold of residents from Ireland, most of whom lived in wood-framed tenement buildings and lodging houses. Here John ("Honey Fitz") Fitzgerald, the grandfather of a future President of the United States, received his political indoctrination as the local ward boss. Because he often spoke so lovingly of the "dear old North End" in his speeches, his political opponents frequently referred to Fitzgerald and his supporters as the "Dear-o's."

Between the 1890s and the 1920s, large numbers of new immigrants from southern and eastern Europe arrived in the North End. At first Poles and Russian Jews took the place of the Irish, lining the streets with kosher markets, Hebrew schools, and synagogues. But it was the coming of the Italian immigrants that completely changed the ethnic character of the old North End. By 1920 about 90 percent of the North End population was Italian, and the district became popularly known as Little Italy. Well into contemporary times the streets of the North End were lined with grocery stores, fruit stands, bakeries, butcher shops, restaurants, and espresso bars, reminiscent of the Old Country. The neighborhood's colorful religious festivals and processions, complete with marching bands, statues of favorite saints, and elaborately decorated floats, never failed to attract visitors from all over the Greater Boston area.

The often badly planned renovations in Boston, brought about by a variety of urban-renewal projects during the 1950s and 1960s, caused extensive changes in the traditional character of the North End. The construction of the overhead Fitzgerald Highway actually cut the district off from the major portion of the downtown area of Boston. The rising prices of homes and rental properties forced many older Italian families to leave the familiar neighborhood, while gentrification also caused younger families to look elsewhere for affordable housing. By 1990 it was reported that only 43 per-

cent of the residents of Boston's North End were of Italian de-
scent—only half the concentration at its peak, but enough to preserve some of the area's distinctive character.

Northeastern University

Today the largest private university in the United States, Northeastern University began in 1896 as an outreach program of Boston's
Young Men's Christian Association (YMCA). In an effort to make a
college education available to young workingmen of the city, the
YMCA established an "Evening Institute for Young Men." It was
located in a building at the corner of Boylston and Berkeley streets
when in 1909 the project became the Northeastern College of the
YMCA, offering to make "a good education possible to every young
man." In 1898 Northeastern established a Department of Law,
which provided evening law courses at a tuition of $30 a year, in-
cluding membership in the YMCA. Similar programs of evening
education were later offered in the fields of business and technical
training to prepare young men of modest means to qualify for professional positions.

In 1909 Frank Palmer Speare, the Evening Institute's original director, became the first president of Northeastern, holding that position until 1940—one of the longest tenures in the history of American education. In addition to starting a number of day programs,
Speare also organized the college around the theme of the "Cooperative Plan of Education." This method of education linked paid employment to a traditional program of academic study so that the
children of immigrant working-class families could work their way
through college. The Cooperative Plan was initiated with the College of Engineering in 1909, and was subsequently adopted by the
College of Business Administration in 1922 and by the College of
Arts and Sciences in 1935. After that the plan was implemented by
all colleges, in both day and evening programs. Students spend half
of the year in school, and the other half working in their field of

study. Over the years, many Boston-area employers have come to rely upon a steady labor supply of Northeastern students.

In 1922 the name of the college was changed to Northeastern University and a number of new colleges were founded, including the College of Business Administration. With the rapid expansion of Northeastern as a major university in its own right, the official separation from the YMCA was arranged in 1936. Carl S. Ell, who served as Northeastern's second president from 1940 to 1959, was responsible for the move from the Berkeley Street location to a site on Huntington Avenue. Completion of the new campus was effected under Ell's successor, Asa Knowles, who was also responsible for establishing the university's first doctoral programs as well as expanding many of the institution's academic programs.

Throughout its history, Northeastern University has continued to respond to a variety of community needs and expectations. Following World War II, for example, a College of Education was created in order to provide new teachers for expanding school systems, and when the Harvard teaching hospitals complained of a lack of nurses, Northeastern established its School of Nursing. Although it closed its Law School temporarily in 1953, at a time when there was little demand for lawyers, it later opened a new Law School that functioned through its Cooperative Plan of Education. In 1975 Kenneth Ryder succeeded Dr. Knowles as president of Northeastern, and through the College of Business Administration developed a variety of graduate programs in business and engineering relating to the modern-day problems of the local high-technology industry. Dr. Ryder also maintained close relations with the Greater Boston community, and through student exchange programs with such institutions as the Boston Conservatory of Music and the Museum of Fine Arts was responsible for promoting the importance of the arts in education. Northeastern University and its pioneering cooperative plan continue to serve as a model for educational institutions throughout the world.

Old State House

Old Corner Bookstore

The building that was once the famous Old Corner Bookstore is located on the corner of School and Washington Streets in downtown Boston. It actually occupies a piece of property that once belonged to Anne Hutchinson until she was forced into exile in 1638. After the old Hutchinson house was burned to the ground in a fire that struck Boston on October 3, 1711, the site was immediately purchased by Dr. Thomas Crane, who built the present brick structure about 1712 as a combination residence and apothecary shop.

The building survived many subsequent owners, who used it for a variety of purposes until 1828, when it was leased to a firm of booksellers known as Carter & Handee. Five years later it was acquired by a book publisher named William Ticknor, who made a fortune by taking in as a junior partner an imaginative young apprentice named James T. Fields. By 1845 the firm was called Ticknor & Fields, and the two men had established the Old Corner Bookstore as the headquarters for a new magazine called *The Atlantic Monthly*. They turned the bookstore itself into a haven for some of America's greatest authors.

During the 1840s and 1850s Boston was the unquestioned literary capital of the United States. The Old Corner Bookstore became the place where Ralph Waldo Emerson, Henry David Thoreau, Harriet Beecher Stowe, Louisa May Alcott, Henry Wadsworth Longfellow, Nathaniel Hawthorne, Margaret Fuller, and many other members of the local literati came to meet, to read each other's works, and to share their latest compositions. It was the favorite meeting place for all the great writers of New England, and an attraction for writers from farther away when they were passing through Boston.

After its literary heyday, the Old Corner Bookstore gradually fell into unsightly disrepair, finally becoming something of an eyesore at its prominent location on the corner of Washington and School streets. During the early 1960s, Boston's plans for extensive redevelopment of the downtown area called for the Old Corner Bookstore to be torn down and replaced either by a high-rise motel or a new federal office building. Learning of this, Bostonians rose up in anger, founded a nonprofit organization called Historic Boston, and almost overnight raised the money necessary to save the old building from demolition. The brick exterior of the original building was restored, and the Old Corner Bookstore (now called the Globe Corner Bookstore) was preserved. It is now a stop on the Freedom Trail, and it still houses a bookstore on the street level along with *Boston Globe* offices on the second floor.

The Old Howard

Ironically, the site of the building that became known as Boston's "Temple of Burlesque" in the heart of Scollay Square was first occupied by a church. The original structure was a wooden Tabernacle built to house the followers of a traveling evangelist named William Miller, who preached that the second coming of Christ would take place on April 23, 1853. When the fateful event failed to take place, the movement gradually faded away and the so-called Millerites turned to other faiths. The wooden temple was replaced by a Gothic-style granite structure by Isaiah Rogers. Designed as a legitimate theater, its richly decorated interior was furnished with the first cushioned theater seats in Boston.

For years, the Old Howard Theater was a fashionable playhouse, where grand operas and dramatic productions were presented—until 1870, when it became a vaudeville theater where ladies attired in skintight costumes adorned the stage as "living pictures." By the turn of the twentieth century, the Old Howard had become a center for burlesque performances that attracted an audience of young and old from all parts of the city and from out of town. By the 1930s the striptease show, complete with a stage orchestra, a chorus line, and a series of popular burlesque comedians, became the leading attraction of the Old Howard, drawing high school students after school hours as well as businessmen and old Harvard graduates, who watched the performances from "bald-headed row." One headline stripper, Ann Corio, recalled that young Jack Kennedy, during his Harvard years, was one of the "regulars." If the Old Howard was booked, or had been temporarily shut down by the city censors, the Crawford House on nearby Brattle Street offered an alternative location where customers could see Sally Keith twirl her tassels or Sally Rand wave her famous fans.

After World War II, with fewer servicemen coming to Boston, and with the area around Scollay Square rapidly deteriorating, the Old Howard's days were numbered. In 1961, as the administration of Mayor John Collins prepared for a wholesale clearance of the Scollay Square district for its new Government Center Project, a number of Bostonians hoped that the Old Howard Theater could somehow be preserved as a historic and sentimental site. The question of the theater's survival became moot, however, when on June 25, 1961, a three-alarm fire burned the old theater to the ground, much to the chagrin of loyal fans, who suspected foul play. "Some Coward / Closed the Old Howard / We don't have Burley any more" mourned Francis W. Hatch (Harvard class of 1919), in a piece of doggerel verse that expressed the sentiments of many old Harvard grads who as young men had enjoyed the pleasures of the famous burlesque palace in the heart of old Scollay Square.

Old North Church

Christ Church, better known as the Old North Church, was the second Anglican church in Boston, originally established to serve the overflow of parishioners from King's Chapel. It was built in 1723 on Salem Street in Boston's North End by two masons, James Varney and Ebenezer Clough. The architect is thought to be William Price, who designed the beautiful steeple that still dominates the area. The spire, which served as a landmark guiding vessels into Boston Harbor, was built with funds contributed by so-called Honduras merchants, who had become prosperous carrying cargoes of dogwood and mahogany from South America to the London market. In the tower of the church are eight original bells, hung in 1744, which were made in Gloucester, England. During colonial times they were used to toll the curfew and for other occasions, and are still often rung today.

The belfry of the Old North Church was made famous by Henry Wadsworth Longfellow's poem "Paul Revere's Ride." Generations of Boston schoolchildren have memorized the verses telling how two lanterns were hung in the belfry on the evening of April 18, 1775, as a signal—"one if by land, and two if by sea"—that the British regulars were marching to Lechmere Point to ferry to Cambridge on their way to Concord. In 1804 the steeple of the Old North Church was blown down by a hurricane, and a new one was erected by Joseph Tucker in 1807 from a design provided by Charles Bulfinch. A century and a half later, in 1954, another hurricane destroyed the Bulfinch steeple. The present restoration is a copy of William Price's original spire, and is surmounted by the original weathervane made in 1740 by Shem Drowne.

The interior of the Old North Church seats more than five hundred persons. It has box pews with paneled doors and narrow wooden seats, galleries arranged along the sides, and an organ loft positioned at the opposite end from the altar. The colonial-style high pulpit, with its ascending steps and sounding board suspended above, is a restoration, and the large arched window above the altar table has been restored. The so-called Bay Pew was set apart in 1727 for the use of "The Gentlemen of the Bay Honduras" who had donated the steeple. In 1808, twenty-five years after Independence, Paul Revere's son, Joseph Warren Revere, purchased pew number 54 as a member of the congregation.

The Old North Church is the oldest church building now standing in Boston, and the only one which has had one form of worship and continuous religious services, interrupted only during the Revolutionary period of British occupation, when the church was closed by order of the British authorities. Since that time, the Old North has embraced persons of various denominations, and its pulpit has been open to speakers of all political and social views.

Old South Meeting House

The original Old South Meeting House was a wooden structure, constructed in 1669 as a Congregational house of worship. In 1706 Benjamin Franklin was baptized in this building. Located on a site that was originally part of Governor John Winthrop's garden, it stands today on Washington Street at the corner of Milk Street in downtown Boston.

In 1729 the original structure was replaced by a more substantial building of American brick, constructed by a well-known mason named Joshua Blanchard and designed by the architect Robert Twelves. The members of the congregation wanted their meeting-house to be plain, simple, and unadorned, in the true Puritan fashion. The exterior of the building was long and low, and the windows were made of clear glass—no colorful stained glass here! Inside, the main floor contained both long, narrow pews and private boxes. The box pews were rented to wealthy families, who outfitted them with special fabrics and personal conveniences. The two layers of upstairs galleries included seating for "less desirable" elements of the town, such as servants, poor people, and slaves.

The Old South Meeting House continued its dual function as a regular place of Congregational worship and a center of civic activities throughout the colonial period. It attained perhaps its most famous claim to fame during the tea crisis of 1773, when thousands of inhabitants of Boston and surrounding towns met there to vent their anger and to plan their response as the hated British tea ships sailed into Boston Harbor. On December 16, 1773, more than 5,000 local residents crowded into the Old South, agreeing that they would prevent the landing of the tea—regardless of the consequences. Later that evening, when the ship captain reported that Governor Thomas Hutchinson had refused to recall the tea, the

Meeting House reverberated to the cries of "A mob! A mob!" From the gallery came sounds of war-whoops from a small group of men, crudely disguised as Mohawk Indians, who led a resolute mob down Milk Street and off to Griffin's Wharf, where the tea ships were at anchor. The "Tea Party" that night set the rebellious colonials on a path from which there was no return, and gave the Old South Meeting House a distinctive place in the history of American freedom. During the subsequent military occupation of the town, British soldiers used the building as a riding academy—an act of desecration that particularly infuriated Bostonians.

As the years went by, the congregation of the Old South Church dwindled. Some members moved away to better homes in the West End or to the new development on Beacon Hill; others were won over to the more liberal doctrines of Unitarianism, which gathered considerable converts during the early nineteenth century. During the Civil War years the building served as a recruiting station, and was later used temporarily as a post office. Although the old structure narrowly escaped destruction in the Great Fire that leveled much of downtown Boston in 1872, most of its remaining congregation moved to the Copley Square area, where a New Old South Church was constructed.

Plans were actually well under way to tear down the aging building on Washington Street when a public outcry put a halt to its demolition. The philanthropist Mary Hemenway not only furnished money to renovate and maintain the historic structure, but also established an educational program in American history at the Old South to benefit local teachers and students. A number of Boston's great literary figures, including Wendell Phillips, Julia Ward Howe, Ralph Waldo Emerson, and Louisa May Alcott, joined in the movement, reading their works to the public from the pulpit of the Old South and pleading for the building's preservation. Local citizens, especially prominent women, organized countless fairs and fundraisers to save the Old South. Finally, in 1877 the private, nonprofit Old South Association was formed to operate the Old South Meeting House as a historic site and museum, preserving this piece of colonial Boston as a permanent part of the city's history.

Old State House

Early in 1658, only twenty-eight years after the town of Boston had been founded, the settlers built a wooden structure as a central town house, where merchants could meet and government officials could assemble. When the original structure burned down in 1711 the citizens replaced it with a handsome brick building. Although the new structure was variously called the Court House, the Second Town House, and the Province House, it was most frequently referred to as the Town House. It is the oldest public building in Boston.

In typical Puritan fashion, the Town House was designed to serve more than one purpose: it functioned both as the colonial capital and as the commercial center of the port of Boston. On the first floor was a "merchants' walk," where the merchants congregated and ships' captains reported. The second floor provided meeting chambers for the various bodies of colonial government. The Royal Governor met with the twenty-eight Councilors in the Council Chamber at the east end, where a small balcony overlooked King Street. In the center of the Town House was an impressive chamber called Representatives Hall. This was where the General Assembly of the Province, with representatives from each town, met to frame legislation. At the west end of the structure was a smaller chamber where the Court of Suffolk County, which eventually became the Supreme Judicial Court of Massachusetts, together with various inferior courts, held sessions until 1742, when they moved to Faneuil Hall. "There is most perfect harmony in the government of this Province," wrote Governor Francis Bernard upon his arrival in Massachusetts shortly after the accession of King George III.

This "perfect harmony" proved to be short-lived, however, as the Town House became a vital center for local patriots' displays of resentment against practices that threatened American freedoms. It was the place where in 1761 young James Otis led the fight against the hated writs of assistance. It was outside the Town House in

1765 that angry Bostonians demonstrated against the Stamp Act. It was here that the General Assembly, meeting in Representatives Hall, passed a motion to create a circular letter to all the other colonial assemblies. And it was just outside the Town House, on the evening of March 5, 1770, that British troops fired into a threatening mob of Bostonians in a historic clash that became known as the Boston Massacre.

On July 18, 1776, Thomas Crafts, Jr., the county sheriff, read a copy of the Declaration of Independence from the balcony of the Town House to a crowd of jubilant Bostonians. When the reading concluded, wrote Abigail Adams to her husband John, the cannon was discharged and all the people shouted "God save our American states!" Festivities continued late into the night, when elated citizens tore down the lion and the unicorn—symbols of royal authority—from the east gable of the building.

After the Revolution, when American independence had been won, the Town House continued to be used for government business. But it soon became clear that Bostonians wanted a separate building of their own from which to govern their state. In accordance with a resolve of the General Court dated February 16, 1795, plans were set in motion for the construction of a new State House on Beacon Hill overlooking Boston Common. When the new Bulfinch State House was completed, the General Court assembled on State Street on Thursday, January 11, 1789, for the last time in what was now called the Old State House. At 11 o'clock, the two houses were joined by Governor Increase Sumner and the members of his Council, and the assemblage marched in procession to the new State House on Beacon Hill, where the business of government was begun anew.

Fortunately, the handsome Old State House was not razed or demolished. It was left standing, as one writer put it, "as a memorial of the stirring scenes which took place in and about it"—demonstrating that our ancestors had "a vein of sentiment and veneration for an historic public building." Unfortunately, over the years the Old State House experienced a series of changes, renovations, alterations, facelifts, and fires. By the end of the nineteenth century the old structure had fallen into such neglect and disrepair that many citizens felt it should be torn down completely. At one point in the late 1870s the city of Chicago offered to purchase the old structure and reconstruct it on the shores of Lake Michigan, as a national shrine "for all America to revere." Fortunately, Bostonians came to the rescue and salvaged the structure. Although the building continued to be owned by the City of Boston, the Bostonian Society has operated the Old State House as a museum since that time.

In November 1989, after more than two years of preparation involving the National Park Service, the City of Boston, and the Bostonian Society, the Old State House was closed for a period of some eighteen months for an extensive $7 million renovation project. A new heating and air-conditioning system was installed, structural problems and serious water damage were repaired, and increased space was provided for storage and exhibit areas. The Old State House was reopened to the public as both a museum and a center for permanent exhibits, rotating displays, and educational programs relating to the history of Boston.

John Boyle O'Reilly

The son of an Irish schoolteacher, John Boyle O'Reilly was born June 28, 1844, in County Meath, on the outskirts of Drogheda, the town where in 1649 Oliver Cromwell had savagely massacred large numbers of Irish Catholics. As a young man O'Reilly traveled to England to work as a printer's apprentice and later enlisted in the British army, where he worked to convert Irish soldiers to the cause of Irish independence. Once his activities were uncovered, O'Reilly was shipped off to a penal colony in Australia. He made a daring escape, however, and eventually made his way to Boston, where he found work as a writer for the weekly Irish newspaper *The Pilot.*

Although O'Reilly was an advocate for the Fenian cause when he first arrived in the United States, he quickly developed an intense American patriotism, and criticized the violence that marked Irish nationalism. He called upon Catholics and Protestants in the United States to put aside their differences and work together. His graceful writing style, staunch patriotism, and conciliatory attitude toward native Bostonians soon made O'Reilly a favorite in local literary and social circles. In 1872 he was invited to join the exclusive Papyrus Club; he was later installed as a charter member of the St. Botolph Club and in 1881 was elected to the Dartmouth College chapter of Phi Beta Kappa. In 1882 he composed and delivered a poem called "America" before former General Ulysses S. Grant at the reunion of the Army of the Potomac; in 1888 he published a poem eulogizing Crispus Attucks, the black patriot killed during the Boston Massacre; the following year he delivered the main address at the dedication of the Pilgrim Monument at Plymouth.

While establishing his literary reputation with Boston's Brahmin community, however, John Boyle O'Reilly was also eager to demonstrate his commitment to the Catholic Church. He was on friendly terms with Archbishop John Williams, helped found an organization of Catholic laymen called the Catholic Union, and in 1876 accepted the position of editor when the archbishop took over management of *The Pilot* at a time when it was in economic distress following losses during the Great Fire of 1872.

As editor of *The Pilot,* O'Reilly charted new and more idealistic directions for the weekly Irish Catholic newspaper during the 1880s. Although he continued to denounce England and agitate for home rule in Ireland, he urged Irish Americans to moderate their activities on this side of the Atlantic. He spoke out strongly in the columns of the paper for the neglected interests of Native American Indians, and became a vigorous advocate for the civil rights of African Americans. He often pointed out the tragic similarities between the discrimination practiced for so long against Irish Catholics and the oppression visited upon black people and other minorities in the United States.

The sudden and unexpected death of John Boyle O'Reilly in 1890 at the comparatively young age of 46 was termed by Cardinal James Gibbons as a "public calamity." His passing was described by the recent Boston author Mark Schneider as a lost opportunity for productive dialogue between Irish Catholics and African Americans in Boston at a time when virtually none existed.

Public Garden

Park Street Church

The Park Street Church was founded in 1809 by thirty Congregationalist members of the Old South Church who found themselves a decided minority during a citywide groundswell for the more liberal doctrines of Unitarianism. Determined to preserve the stricter doctrines of the Congregational orthodoxy in a church of their own, they selected a site on the corner of Park and Tremont Streets, overlooking the Boston Common in one direction and the Old Granary Burying Ground in the other, and commissioned the architect Peter Banner to design "the sightliest building in the country."

Peter Banner might, indeed, have accomplished just that. Basing his design on Christopher Wren's concept for St. Bride's in London, Banner created a lovely building whose graceful white spire still dominates its surroundings. Solomon Willard, the man who designed the obelisk for the Bunker Hill monument, hand-carved the wooden capitals of the church, which stands at what has become known as "Brimstone Corner." There are those who say that it acquired that title during the War of 1812, when the church is supposed to have stored in its basement crypt a supply of brimstone, an ingredient used in the making of gunpowder. Others maintain that the corner is so called because the old-time Congregationalist ministers gave terrifying sermons that called down "hell-fire and brimstone" upon unrepentant sinners. In either case, the church is a sparkling sight for all those commuters who come up from the underground subway at Park Street and see the gleaming white steeple at the top of the stairs.

Once construction of the building was completed, the Park Street Church became very active in movements for social and humanitarian reform. In the year of its opening in 1810, for example, it became the organizing site for the American Board of Commissioners for Foreign Missions, and in 1815, for the American Education Society; in 1819 it sent the first missionaries to Hawaii; in 1824 it was the meeting place for the Prison Reform Society; in 1826 it was the center for both the American Missionary Association and the American Temperance Society. On July 4, 1831, at a children's holiday party in the church, the youngsters gathered on the front steps and sang a song that began with the words "My country, 'tis of thee." Although the new song "America" was set to the music of an old English tune that praises the English monarch ("God save our gracious King"), its fervently patriotic words made it virtually the national anthem for many years.

❖

Parker House

Constructed on the corner of Tremont and School Streets, directly across from historic King's Chapel, the Parker House opened its doors on October 5, 1855, the day Harvey D. Parker hung the simple sign "Parker's" atop his five-story, white marble building. The hotel was built from plans by the well-known architect Gridley J. F. Bryant.

The proprietor, Harvey Parker, was one of the last in Boston to keep the custom of greeting his guests personally upon their arrival. In an atmosphere of hospitality and comfort, poets, philosophers, and politicians congregated at the hotel. Merchants from State Street came in their carriages to drink Sherry Cobblers and dine on Scotch grouse and leg of mutton in the Parker House's celebrated dining room. During the 1860s and 1870s, Oliver Wendell Holmes often gathered with his friends Emerson, Lowell, Longfellow, Whittier, and Hawthorne at meetings of the literary Saturday Club. Charles Dickens joined them for a time, during his second visit to Boston in 1868, taking up residence in Suite No. 338, where he reported that he had been furnished with "a parlour and little bedchamber." It was, indeed, an impressive collection of artists. "Such guests!" recalled Holmes nostalgically. "What famous names its record boasts, / Whose owners wander in the mob of ghosts!" During the Civil War years, Generals Grant, Sherman, Hancock, and Garfield came at various times to stay at the Parker House, as did Sarah Bernhardt, Edwin Booth, and his brother John Wilkes Booth, just eight days before he went to Washington to assassinate President Lincoln.

In the 1890s the Joseph R. Whipple Corporation took over the sprawling complex of buildings that had grown up over the years, and in 1925 most of the existing structures were demolished to make way for more modern structures of steel and granite, completed in 1927. The stock market crash of 1929, however, brought mortgage foreclosure and a transfer of ownership to Glenwood Sherrard, who operated the property until 1958.

In 1968 the hotel, which by that time had fallen into disrepair, was acquired by members of the Dunfey family, who initiated a $12 million long-range restoration program. Soon it offered 530 restored guest rooms and 14 function rooms, with names like Whittier, Longfellow, and Emerson, that were able to accommodate gatherings of 400 people. The oldest continuously operating hotel in the United States, the Parker House in downtown Boston was owned and operated by the Dunfey family until 1968, when it was taken over by the Omni Hotels subsidiary of Wharf Holdings Ltd. of Hong Kong.

Elizabeth Palmer Peabody

American parents who look forward to the day when they can pack snacks for their five-year-old children and send them off to kindergarten for a few hours have a Boston woman to thank for that brief but welcome interlude of peace and quiet.

Elizabeth Peabody was born May 16, 1804, the eldest of seven children. Her father was a dentist in Salem who taught her Latin and inspired her to go on to master ten languages. Her mother, a Salem schoolteacher, developed in Elizabeth an abiding interest in such disciplines as theology, philosophy, history, and literature. Elizabeth herself became a schoolteacher in her teens, first in Salem, later in Maine, and still later in Brookline, where she became acquainted with such prominent intellectuals as Ellery Channing,

Bronson Alcott, and Ralph Waldo Emerson. During the 1820s and 1830s, Channing became a sort of mentor to the young woman, introducing her to the ideas and writings of the great European philosophers of the day, whose theories were influencing American Transcendentalism. In 1837, Peabody took her place alongside Margaret Fuller as the only other female charter member of the Transcendental Club.

In the heady intellectual atmosphere of Boston during the 1830s, Elizabeth Peabody encountered other creative figures who helped shape her own ideas and ambitions. Her ideas about education, for example, were influenced by those of Horace Mann, who started the Boston public school system and who later married her sister Mary, as well as by Bronson Alcott, whose avant-garde educational theories were put into effect at Brook Farm. She developed a close relationship with Ralph Waldo Emerson, who had tutored her in Greek, and maintained a friendship with Nathaniel Hawthorne, whose Salem family she had known from childhood, and who married her sister Sophia.

In 1840 Elizabeth Peabody moved to Boston, where, in the front parlor of 13 West Street, she opened what one biographer has called "the most unusual and influential bookstore in American history." Specializing in foreign books and periodicals, her store became a headquarters for local Transcendentalists. On Wednesday evenings, Margaret Fuller would hold her famous "Conversations" there, and throughout the week figures such as George Ripley, his wife Sophia, Theodore Parker, and Emerson himself would discuss ways to save the *Dial* magazine or methods to enhance the academic curriculum at Brook Farm. As a publisher, Peabody's output included a pamphlet by her friend William Ellery Channing on emancipation; several other antislavery booklets; three of Hawthorne's children's books; and Henry David Thoreau's radical essay on "Civil Disobedience," which would eventually inspire the activities of Gandhi and Martin Luther King, Jr. For a brief period of time, Peabody also published the *Dial,* the "house organ" of New England Transcendentalism, when the original publisher failed in 1842. Elizabeth Peabody thus established herself as the first woman publisher in Boston and, it appears, in the nation.

The education of young children, however, was Elizabeth Peabody's central concern. She was convinced an ideal society could be created only by "educating its children truly." After the Transcendental movement had faded away, she closed her bookstore in 1850 and went off to teach school at various locations, and eventually to write some ten books about the goals and purposes of education. In 1859, she heard about the kindergarten ("children's garden") movement that had been founded in Germany by Friedrich Froebel. A year later she started in Boston the first formally organized kindergarten in the United States. She was eager to learn more about the system at firsthand, and in 1867, with money saved from her lectures, she paid her way to Europe to observe kindergartens conducted on the Froebel model. Upon her return to Boston, she established and edited a journal called the *Kindergarten Messenger*.

As Elizabeth Peabody passed into old age, her increasing stoutness, her failing eyesight, her careless dress, and her eccentric habits tended to distract people from the significant influence she had on American life and culture. As a result of her own considerable intelligence, as well as her wide range of associations with leading American intellectuals and her publishing activities, she was able to transmit to others a remarkable vision. Peabody died in 1894 at her home in Jamaica Plain at the age of 90, and was buried in Sleepy Hollow Cemetery in Concord, the final resting place of Emerson, Thoreau, and the Alcotts. Two years later, as a tribute to her lifelong dedication to education, a group of her friends established in Boston a social settlement called the Elizabeth Peabody House, which relocated to Somerville in 1978 and is still in operation.

Perkins School for the Blind

The task of educating blind persons began to receive attention during the "ferment of reform" that took place during the early 1830s. Educational institutions for the blind were founded in New York and Philadelphia, but the most advanced and influential was the one established in Boston by Dr. Samuel Gridley Howe, a physician, humanitarian, and indefatigable social reformer.

Dr. Howe persuaded Colonel Thomas Handasyd Perkins, a wealthy Yankee merchant, to donate his personal estate on Pearl Street in downtown Boston for use as a school for the blind. Early in 1839 the Mount Washington House, a hotel constructed only a few years earlier on the corner of Broadway and H Street on the peninsula of South Boston, was offered to the trustees of the Perkins Institution in exchange for the property on Pearl Street. The exchange was agreed upon, and during May 1839 the school was moved from one site to the other, with the expenses paid by private contributions from Samuel Appleton and several other prominent Boston gentlemen.

From that time on, the Perkins Institution for the Blind became a well-known feature of the South Boston landscape, attracting visitors from around the country as well as from Europe. They came to observe the various mechanical devices and experimental techniques Dr. Howe used to educate blind persons, and to marvel at the progress he made with Laura Bridgman, a young woman born without hearing or sight. In 1849, a large three-story workshop was erected adjacent to the main building, where students were provided with occupational training in such manual skills as furniture upholstery, mattress stuffing, and the manufacture of fiber mats. Dr. Howe established this workshop with some reluctance, because he had observed in Europe that most blind adults spent their entire lives in sheltered workshops. He hoped that his workshop would prepare Perkins students to go out into the world and "earn a livelihood by honest work."

Dr. Howe made his home for a number of years in South Boston with his five children and his wife, Julia Ward Howe, who later gained fame as the composer of "The Battle Hymn of the Republic." Howe died in 1876 at the age of 74, and was succeeded by a close friend, Michael Anagnos, who had emigrated from Greece. One of his innovations was a "kindergarten for the blind," located in the Jamaica Plain section of town, which accepted pupils before the age of 8 and offered the first six grades of school. It was Anagnos who sent Annie Sullivan, a recent Perkins graduate, to work with the young deaf-blind child Helen Keller in Alabama.

Dr. Edward Allen, who succeeded Anagnos, moved both the original South Boston school and the more recent Jamaica Plain school to the more spacious grounds of the Stickney Estate in Watertown. Three years later, he moved both schools to their present site on a 38-acre campus overlooking the Charles River in Watertown. Several other directors have followed, each making a distinctive contribution toward keeping the Perkins School for the Blind (as it was renamed in 1955) a pacesetter in the field of education for the blind. Supported by private endowment, supplemented by state subsidies, Perkins continues to function in ways reminiscent of its early Boston origins. Gubernatorial appointees sit on the board of trustees, but the majority of trustees are chosen by the members of the corporation, most of whom represent Boston's oldest and most prominent families. Engraved in the impressive Gothic tower that presides over the school is a lantern, a symbol of light that reflects the Perkins philosophy.

Pine Street Inn

In the South End, on Bristol Street (later renamed Paul Sullivan Way), between Albany Street and Harrison Avenue, stands a magnificent tower, built as a replica of the Palazzo Vecchio in Florence, Italy. This structure is the work of the city architect Edmund March Wheelwright, who designed it in 1894 as the Bristol Street fire station. In 1920 it became the headquarters for the Boston Fire Department. For many years the building served as a training school; cadets were taught to scramble up the sides of the building and then leap from the tower into safety nets below. The tower was also perfect for hanging long fire hoses out to dry.

In 1961 the Boston Fire Department moved its headquarters to a new location on Southampton Street, leaving the building unused until 1980, when the City of Boston invited the Pine Street Inn to use the structure as a shelter for homeless men and women. The original site of the shelter had been on Pine Street, not far from the Dover Street area of the South End, between Tremont and Washington Streets, which during the 1930s and 1940s had become Boston's "skid row" district. In this part of town an increasing number of poor, homeless, and indigent persons, many of them alcoholic, drug-addicted, or mentally ill, wandered the streets, slept in the alleyways, and collapsed in the gutters.

The new Pine Street Inn opened in 1980 to care for these homeless people, but soon found itself overwhelmed by their sheer numbers. Mayor Raymond Flynn made substantial efforts to provide additional resources; with increased public funding, private donations, and thousands of hours of volunteer service, the Pine Street Inn was able to expand its facilities. By 1991 it was operating four shelters that provided food, lodging, and medical care for up to 1,000 men and women. In addition, it operated 186 "permanent" housing units in 11 buildings in Boston and Brookline. The number of homeless families in the city continued to increase, however, and it is estimated that there are now at least 5,000 persons without housing in Boston. The Inn currently serves more than 1,100 people each night at 25 locations throughout the area.

By the 1990s, the Pine Street Inn moved "beyond shelter," and inaugurated a series of transitional programs that attempted to address the basic conditions underlying such problems as alcoholism, drug addiction, and depression. In addition, the Pine Street Inn provides vocational training for those who satisfactorily complete the transitional programs and are prepared to return to the working world.

The Police Strike

As the First World War came to an end, the cost of living rose to double what it had been only five years earlier, and all over America many working people found their incomes were falling behind. Throughout 1919 the frustration of workers spawned protests, demonstrations, and strikes from one part of the country to the other. In August 1919 more than nine hundred Boston policemen, in protest against low wages and intolerable working conditions, voted to join the American Federation of Labor (AFL) in an effort to force city officials to respond to their repeated demands for change.

Police Commissioner Edwin Upton Curtis, furious at the idea of policemen joining the AFL, promptly dismissed nineteen patrolmen he considered to be the ringleaders. Policemen, he said, were state officers; affiliation with a labor union would compromise their sworn duty to impartially carry out law enforcement. On Tuesday, September 9, 1919, the policemen voted overwhelmingly to strike: 1,134 men voted for the strike and only 2 against. As news of the strike vote got around, policemen put their uniforms in their lockers and walked out of station houses all over Boston.

Left without organized police protection, the city of Boston found itself virtually defenseless against the violence of vandals, rowdies, and troublemakers. On the first night, trouble broke out in the downtown area, as mobs went along Washington, Tremont, and Boylston Streets smashing windows, looting clothing stores, and breaking into jewelry shops. Quickly the violence spread into residential neighborhoods, where troublemakers took advantage of the absence of police protection to start bonfires, break streetcar windows, and ransack grocery stores.

In an effort to prevent another night of violence, the next morning Mayor Andrew Peters called out the state guard, although he was already being assisted by a makeshift volunteer militia force made up of prominent Back Bay Brahmins, old-time Beacon Hill residents, and about fifty Harvard undergraduates. Later that afternoon Governor Calvin Coolidge, proclaiming "There is no right to strike against the public safety anywhere, anytime," called up additional regiments of the National Guard and ordered them to immediate duty in Boston.

While some vandalism continued for several more nights, the arrival of helmeted National Guard units in Boston, equipped with rifles, bayonets, and live ammunition, clearly turned the tide. Taking up positions in the heart of the downtown business district, as well as in the neighborhoods, the troops quickly dispersed troublemakers and restored order in the streets. By Thursday morning, the state guard was in complete control of the city. On December

21, 1919, the last units of the state guard were finally relieved of their patrol duties, and the police strike was officially over. Not one of the striking policemen was ever rehired by the City of Boston. A completely new Boston Police Department was organized, recruited in large part from young men who had been recently discharged from military service in World War I.

❖

The Ponzi Scheme

During the summer of 1920, Boston newspapers were carrying the exciting news of a fabulous investment scheme being promoted by a man named Charles Ponzi. An Italian immigrant who claimed to have come from a wealthy family and studied at the University of Rome, Ponzi was a diminutive (five-foot-two), fast-talking, sharply dressed confidence man. He had landed in Boston in 1903, did various odd jobs all the way down the East Coast, and in 1917 returned to Boston, where he worked in a local brokerage house before taking over a small grocery store business.

In August 1919 Charles Ponzi came up with a scheme involving foreign postal-reply coupons. Pointing out that he could purchase such a coupon in a Spanish post office for 30 centavos and then exchange it for a U.S. postage stamp for 5 cents, Ponzi insisted that he could make a 10 percent profit on every exchange. On this basis, he argued that he could make a financial killing by purchasing huge quantities of these coupons in foreign markets and then, by redeeming them with a stronger currency, make a profit for those who invested in the enterprise. Calling his new business the Securities Exchange Company, Ponzi persuaded thousands of Bostonians to invest money so that his overseas agents could corner the market in postal coupons all over Europe.

Ponzi did not have any overseas agents, however, nor was he using his investment funds to purchase any postal coupons abroad. There was no investment going on at all. Ponzi used a network of local salesmen, working on a 10 percent commission, to promote the get-rich-quick scheme and bring in new investors in a "pyramid" scheme that took money away from today's investors to pay off yesterday's investors. Ponzi himself became a well-known figure in Boston, as he met with all kinds of people, attended bocce games in the North End, and lured additional investors with his elegant lifestyle. He dressed in fine clothes, bought expensive jewelry for his wife, built a twelve-room mansion in the suburb of Lexington, and even took over the Hanover Trust Bank. At the peak of his success, it is estimated that Ponzi had raked in some $15 million by persuading gullible Bostonians to invest in his scheme.

Ponzi's house of cards came crashing down almost as quickly as it had gone up. In February 1920 United States postal and legal authorities began looking into his operations, and on August 2, 1920, the *Boston Post* reported that Ponzi was over $2 million in debt—$4.5 million if interest were included. Despite efforts by Ponzi to calm the growing anxiety of his investors, further reports by the *Post* revealed that the confidence man had served time in Canada for forging checks, and had served a prison term in Atlanta for smuggling Italian aliens into the United States. A short time later a government audit reported that Ponzi was $3 million in debt—a figure later revised to $7 million.

Charles Ponzi was arrested and eventually convicted on federal charges of using the mails to defraud. After serving three and a half years on that charge, he was later convicted on state fraud charges, which sent him to the Charlestown state prison. When he finally emerged from jail in 1934 at the age of 52, Ponzi was deported to Italy, where he worked for an airline doing business between Italy and Brazil. On January 18, 1949, Charles Ponzi, the onetime millionaire, died virtually penniless in a charity hospital in Rio de Janeiro, his only legacy the name he gave to pyramid schemes like his most famous con.

The Pops

In recent years, the so-called Friday crowd from Beacon Hill and the Back Bay that regularly came to the afternoon performances of the Boston Symphony Orchestra has begun to dwindle. "You don't see as many of the old Brahmins as you used to here because they're dying off," said one observer, pointing to the high average age of the longtime symphony-goers. Hundreds of patrons now arrive in minivans from nearby retirement facilities, or in chartered buses from estates in the North Shore or in Cape Cod. There are some who hope that the Boston Pops concerts, with an audience whose average age is 45, might help bring in a newer and younger audience to Symphony Hall.

On Saturday evening, July 11, 1885, a large and fashionable crowd showed up at the old Boston Music Hall, located between Washington and Tremont streets in downtown Boston, to attend what was advertised as a program of "light music of the best class" presented by the Music Hall Promenade Concert. This was another idea from the fertile musical imagination of Henry Lee Higginson, who proposed this series in hopes of recreating the concerts of pleasant and light-hearted melodies he had attended in the gardens of Vienna, where he had been a music student.

The new Promenade Concerts interspersed the compositions of classical composers with such popular works as the waltzes of Victor Herbert and the rousing marches of John Philip Sousa, and audiences took to them right away. In 1900 the Promenade Concerts officially became known as the Pops. They were led by a series of European conductors until 1929, when a 35-year-old BSO violinist, the Boston-born Arthur Fiedler, was named the Pops' conductor. Over the course of the next fifty years, Fiedler built the Boston Pops into a national institution with an international reputation, combining popular musical favorites with traditional classical works in such a way as to introduce the public to the beauties of music.

Pops concerts, with their familiar format of three sections, divided by two intermissions, are performed at Symphony Hall from the end of April through the month of June. On July 4, 1929, Fiedler inaugurated a new series of free open-air concerts, called the Esplanade Concerts, held along the east bank of the Charles River. In 1940 the Hatch Memorial Shell was constructed as a permanent site for the concerts. In January 1980, after the passing of Arthur Fiedler, the composer John Williams, creator of notable musical scores for American films, became the conductor of the Pops.

He retired in 1993, and in February 1995 Keith Lockhart was named twentieth conductor of the Boston Pops Orchestra. The Pops' recording *The Celtic Album* made history in 1999 by becoming the first Boston Pops Orchestra recording nominated for a Grammy Award. The Pops continues to carry out its mission of introducing younger listeners to classical music and entertaining a national audience through television broadcasts and recordings.

The Pru

At a time in the mid-1950s when other major American cities were putting up skyscrapers, the only high-rise structure along the entire Boston waterfront was the Custom House Tower. The city's unsavory political reputation had discouraged both government funding and private investment in building. The unpleasant experience of the John Hancock Life Insurance Company with city tax assessors when it opened its 26-story office building in 1947 near Copley Square further discouraged construction in Boston.

In 1949 James Michael Curley was defeated in the city mayoral election by John B. Hynes, who appeared to be an honest mayor with optimistic visions for a "New Boston." When Hynes learned that the Prudential Insurance Company was looking to build a regional office in the northeast, he offered a 28-acre parcel of unused railroad lands in the Back Bay as a possible site. But Prudential insisted on tax concessions that Hynes could not deliver, and negotiations seemed stalemated.

When Prudential itself purchased title to the railroad lands in 1956, Hynes renewed discussions with the company and eventually worked out a special tax formula. On January 9, 1959, Hynes joined the Prudential president, Carroll Shanks, in supervising the destruction of old Mechanics Hall on Huntington Avenue and the beginnings of the $150 million Prudential Center. Late in 1959, however, only a short time after the election of Hynes's successor, John F. Collins, as mayor of Boston, the Massachusetts Supreme Judicial Court struck down the city's special tax formula as unconstitutional. At that point it looked as though the Prudential project was gone forever, until Edward Logue, Mayor Collins's redevelopment expert, took the project out of the city's hands. Declaring the unused railroad lands to be a "blighted area," he used the federal urban-renewal powers of the Boston Redevelopment Authority (BRA) to turn the project over to the Prudential Company to develop for the public benefit.

Once the court approved this new arrangement, construction began in earnest. The master plan, designed by Charles Luckman, appeared heavily influenced by the Swiss architect Le Corbusier, with its severe lines and modernistic use of glass and steel. The complex sat on a concrete platform, with the 52 stories of its central building, the "Pru," rising to a height of 743 feet, surrounded by a cluster of flat-roofed buildings. Most residents hailed the success of Mayor Collins in getting this new enterprise under way as the turning point in the movement to transform the old, rundown city into the beginnings of a "New Boston." Although some residents feel its design ignored its surroundings, the Pru has become an instantly recognized landmark in a Boston skyline that is now dominated by skyscrapers.

Public Garden

In 1795, a series of long, one-story buildings called ropewalks, where ropemakers laid out their heavy hawsers and cables, were constructed on the salt marshes just beyond the west side of the Boston Common, along what is today Charles Street. In 1837, Horace Gray, an amateur horticulturist, thought the area would be an excellent spot for a public botanical garden like those he had seen in European cities. In February 1830 Gray and several other Bostonians were incorporated by the state legislature as Proprietors of the Botanical Garden in Boston. The group constructed an immense conservatory near the corner of Charles and Beacon Streets to house exotic plants and rare birds. Although the structure was destroyed by fire shortly after it was built, the idea of a public garden remained alive. As work was begun during the 1850s to fill in the marshlands of the Back Bay, twenty-four acres were set aside for a Public Garden.

The original plans for the Public Garden were based on the gardens at Versailles, with walks, grass plots, flowerbeds, trees, and a fountain. The first bed of tulips in the United States was planted in the Public Garden, a gift of Horace Gray, and inaugurated an annual spring tulip season that has brought many visitors to the city. The twenty-four acres of the Public Garden contain fifty-seven flowerbeds planted with colorful pansies, tulips, roses, and begonias. Seven hundred and fifty trees and shrubs, along with twenty weeping willows, surround the garden's three-acre artificial lagoon, an idyllic English-style pond that was added in 1861. Populated by ducks and swans, the lagoon is spanned by the decorative curving cables of a span that is known as the world's smallest suspension bridge. It was also in 1861 that a competition was held for the design of an elaborate iron fence around the perimeter of the Garden, alongside which a number of memorial statues and monuments were placed. In 1869 the first equestrian statue in Boston, a rendering of George Washington by the sculptor Thomas Ball, was erected inside the Commonwealth Avenue gate.

In winter, the frozen pond becomes a popular skating rink for both children and adults; in spring, the gardens of dahlias, pansies, heliotropes, and cannas attract thousands. The flowers in the Public Garden are changed according to the season, and in summer, the Garden's famous Swan Boats become a favorite part of this urban oasis. Designed in 1877 by Robert Paget of Jamaica Plain, an English immigrant who worked as a shipbuilder at the Charlestown Navy Yard, the original craft was a catamaran, powered by a paddle wheel, covered by a decorative larger-than-life swan, that is driven by the operator's pedaling. Inspired by Richard Wagner's opera *Lohengrin*, Paget called the vessels Swan Boats. The Swan Boats have continued to be owned and operated by members of the Paget family—at the present time by Robert's grandson Paul.

Quincy Market

Quabbin Reservoir

Obtaining a supply of clean drinking water was a serious concern for Bostonians from the very start. In April 1630 John Winthrop and his Puritan followers settled briefly at Charlestown, but the lack of fresh water in that location forced them to move across the Charles River to the Shawmut Peninsula, where the Reverend William Blackstone (Blaxton) assured them they would find an "excellent spring" on the western slope of what is now Beacon Hill.

Over the years, the provision of clean water was largely an individual enterprise, with the Charles River serving as the natural source of Boston's water. Residents usually drew their water either from private wells and public cisterns or from community pumps located in various parts of the town.

By the early 1800s, however, two developments raised questions about the future of the town's water supply: First, Boston's population had grown remarkably after the Revolution, rising from 18,000 in 1790 to well over 30,000 in 1810, with no sign of a letup. Second, during the same period, attempts to dam the river for mills and factories caused the Charles to dry up, and its polluted and foul-smelling waters raised the dangers of disease. The combination of an increasing demand for water and a diminishing supply of the indispensable liquid made it clear that some sort of public arrangement would have to replace the haphazard system that prevailed.

Boston responded by developing one of the country's earliest municipal water systems, drawing water from Jamaica Pond and distributing it through the town by a system of wooden pipes. By later in the nineteenth century, however, immigration, landfill, and annexation caused both Boston's population and its geographical area to expand dramatically. As a result, the city was forced to extend its search for water some 17 miles to the west to Lake Cochituate, and later nearly 25 miles in the same direction to the Sudbury River. By this time it had become clear that a regional approach was needed to construct larger reservoirs and accommodate new water system technologies. In 1895 the state legislature created the Metropolitan Water District (MWD).

The new MWD selected an area near the towns of Boylston and West Boylston, about 40 miles west of Boston, and expanded a small local reservoir into what eventually became the Wachusett Reservoir, with waters drawn from the nearby Nashua River. It soon became apparent that the Wachusett Reservoir was insufficient for the demands of the growing metropolitan area, and so by 1928 the MWD looked even farther to the west—this time to the Swift River Valley, where the towns of Dana, Enfield, Prescott, and Greenwich were located. Formed by a tributary of the Connecticut River, the Swift River Valley was a low-lying area, surrounded by a series of rugged hills that created a natural basin ideally suited for collecting water. After displacing a population of some 3,500 farm people and razing their small communities, in 1928 the MWD began construction on a twenty-year project that would become the Quabbin Reservoir. The work, requiring the building of two huge tunnels to divert the waters of the Swift River away from the dam sites, was completed in 1939. It was not until 1946, however, that the Quabbin Reservoir was filled for the first time, furnishing a whole new supply of water for the Boston metropolitan area and drowning the remains of the old towns in the process.

According to the historian Thomas Conuel, the Metropolitan District Commission (MDC) now manages the water stored in the Quabbin Reservoir, which supplies almost half the fresh water used in the Commonwealth of Massachusetts. But it is a new state agency, the Massachusetts Water Resources Authority (MWRA), that actually distributes the water to some 2.5 million residents in forty-four Bay State communities. The Quabbin Reservoir, which has also become an extensive wildlife refuge and superb fishing ground, provides what appears to be a permanent source of fresh water for Boston well into the foreseeable future.

The Quebec Act

Ever since it defeated France in the Seven Years War (1756–1763), Great Britain had been faced with the problem of how to deal with its newly acquired territory in Canada. Where should the boundary lines be drawn? Should the French people be permitted to retain their language and customs? Should French legal practices be changed to conform to English law? Should an attempt be made to suppress the Catholic Church in accordance with the laws of Great Britain? Such questions were carefully weighed.

After many years of committee work, in 1774 Parliament finally worked out what it considered a final solution to the problem, in what became known as the Quebec Act. Though by coincidence this resolution occurred at exactly the same time Parliament was also taking punitive action against the American colonies with the Coercive Acts, it had in no way intended that the two actions be regarded as one. The Americans, however, considered the Quebec Act to be but another of Parliament's "Intolerable Acts." As one historian later noted, it was "a good law in bad company."

Under the terms of the Quebec Act, Parliament worked out the political, cultural, and territorial future of what was now British Canada. It provided the French inhabitants with a central government in which legislative authority was vested in a council appointed by the Crown, and provided that acts of the council were subject to the royal veto. In many other areas, however, the French were permitted a wide degree of latitude. Civil cases were to be tried without benefit of a jury, the French people were permitted to retain their language and customs, and the Catholic Church was granted a privileged position. The southern portion of Canada (Quebec) was ruled to extend south all the way into the Ohio Valley. Thus, the St. Lawrence River would become a central artery connecting the inland areas with the Atlantic Ocean, making the entire region more valuable to Great Britain.

In many respects the Quebec Act was a wise, tolerant, and far-sighted policy on the part of Great Britain, and would go far toward retaining Canada's loyalty at a later date. From the viewpoint of the Americans, however, the Quebec Act flew in the face of their hopes and expectations. The idea that the vast Ohio Valley would become the property of the detested French Canadians was totally unacceptable to the frontiersmen of western Virginia and Pennsylvania, who claimed this region as their own. To New Englanders in general, and to Bostonians in particular, the Quebec Act once again raised the old fears of a Catholic Menace. That Great Britain had permitted Catholicism to officially exist in Canada was bad enough. But to learn that by extending Canada's boundary southward it had also allowed Papists to spread their evil doctrines into the Ohio Valley caused grave anxieties throughout New England. Their Puritan forefathers, after all, had fled England chiefly because the Church of England too closely resembled the Catholic Church. Had the Puritans braved the dangers of the Atlantic crossing and the perils of the wilderness only to have Catholicism follow them to the New World?

When Bostonians first learned that Great Britain was thinking of allowing the Catholic religion to exist in Canada as "a harmless and indifferent thing," they protested vigorously. In a lecture "against popery" in the chapel of Harvard College on May 8, 1765, the Reverend Jonathan Mayhew, pastor of West Church, referred scornfully to members of the Church of England as "half-Papists" who conducted Masses instead of holding Meetings as good Protestants should. "May this seminary of learning [Harvard], may the people, ministers, and churches of New England," he pleaded, "ever be preserved from popish and all other pernicious errors."

The final passage of the Quebec Act in 1774 confirmed the worst fears of Bostonians. This official establishment of "Popery" so close to their borders showed that Parliament was willing to use religion—along with other Coercive Acts—as one more weapon to crush the independent colonial spirit. Throughout Boston, the pastors of the various Congregational churches observed December 15, 1774, as a day of humiliation, prayer, and thanksgiving. Congregation after congregation listened as its minister promoted the Whig ideology, praised the Continental Congress, and loudly denounced the establishment of Catholicism in Quebec. Unwittingly, it would seem, the British had handed the Americans a strong religious justification for a war to protect their spiritual liberties as well as their civil rights.

Quincy Market

When the first Puritans settled on the Shawmut Peninsula in 1630, they congregated along the southern part of the waterfront at an inlet known as the Town Cove that effectively divided the north and south ends of the peninsula. Close to such centers of government activity as the Town House and Faneuil Hall, the area around the cove also became the focus of the town's early commercial activities.

As time went on and the population grew larger, the Faneuil Hall market district became increasingly congested, a jostling mass of people making their way among butchers cutting their meat in the Hall, venders peddling their fruits and vegetables under wooden sheds along the outside walls, and fishmongers stationed behind long wooden benches lined with large tubs filled with all kinds of seafood. On "high market days," customers and pedestrians were in constant danger of being knocked down by stagecoaches or bowled over by droves of pigs being hustled to market.

In addition to the congestion in the market district, visitors were repelled by the abominable stench, combining the oily smells from the docks and the sickish odors of mudflats at low tide with the repulsive reek of uncollected street refuse and rotting garbage. The Town Dock, the pond directly behind Faneuil Hall, had become a stagnant receptacle for all kinds of filth and rubbish. In 1805 one member of the Night Watch recorded in his logbook that the pond was full of "putrid fish and dead dogs and cats."

When Josiah Quincy became the second mayor of Boston in 1823, one year after the town had been transformed into a city, he determined to take action against this "generated pestilence." Rich people could move out of town in the summer months and find refuge in "purer atmospheres," he wrote. But poor people were forced to remain in the city and inhale the "noxious effluvia." In a dramatic demonstration of executive authority, this "Great Mayor," as he later came to be known, took whatever steps he thought necessary to clean up the mess. Mayor Quincy appointed professional administrators who reported to him personally, and put them in charge of having the streets cleaned, the refuse collected, and the sewers brought under control. He customarily conducted tours of inspection on horseback at 5 o'clock every morning to be sure that his orders were being carried out. He drained the Town Dock, moved the sewer outlets out to the mudflats, brought in fresh landfill, created new streets, knocked down old houses, and put up new ones. In 1826 Mayor Quincy had Alexander Parris design a new granite market-house, directly behind Faneuil Hall. It was two stories high and more than 500 feet long, with a classical portico at each end in Greek Revival fashion, and a copper-sheathed dome gracing the center. Two matching granite warehouses were constructed on either side of the central market building to house the products that came into the port of Boston from all over the world.

The Quincy Market Building continued to be the center of Boston's business activities well into the nineteenth century, until newer buildings and more up-to-date companies in the vicinity of Washington and Summer Streets began to draw retail business away from the old market district. By the early twentieth century, the old Faneuil Hall market district was once again a congested and discordant mixture of horses, carts, wagons, and pushcarts. The Quincy Market Building itself had become neglected, discolored, and dilapidated, a sad reminder of its earlier splendor. Indeed, so painfully run down had the structure become that when the post–World War II process of urban renewal moved toward the waterfront, there was a general assumption that the central market building and the adjoining warehouses would all be demolished.

Fortunately, however, in 1963 BRA director Edward J. Logue was convinced that the buildings were a valuable part of the city's historical tradition that should be saved and restored. By 1970, after Kevin H. White had become mayor of Boston, the city had begun the actual physical restoration of the rundown market buildings. Over the next five years, the old granite buildings were gutted and transformed into attractive and usable structures. At the suggestion of the architect Benjamin Thompson, Mayor Kevin White made contact with James Rouse of Maryland for plans to transform the refurbished marketplace into a lively urban shopping center in the heart of the historic Faneuil Hall district, where food stalls, restaurants, shops, and pushcarts would be operated by local merchants. Despite negative reactions from critics who insisted it would be impossible to bring people back into the central city from the outlying suburban shopping malls, the Quincy Market proved to be an outstanding success that attracted visitors, tourists, and local residents to its colorful shops, boutiques, and restaurants.

At the opening ceremonies of the restored and refurbished Market on August 26, 1976, speakers unveiled a seven-foot stone monument honoring Josiah Quincy, Boston's "Great Mayor," who had dedicated the original market himself nearly 150 years earlier. Quincy Market is still owned by the City of Boston and leased to the company that developed it.

"The Rascal King"

"The Rascal King"

Undoubtedly the most colorful and charismatic Irish politician in Boston history, James Michael Curley has been dubbed "The Rascal King" by his most recent biographer, Jack Beatty. Born November 20, 1874, on Northampton Street in Boston's Roxbury section to immigrant parents from Galway, Curley grew up in the Irish colony that settled just beyond the mudflats of the South Bay. After his father died suddenly, 10-year-old Jim worked at a variety of jobs while attending school—delivering groceries, peddling newspapers, helping at the drugstore. He spent most of his evenings at a local tobacco shop, where he listened to old-timers swapping fascinating stories about local Ward 17 politics. He continued to broaden his reading and improve his public-speaking skills, and before the age of 20 James Michael Curley had decided to make politics his career.

Meeting people and trading favors, young Curley worked his way up the echelons of ward politics. In 1899 he won a seat in Boston's Common Council, and a year later took control of the Ward 17 Democratic committee, becoming the youngest ward boss in the city. In 1901 he moved up the political ladder to serve a single term as a representative in the state legislature, and in 1903 ran for a seat on the city's Board of Aldermen. Despite serving a sentence in the Charles Street Jail for having taken a Post Office examination for someone else ("I did it for a friend," he explained), Curley won his campaign for alderman, and later moved back onto the Common Council. In 1910 Curley ran successfully for a seat in the United States Congress from the Tenth Congressional District and moved his family to Washington to serve two uneventful terms in the House.

Clearly uncomfortable in the nation's capital, in 1914 Curley decided to return to Boston and run for mayor. Deliberately bypassing the two traditional nominating channels—the Yankee Good Government Association and the Irish Democratic City Committee—Curley used a combination of wit, bravado, and political power to win his first mayoral election. The only thing his political enemies could do to impede his progress was to pass a state law in 1918 prohibiting the mayor of Boston from serving two consecutive terms.

Despite such roadblocks, James Michael Curley moved in and out of City Hall every four years with remarkable regularity, establishing himself as a major political force. The power of his mellifluous speaking voice, the devoted loyalty of his working-class ethnic supporters, and his absolute personal control of citywide patronage allowed Curley to wield his political influence to provide the poor and immigrant populations of Boston with the economic benefits and social amenities he felt had long been denied them by the entrenched Yankee-Republican establishment. To combat the effects of the Great Depression, as well as to furnish jobs for Irish workers, Curley undertook a series of public works programs in Boston. He laid out numerous beaches, bathhouses, parks, and playgrounds; he built branch libraries, health centers, and municipal buildings; he repaved streets, widened roadways, and constructed bridges. Under his direction the Callahan Tunnel was completed, the Kenmore MTA Station was built, and the subway from Boston to Logan Airport was constructed.

After serving a single two-year term as Governor of Massachusetts, from 1935 to 1937, Curley's local political career went into decline. Defeated in a 1936 U.S. Senate race by Henry Cabot Lodge, Jr., the following year he suffered a disappointing upset by young Maurice J. Tobin of Roxbury in yet another bid for the mayor's office. In 1938 he lost the governor's race to the Republican Leverett Saltonstall, and in 1941 he lost a second mayoral race to Maurice Tobin. After his election to a term in the U.S. Congress, from 1943 to 1946, it looked as though Curley's political career in Boston might be coming to an end.

Yet the days of James Michael Curley were not over. When Maurice Tobin retired as mayor to run for governor, Curley returned from his congressional seat in Washington to run for the vacant office himself. Despite being under indictment on a charge of mail fraud, the 70-year-old politician swept the field and took office as Mayor of Boston in January 1946. A year later he was sentenced to 6-to-18 months in the federal penitentiary in Danbury, Connecticut, leaving Boston in the hands of the City Clerk, John B. Hynes, who was appointed temporary mayor. Thanks to a pardon by President Harry Truman, Curley served only five months of his sentence, making a triumphant return to Boston the day before Thanksgiving 1947. After his first day back at his City Hall office, he boasted proudly: "I have accomplished more in one day than has been done in the five months of my absence."

Curley's offhand remark so infuriated John B. Hynes that he retaliated by running against Curley in the 1949 mayoral race. For a man who had no money and no political organization, and who had never run for political office in his life, Hynes engaged in this David-and-Goliath struggle with remarkable success. Hynes not only used longtime enemies of Curley to construct a new organization, but he also brought in new sources of political support. Large numbers of young war veterans, an increasing representation of female voters, and organized groups of college students swelled the ranks of Hynes supporters. With their assistance, Hynes went on to defeat Curley in November 1949 in a close race that was decided by the small margin of only 11,000 votes.

Despite the closeness of the 1949 contest, it was apparent to most Bostonians that this was Curley's "Last Hurrah." Although Curley would run for mayor two more times, each time the growing margin of his loss showed his declining influence. With the rise of federal patronage, the transformation of the old ethnic neighborhoods, and the advent of a younger generation in Boston politics, it was clear that "Old Jim's" days were finally over. James Michael Curley died on November 12, 1958, and thousands of his faithful followers viewed his body as it lay in state in the rotunda of the State House on Beacon Hill.

Paul Revere House

The house in which Paul Revere lived, located at 19 North Square in Boston's North End, was nearly a hundred years old by the time the famous Revolutionary patriot moved in. Originally the site was the dwelling place of Reverend Increase Mather, minister at the nearby Old North Meeting House. Mather's house was destroyed by the great fire of November 27, 1676, which also burned down the Meeting House and dozens of other buildings in the area. On the site of the old Mather house was built a new two-story wooden house in what is called the "folk Gothic" style, with a steep-gabled roof, clapboard siding, and leaded casement windows with dia-mond-shaped panes. The new house's first owner was a successful merchant named Robert Howard, who bought it in 1681. Over the years it changed hands several times, and during the mid-1700s a third story was added.

In 1770 the house was purchased by Paul Revere, who lived in it for ten years with his large family—he eventually had sixteen chil-dren by two wives. Between 1780 and 1800 Revere rented it out: in 1780 to George De France, and in 1784 to a local painter named Jo-seph Dunkerly. In 1800 he sold the house and moved to nearby Charter Street. After Revere's death in 1818 the three-story build-ing was converted into a tenement, with its first floor used for a vari-ety of commercial tenants, including a candy store, an Italian bank (La Banca Italiana), a cigar factory, a Jewish grocery store, reflecting the changing ethnic nature of the community.

The passage of time and neglect caused the historic house to de-teriorate badly, but in 1907, led by Revere's great-grandson John P. Reynolds, Jr., a civic organization called the Paul Revere Memorial Association acquired the house and authorized extensive restora-tions under the direction of the architect Joseph Chandler. In its renovated form, the Paul Revere House is a fairly accurate repro-duction of the seventeenth-century building, preserving its original structural skeleton. It provides tourists and visitors with a good ex-

ample of the domestic architecture prevalent in early colonial
Boston. Today the building is open to the public, and serves as a
historic house museum along Boston's Freedom Trail.

The Rise of Silas Lapham

Published in 1885, *The Rise of Silas Lapham* became one of the
most controversial novels of its time. Although he was born in Martin's Ferry, Ohio, its author, William Dean Howells, moved to
Boston in 1867 to pursue a writing career. After serving as editor of
the influential *Atlantic Monthly* for several years, he left to devote
more of his time to writing fiction. Later he served more than two
decades as a columnist and critic for *Harper's Monthly*. In time,
Howells became more of a Proper Bostonian than most native Bostonians.

The Rise of Silas Lapham stands out as Howells's most famous
and lasting novel—one of the earliest generally sympathetic fictional
treatments of the modern American businessman. Writing in the realistic style of late nineteenth-century literature, Howells depicts the
class conflicts and social differences between the established elite of
Boston and the newly rich family of a hard-working and upwardly
mobile paint manufacturer.

Only Penelope, Silas Lapham's literary daughter, is finally accepted into the city's highest circles through a marital alliance with
one of the old families. Howells presents this as an instance of the
way in which an increasing number of outsiders, representing new
social classes, different cultures, and more prosaic forms of economic enterprise, would gradually make their way into the more exclusive echelons of Boston society by the opening of the twentieth
century.

Ritz-Carlton

On May 18, 1927, the Ritz-Carlton, modeled after the Ritz in Paris, was opened in Boston by the real estate developer Edward N. Wyner. Located on the corner of Arlington and Newbury Streets, directly across from the Public Garden, the hotel's combination of Regency and Art Deco styles signaled its aspiration to grandeur and elegance. The original charge for a room at the Ritz was $15 a night, and it was one of the first American hotels to include private baths in the guest rooms.

Wyner never granted a reservation at the Ritz without first researching the customer's background and reputation. Rooms were given only to those listed in the *Social Register, Standard and Poor's Directory of Executives,* or *Who's Who in America.* Over the years the Ritz acquired a colorful and sophisticated reputation. In 1930 the Broadway composer Richard Rodgers is said to have composed the song "Ten Cents a Dance" on a piano in a Ritz-Carlton suite, while the playwright Tennessee Williams is reported to have written portions of *A Streetcar Named Desire* while staying at the Ritz. During the 1930s and 1940s, when Boston was a principal town for tryouts of theatrical productions on their way to New York, it is said that more Broadway plays were revised, rewritten, and restaged at the Ritz than at any other single location in the country. Famous figures such as Charles Lindbergh, Winston Churchill, and John F. Kennedy are among notables who have slept at the Ritz. The final bastion of good taste, the Ritz was determined to maintain its strict code of dress and manners, even to the point of putting up a sign in the 1960s that cautioned: "Turtlenecks on Men, Pants on Women, and Mini-Skirts on All But Children, Are Forbidden."

In 1964 Edward Wyner sold the Ritz to Cabot, Cabot, and Forbes; in 1983 the chairman Gerald Blakely sold the hotel to W. B. Johnson Properties, Inc., in Atlanta. After the Ritz-Carlton Company was founded, the Boston hotel became the flagship for a chain of some thirty-two hotels known for their exacting standards of hotel management. In 1997, however, most people were surprised to learn that Sumitomo Bank announced plans to sell the mortgage of the 275-room Ritz-Carlton at auction in order to regain the interest and penalties on a $136.5 million mortgage. The mortgage was subsequently sold for $75 million to a subsidiary of the Blackstone Group, a privately held New York investment firm.

Many Bostonians were startled to read in their morning newspapers on October 20, 1999, that Millennium Partners, a New York development firm, had not only purchased the Ritz-Carlton Hotel for the sum of $122 million, but also had plans to construct a second Ritz-Carlton Hotel in Boston in the next year. The second hotel it to be located in downtown Boston, facing Boston Common, within the two city blocks bounded by Washington, Tremont, and Boylston streets. The new hotel is planned as part of a $500 million Millennium Place project that will include 270 condominiums, a movie theater, a fitness club, and 85 apartments.

❖

The Sarah Roberts Case

In the fall of 1849 an African American resident of Boston named Benjamin F. Roberts brought suit against the City of Boston on behalf of his 5-year-old daughter Sarah. Sarah Roberts had been denied admission to a nearby white school solely on the basis of her color.

Back in 1789, when their numbers were small and they received no public support, Boston's black citizens had set up a school of their own in the home of a prominent black resident named Prince Hall. In 1806 they transferred the school to the African Meeting House and then, in 1835, constructed a new school with money from a wealthy merchant named Abiel Smith. The Boston School Board agreed to take the Smith School under its jurisdiction, but designated it as a primary school exclusively for black children.

Starting in 1844, a group of African Americans began petitioning the School Board to allow black children to enroll in other schools of the city, especially when they were located much closer to the children's homes. In this effort they were supported by local aboli-

THE SARAH ROBERTS CASE

tionist leaders, who informed black citizens of their constitutional rights and offered legal assistance in securing "the full and equal enjoyment of the public schools." The Boston School Board, however, refused to yield. The members insisted that it was the Board's responsibility to keep apart the two races which "the All-Wise Creator had seen fit to establish."

The Roberts case was eventually argued before the Supreme Judicial Court of Massachusetts, with Charles Sumner, the prominent abolitionist, representing Sarah Roberts, and with Robert Morris, a black attorney, serving as assistant counsel. Despite Sumner's appeal for "equality before the law," and his argument that both black and white children suffer from attending separate schools, Chief Justice Lemuel Shaw decided against the black plaintiffs.

Although they had lost the Roberts case in the courts, black and white abolitionists renewed their efforts to desegregate the public schools in Boston. Switching from the judicial chambers to the political arena, they were able to bring enough pressure to bear on members of the state legislature to persuade them to repudiate the decision of the court. On April 28, 1854, the General Court of Massachusetts passed a law stating that no child, on account of "race, color, or religious opinions," could be excluded from any public school in the Commonwealth. Following the passage of this law, a number of boys from the all-white Phillips School were transferred to the all-black Smith School, while a corresponding number of black boys from the Smith School walked over to the Phillips School to take their seats.

It is difficult to read about this first and apparently uneventful interchange of students to create a more equitable racial balance in Boston's schools without comparing it to the turmoil and violence that accompanied similar efforts to desegregate Boston's public schools 120 years later. Only six years before the Civil War, Boston had further enhanced its reputation as the "Cradle of Liberty" by declaring its public schools open to all students, regardless of race, religion, or ethnic origin. The city's refusal to abide by this idealistic principle a century later disappointed many of its admirers, and gave it a reputation for racial bigotry that would take many years to overcome.

Scollay Square

Sacco and Vanzetti

At 3 o'clock in the afternoon of April 15, 1920, two armed men robbed and killed a paymaster and his guard in the town of Braintree, Massachusetts, and got away in an automobile with two tin boxes containing $15,765. Two weeks later, two Italian immigrants of avowed socialist and anarchist sentiments were arrested. A year later they were tried, found guilty, and sentenced to be executed. At the time the incident was regarded as a local crime of little general significance. By the time the executions finally took place in 1927, however, sympathy for the two defendants had assumed worldwide proportions, and among a variety of liberal, socialist, and left-wing organizations Nicola Sacco and Bartolomeo Vanzetti had become the symbols of a major human-rights crusade.

For six years the names of Sacco and Vanzetti were carried in the headlines of Boston newspapers as appeal after appeal was made on their behalf. Literary celebrities like Dorothy Parker and Robert Benchley led pilgrimages from New York to Boston to plead their cause; Justice Felix Frankfurter declared that they had been unfairly tried; the Episcopal Bishop William Lawrence spoke out on their behalf. Claiming that Sacco and Vanzetti had not had an adequate defense, that their lack of English and their foreign birth were used against them, and that the presiding judge, Judge Webster Thayer, had exhibited extreme prejudice when he vowed to punish the "anarchist bastards," supporters demanded a new trial.

Massachusetts Governor Alvin T. Fuller finally decided that the case should be reviewed, and appointed a blue-ribbon board to consider the case: Judge Robert T. Grant of the probate court; Samuel W. Stratton, head of the Massachusetts Institute of Technology; and A. Lawrence Lowell, president of Harvard University. Although the members of the board conceded that the trial judge had been guilty of a "grave breach of judicial decorum," they reported that on the basis of the evidence they could see no reason the original guilty verdict should be overturned or the two men should be granted clemency.

Despite a renewal of angry petitions and public actions, Sacco and Vanzetti were executed on August 23, 1927. Boston erupted with demonstrations of sympathy for the two men, as huge crowds attended the large funeral procession that made its way through the city on the way to Forest Hills Cemetery. Even today there is considerable controversy over whether the two men were executed because they were cold-blooded murderers or because they were foreigners whose unfamiliar social customs and radical political views ran contrary to the nationalism of a time, just after World War I, when "100-percent Americanism" was the ideal.

In 1977, fifty years after their executions, Massachusetts Governor Michael Dukakis issued a proclamation declaring that Sacco and Vanzetti did not get a fair trial, and in August 1997 a memorial committee presented a bust of the two men to the city of Boston. The bas-relief is housed in the Boston Public Library, along with a donation of materials including a metal drum containing the ashes of Sacco and Vanzetti, which is locked in a vault. An Italian cultural society in Cambridge plans a conference on the subject, and two operas on the subject are in the planning stages—one by Anton Coppola, uncle of the motion picture director Francis Ford Coppola.

The Sacred Cod

A replica of a codfish, four feet ten inches long and carved from a solid block of pine, was mounted in the Old State House in 1784 as "a memorial to the importance of the cod fishery to the welfare of the Commonwealth." Salted or dried cod had become the first export of the Puritan residents of Boston, and for many years was their main source of outside revenue. It was actually the cod that started the shipyards, which produced the first ships for fishermen and went on to build larger vessels for coastal trade and traffic with the West Indies and Europe. At the suggestion of John Rowe—Grand Master of St. John's Lodge of Masons, an active fisherman, owner of Rowe's Wharf, and a member of the House of Representatives—in

1798 the wooden fish was moved with much ceremony from the Old State House to the new Bulfinch State House on Beacon Hill.

Over the years the fish took on the stature of a mascot. Indeed, the representatives began to take it so seriously that they appointed a special commission to carefully move the Cod to the new chambers that were provided for the House in 1895. An escort of fifteen men wrapped the Cod in an American flag and solemnly carried the object to the new House chambers.

Since that time, the Sacred Cod has hung suspended over the center gallery in the chamber of the House of Representatives in the Great and General Court—except when it becomes a victim of a periodic university prank known as "codnapping." In 1933, for example, members of the Harvard Lampoon stole the relic as a college prank. For three days the Sacred Cod was missing, and the members of the state's House of Representatives refused to meet in session until the sacred symbol was returned.

John Singer Sargent

This most Bostonian of artists was actually born in Florence, Italy, on January 12, 1856, and did not come to the United States until he was 20 years old. His mother was an amateur painter who had persuaded her husband, a Philadelphia physician, that the climate of Europe would suit her delicate constitution. Educated at home in several European languages, John Singer Sargent remained an expatriate for the rest of his life, visiting America only on rare occasions.

When the Sargent family moved to Paris, young John's talents came to the attention of the art community. After a period of study with local painters, he was ready by the age of 22 to submit some of his own works to the annual showing of the Parisian Salon. Each year Sargent would offer the Salon judges at least one major portrait, along with a sampling of colorful scenes based on his travels to such exotic locales as Spain and North Africa. In 1881 he was awarded a medal for one of his portraits, and the following year won great acclaim for *El Jaleo,* the dramatic painting of flamenco musicians and Spanish dancers that was later to hang in Isabella Stewart Gardner's *palazzo* in Boston's Fenway.

Sargent's ascendance in the Paris art establishment came to a crashing halt in 1884, when he scandalized conservative art critics with his striking portrait of Virginie Gautreau, which came to be known as *Madame X.* Her heavily powdered skin, bare shoulders, ample bosom, and distinctively haughty manner caused such a stir that he had to give up hopes of establishing himself as a portrait painter in Paris.

In 1886 Sargent moved to London, where his hopes for acceptance were realized as a result of the popularity of his *Carnation, Lily, Lily, Rose,* a charming painting of two young girls in white dresses lighting Chinese lanterns in a garden. His ambition to become a successful portrait painter was further advanced when he was invited to come to America in 1887 to paint the wife of a wealthy New York banker. Doors were opened to more commissions, and Sargent soon found himself in great demand by powerful men and beautiful women. Theodore Roosevelt, Woodrow Wilson, John D. Rockefeller, and Isabella Stewart Gardner were among the famous personalities of the day who chose Sargent as their portraitist.

After years of steady work, in 1907 Sargent announced he would no longer paint portraits. He returned to depicting landscapes and outdoor figures, as he resumed his travels to many parts of Europe. With the outbreak of World War I he went to the Western Front, where he painted Allied soldiers on the battlefield. After the war he produced a pair of murals for the Widener Memorial Library at Harvard University, symbolizing the involvement of the United States in the Great War.

Increasingly, John Singer Sargent turned to murals as a permanent way to secure his artistic renown. He devoted a great deal of time to a series of murals he had promised for the Boston Public Library at Copley Square. The images were painted on canvas in his studios in London or in Boston and then attached permanently, section by section, to the walls. His murals, titled *The Triumph of*

Religion, which fill the third-floor hall leading to the Special Collections Room of the BPL, took some thirty years to complete; the last section was shipped to the library in 1919.

In 1916 Sargent also accepted a commission to paint the rotunda over the main staircase at the entrance to Boston's new Museum of Fine Arts on Huntington Avenue. Drawing upon ancient Greek mythology, paintings and sculptural elements depict Apollo and Athena, as well as other gods and goddesses, in their attempts to preserve Art and Culture from the ravages of Time. On April 14, 1925, John Singer Sargent attended a farewell dinner in London the evening before he was scheduled to sail for Boston to supervise the installation of the last section of his murals at Boston's Museum of Fine Arts. That night, at the age of 69, he died peacefully in his sleep.

In 1999, the Museum of Fine Arts and other Boston institutions collaborated on a "Sargent Summer" that brought the first major exhibit of his paintings at the MFA since his death, along with restoration of the murals at the Public Library and the Museum.

Scollay Square

Scollay Square was an area of downtown Boston between the North End and the beginnings of the retail business section. Named after William Scollay, a frugal Scotsman and wealthy real estate entrepreneur, Scollay Square was located close to the waterfront, the center of government, and the business section of the colonial town. A number of prominent government officials and wealthy merchants made their homes in the district until the early nineteenth century, when they were able to move into more fashionable residential areas on Beacon Hill.

For a number of years Scollay Square continued to serve as an important terminal point at the east end of Washington Street, especially after 1856, when horse cars belonging to the Metropolitan Railroad began operating from Scollay Square across the neck of the peninsula through the South End to Roxbury. As the city's center of balance continued to shift westward—especially after the Great Fire of 1872 prompted many churches and businesses to seek new locations in the Back Bay—the Scollay Square area lost a number of its permanent residents and became home to an increasingly transient population. By the twentieth century the square had become a place where tattoo parlors, barrooms, shooting galleries, shabby movie theaters, hot dog stands ("Joe and Nemo's" was a favorite), and sleazy burlesque houses blighted what had once been a historic district. During World War II it was a favorite destination for sailors docking at Boston Harbor and soldiers visiting the city on leave. "Where's Scollay Square?" was usually their first question on their arrival in Boston.

After the war many city authorities felt that old Scollay Square was no longer compatible with their vision of a modern and progressive city. Once the adjoining West End neighborhood had been cleared for urban renewal, it was only a matter of time before Scollay Square met a similar fate. The plans of Mayor John Collins for his "New Boston" included a multi-million-dollar Government Center Project that encompassed some 60 acres, including most of Scollay Square. In February 1962 the bulldozers came rumbling in, the streets were torn up, the buildings were knocked down, and old Scollay Square ceased to exist—much to the regret of many old Bostonians, who felt that the district had become a cherished part of the city's history. Scollay Square was replaced by the open space of Government Center surrounding a new, modernistic City Hall that became even more controversial than Scollay Square had been a generation earlier—but this time for aesthetic, not moral reasons.

In 1977 a plaque commemorating old Scollay Square was placed by a local businessman at Two Government Center, directly across from the new City Hall. Ten years later, on April 29, 1987, as a result of activity on the part of the local radio talk-show host Jerry Williams, supported by the popular city councilors Albert "Dapper" O'Neill and Fred Langone, Mayor Raymond L. Flynn read a proclamation that officially returned the name Scollay Square to Boston.

Southie

"Southie" is a popular name for the predominantly Irish American, working-class neighborhood of South Boston, situated on a peninsula across the channel from downtown Boston. Originally an extension of the colonial settlement of Dorchester, the peninsula was known as Dorchester Neck. A rustic area with a rich crop of grass that made it ideal for grazing, the district was dotted with fruit orchards and clumps of trees that offered shade for cattle. A small number of wealthy families, including the Wiswells, the Fosters, the Mathers, the Blakes, and the Birds, built permanent and substantial residences on this delightful strip of land that extended out into the Atlantic Ocean. In 1776 the district gained historic significance when General George Washington fortified a series of strategically located hills known as Dorchester Heights and forced the British occupation forces to evacuate Boston.

Dorchester Neck continued its quiet, bucolic existence until the early 1800s, when its prime location came to the attention of a group of real estate developers headed by William Tudor. They purchased a considerable amount of property across the channel, and then petitioned to have the entire peninsula annexed to the Town of Boston. Despite violent protests from the inhabitants of Dorchester, the transfer of ownership took place on March 6, 1804, and what formerly had been Dorchester Neck became South Boston.

The South Boston lands proved to be a valuable investment, as added settlements boosted land values. An orderly street pattern was laid out: streets going from north to south proceed in numerical order; streets going from west to east are in alphabetical order. Because of its fresh salt air and expanses of green pastures, South Boston became the site for a number of medical facilities. In 1792 a special hospital was set up on the peninsula to isolate smallpox patients and those Boston residents who had agreed to receive inoculations. In 1839 the district became the site of the Perkins Institution for the Blind, where Dr. Samuel Gridley Howe became famous for devising techniques for educating persons who were blind. Dr. Howe also became superintendent of a residential facility in the City Point section called the Massachusetts School for Idiots, designed for the care and treatment of retarded and emotionally disturbed young people. South Boston was also the site of a new House of Industry, where what Mayor Josiah Quincy labeled "the able poor" could work for their keep and help defray city costs. Eventually a poorhouse, a lunatic asylum, a house of correction, and a house of reformation for juvenile offenders were constructed on a tract of so-called City Lands in the center of the peninsula. The Carney Hospital, constructed through the bequest of a wealthy Irish immigrant, Andrew Carney, and operated by the Catholic order of the Daughters of Charity of St. Vincent de Paul, became an important South Boston institution, providing medical care for indigent Irish immigrants.

The number of residents in South Boston continued to increase, especially during the 1830s and 1840s, when unemployed Irish immigrants found job opportunities in the "lower end" of the peninsula where it abutted the South End of Boston. Wooden tenements and boarding houses provided inexpensive lodging for Irish residents who worked in the nearby glass factories, iron foundries, blast furnaces, machine shops, shipyards, and locomotive works. These industrial operations worked at full peak during the Civil War years, turning out valuable war materials for the Union cause and supplying much-needed work for Irish immigrants who had come into Boston during the 1850s in the wake of the Great Famine. During the Civil War the population of the peninsula grew from about 22,000 in 1860 to over 30,000 in 1865.

In the years after the war, the character of South Boston became even more distinctively Irish Catholic. In addition to old SS. Peter and Paul's Church, several other churches were constructed to serve the largest concentration of Irish Catholics, in the lower end of the district. In 1874 a new St. Vincent's Church was dedicated on E and Third Streets; in 1884 Our Lady of the Rosary went up on West Sixth Street near D Street. Other churches soon followed the movement of residents eastward toward the City Point area. In

1863 the Gate of Heaven Church was constructed on the corner of Fourth and I Streets; in 1874 St. Augustine's Church was dedicated on Dorchester Street. Public and private life revolved around the Church: Sunday Masses were always crowded; special devotions to the Sacred Heart, the Blessed Mother, and the Saints were numerous; religious organizations for men and women were plentiful. Their own Irish heritage, combined with this strong Catholic influence, created for residents of South Boston a unique socioreligious society whose moral principles guided their community for generations.

Well into the twentieth century, residents of South Boston—as well as residents of Boston's other ethnic neighborhoods—maintained distinct and essentially clannish communities where people lived with their "own kind." Dwelling mostly in two- and three-decker houses, the residents were generally blue-collar workers employed in such local plants as the Standard Sugar Refinery, the Boston Beer Company, and the Walworth Company, or in one of the leather, wool, or coffee warehouses along Summer Street. Others worked for one of the public utility companies—the telephone company, the electric company, the gas company, or the elevated railway—or had jobs with the City in public works or in parks and recreation. For those born and raised there, South Boston was a warm, friendly, comfortable community where people knew one another, shared the same values, enjoyed the same pastimes, and were safe from outside contacts and alien influences.

This "tight little island" atmosphere was threatened by the remarkable growth of Boston's African American population during the 1950s and 1960s, a result of a major migration from the South of unemployed cotton workers seeking jobs during World War II. Since there had been little residential construction in Boston since the 1920s, the expanding black population spread first out of the South End and lower Roxbury into adjacent areas of North Dorchester and upper Roxbury, and then into such traditionally white neighborhoods as Dorchester, Jamaica Plain, Roslindale, and Hyde Park in search of housing. It was not long before the growing black presence ran into resistance from the Irish in South Boston and residents of other white ethnic neighborhoods, who resented the efforts of black people to move out of "their" communities into localities others viewed as exclusively their own. Inspired by the recent civil-rights successes in the South during the mid-1960s, however, black citizens refused to be denied access to public facilities in Boston and increased their demands for better housing, improved employment opportunities, and equal rights in education.

The all-white Boston School Committee, under the leadership of Louise Day Hicks, a popular political leader from South Boston, refused to admit that the Boston school system was segregated—either *de jure* or *de facto*. For nearly twenty years since the Supreme Court decision in *Brown v. Board of Education* the School Committee refused to make any adjustments in the traditional way students were assigned to schools. Finally, in 1971 black residents and the NAACP brought suit against the Boston School Committee to achieve integration. The court case was assigned to federal Judge W. Arthur Garrity, Jr., who for two years studied all aspects of the case. On June 21, 1974, he handed down his decision: the Boston School Committee had "knowingly carried out a systematic program of segregation," and thus "the entire school system of Boston is unconstitutionally segregated." In order to remedy the situation as soon as possible, Judge Garrity ordered a system of busing to go into effect at the beginning of the next school year, in which some 15,000 students would be bused into each other's neighborhoods to develop a systematic program of racial balance in the schools. According to the plan designed by the state Department of Education, most of the children would be bused between schools in South Boston and Roxbury. "To mix Southie and Roxbury," the journalist Alan Lupo later observed, "was not to ask for war, for the war was inevitable, but it was to insure that the war would be bloody."

Opponents of integrated schools in South Boston had already begun building up organizations and associations to oppose enforced busing, the most powerful of which was ROAR—"Restore Our Alienated Rights." Members of these groups were on hand to create a major demonstration on the first day of school, September 12, 1974, when yellow buses brought black students to classes at South Boston High School for the first time in its history. Day after day, month after month throughout the school year, the yellow buses became a familiar sight, rumbling through the streets of the neighborhood morning and afternoon with police motorcycle escorts riding alongside. Despite the parades, demonstrations, rioting, and violence that marked the first year, Judge Garrity refused to be deterred from his purpose, and arranged to have even more students bused the next year. Once more fights, brawls, protests, and boycotts rocked South Boston High School, while community leaders and activist groups continued protest meetings and antibusing demonstrations. Words like "never" and "resist" were scrawled angrily on walls and fences, giving the neighborhood the appearance of Belfast under siege.

Eventually, as time went on, as students graduated, as residents moved away or grew tired of the struggle, the furor over the busing controversy gradually died down. But it took a good ten years, and even then the pain never went away, as evidenced by the bitter responses from neighborhood parents on the occasion of Judge Garrity's death in September 1999—twenty-five years after the first buses had appeared. Although the crisis over busing was a relatively brief episode in South Boston's 300-year history, it was an unusually bitter and violent period that stereotyped the neighborhood forever in the minds of people throughout the nation as a place where beer-bellied men and foul-mouthed women made war on defenseless black children. But the people of South Boston insisted they were fighting to preserve their local institutions, and to protect their schoolchildren from unsafe and crime-infested communities. From their point of view a virtual conspiracy of out-of-town liberals, irresponsible black militants, and radical social engineers were attempting to introduce new social principles and different moral values into their traditional neighborhood. They would go down fighting if they had to, but they would not yield.

With the election of Raymond Flynn, a South Boston native, as mayor of Boston in November 1983, some of the anger and bitterness over busing finally began to recede. In addition to Flynn, several other South Boston political figures moved into positions of power. William M. Bulger, for example, rose to the influential post of president of the Massachusetts Senate, where he remained for many years; Joseph Moakley, another local resident, became an important spokesperson for neighborhood interests in the U.S. House of Representatives; James Kelly served as an inveterate defender of the interests of South Boston on the Boston City Council. During the 1980s South Boston itself began to assume a much more attractive appearance. Streets were cleaned, old houses were sided, trees were planted along major thoroughfares, flowers were arranged in public places, and the beaches were tended with greater care. With its fresh air, beautiful beaches, and lovely walkways, South Boston soon began attracting young professionals who worked in the expanding service economy of the "New Boston." The process of gentrification boosted real estate prices in the peninsula district to astronomical heights, causing some friction with long-time residents, who fear that such economic influences will change the character and values of its traditional working-class population.

Real estate developers and entrepreneurs also began to see the peninsula of South Boston as a natural extension of downtown Boston, which no longer had enough land left for expansive building projects. A new federal court building was erected across the Fort Point Channel, a new hotel has gone up across from an expanded World Trade Center, and plans are under way for an enlarged Convention Center in an area along the South Boston waterfront, where an ambitious complex of hotels, apartment houses, offices, shops, and restaurants is on the drawing board. Local political representatives like Jimmy Kelly have fought vigorously to insure the safety and the interests of the residents of South Boston, and in 1998 succeeded in organizing neighborhood opposition to plans to construct a major football stadium in the district. But it seems almost inevitable that with the influx of new and more diverse residents, as well as with the massive building projects taking place, the traditional social and economic characteristics of South Boston will undergo substantial change.

State House

Throughout the colonial period, the handsome Town House that stood at the intersection of Cornhill and King streets (now Washington and State streets) served as an impressive symbol of Great Britain's imperial rule over the Massachusetts Bay Colony. After the

American Revolution, the old structure continued to function as the center of the new state government as well as the focal point of political life in Boston. It was the home of the legislature, and four successive governors of the Commonwealth frequented the building in the course of their official duties.

It was not long, however, before Bostonians expressed their desire for a State House of their own that would properly reflect their independent status. In accordance with a resolve of the General Court, dated February 16, 1795, Edward Hutchinson Robbins, speaker of the House of Representatives, together with Thomas Dawes and Charles Bulfinch, were appointed agents for the Commonwealth with authority to build a new State House for the "accommodation of all the legislative and executive branches of government." The site selected for the new structure was the "Hancock pasture," two acres of land adjoining the late governor's estate on the south slope of Beacon Hill. The sum of £8,000 was appropriated for the purchase, but a special committee was able to get the land for only £4,000. After the deed was officially signed, Charles Bulfinch was chosen as the architect.

The date chosen for laying the cornerstone of the new State House was, appropriately enough, July 4, 1795—Independence Day. The state officials and their guests assembled in the Old State House, proceeded to the Old South Meeting House, and, after listening to a sermon, marched across the Common to the site of the new building. The cornerstone had been transported to the site on a large truck drawn by fifteen white horses, representing the thirteen original states plus two new ones, Vermont and Kentucky. With elaborate public ceremony, the cornerstone was laid by Governor Samuel Adams, assisted by Paul Revere, William Scollay, and other members of the Grand Lodge of Masons.

The new State House was completed in January 1798, at a cost carefully recorded as $133,333.33—a typically exact Boston figure. On Thursday, January 11, 1798, the members of the General Court assembled for the last time in the Old State House on State Street, and promptly at noon they marched to the new building, accompanied by Governor Increase Sumner, the members of his council, and the architect Charles Bulfinch. The two houses of the legislature, together with the governor and his council, first assembled in the Senate chamber and then proceeded to the House of Representatives, where they heard prayers from the chaplain. After that, the members of the Senate retired to their own chamber, and the business of state government resumed.

The new State House in which the Governor and the General Court took up their official duties was much larger than its modest predecessor, measuring 172 feet across, 65 feet deep, and 155 feet high including its signature dome. The Bulfinch structure was a red-brick edifice, trimmed in white, with balconies on the south and north fronts. It featured tall, white Doric columns, many of which were hewn on the State House lawn from enormous pine trunks. Most of the wood used in the original building came from Maine, which was a part of Massachusetts at the time; the pine cone atop the cupola above the dome symbolizes the importance of the lumber industry to early New England. The original wooden pillars were later replaced by steel and plaster facsimiles because of concern about fire. The 30-foot-high dome, with a diameter of 50 feet, was first constructed entirely of wood, but to safeguard it from the danger of fire and the effects of the elements, in 1802 it was sheathed with copper, purchased from Paul Revere & Son. It was not until 1874 that a covering of 23-carat gold leaf was placed over the copper-sheet base, at a cost of $2,862.50, and the "golden dome" of Bulfinch's State House took on its distinctive appearance.

Visitors to the State House do not use the central front entrance to the building at the top of the main staircase. The main doors are opened only for departing governors to leave the building at the end of their terms, to receive a Massachusetts regimental flag, or for official visits by the President of the United States. Just inside the Beacon Street door on the first floor is a beautiful entrance foyer known as Doric Hall. This room, 55 feet square, is divided into three aisles by rows of ten Doric columns, and its floor is paved with black and white marble squares.

On the second floor are several rooms housing paintings and historic memorabilia. One of the most impressive is the Hall of Flags, which has a series of murals depicting the pilgrims aboard the *Mayflower* sighting land, John Eliot preaching to the Indians, and the Battle of Concord Bridge. In this hall there is a rotating exhibition of the flags Massachusetts regiments have carried into battle, from the Civil War through the Vietnam conflict. The Governor's office, beautifully decorated in Wedgwood blue with white Corinthian pilasters, occupies the southwest corner of the Bulfinch front.

Moving from the original Bulfinch building to the 1895 addition, what was once called the Senate Staircase Hall was renamed Nurses' Hall in 1985, and features a dramatic sculpture by Bela Pratt showing an army nurse tending a wounded soldier during the Civil War. The walls of Nurses' Hall are covered with murals of historic scenes from Bay State history, showing Paul Revere on horseback, the Boston Tea Party, and James Otis railing against the Writs of Assistance. A more recent tribute to the accomplishments of Bay State women was provided when the state legislature authorized a special work of art honoring six Massachusetts women: Sarah Parker Remond, antislavery lecturer and physician: Mary Kenney O'Sullivan, labor organizer and settlement worker; Dorothea Lynde Dix, advocate for the mentally ill and Superintendent of Nurses for the Union Army; Lucy Stone, abolitionist and suffrage leader; Josephine St. Pierre Ruffin, suffragist and leader in the national women's club movement; and Florence Hope Luscomb, suffragist, labor organizer, and advocate for racial equality. The installation, designed by the team of Sheila Levrant de Bretteville and Susan Sellers, was opened to public display in October 1999. A bronze bust of each woman is set in an opening in one of a series of marble panels just outside Doric Hall. Brief quotations from the women's writings or speeches are etched on the panels, which are mounted on a wall covered with official Massachusetts documents.

The House and Senate chambers occupy the entire third floor of the State House, and are richly ornamented rooms in early Federal-classic style, with graceful colonnaded galleries and lofty barrel-vaulted domes.

With the construction of new additions throughout the nineteenth and early twentieth centuries to accommodate the expansion of state government, additional land purchases increased the building's original 1.6-acre lot to its current 6.7 acres, the equivalent of two city blocks. Each of the major new wings, annexes, and renovation projects—completed in 1831, 1851, and 1917—was intended to be architecturally "subservient" to Bulfinch's original design. The red bricks of Bulfinch's structure, for example, which were painted white in 1825 and later changed to yellow, were finally restored to the original red color in 1928 to clarify the distinction between the original Bulfinch building and the wings and annexes added later.

On the grounds outside the State House are a number of statues depicting figures from Massachusetts history. Below the central colonnade are statues of Senator Daniel Webster, the educator Horace Mann, and Civil War General Joseph Hooker, as well as Anne Hutchinson, who was banned for heresy, and Mary Dyer, who was hanged for her Quaker beliefs. In 1990 a statue was placed on the southeast lawn depicting President John F. Kennedy, walking casually toward Boston Common.

Lucy Stone

At the height of the modern feminist movement during the 1960s and 1970s, when young women were choosing either to hyphenate their names with their husbands' or retain their birth names after marriage, a number of "Lucy Stone Leagues" appeared, recalling a female activist from more than a hundred years earlier.

Lucy Stone was born August 13, 1818, on a farm near West Brookfield, the eighth of nine brothers and sisters. Even as a young girl, Lucy resented the inferior position of women in American society, and determined to go to college to study Greek and Hebrew in order to disprove what she considered inaccuracies in the Bible's teaching concerning the subservience of women to men. After studying at Mount Holyoke Female Seminary in South Hadley, in 1843 she enrolled at Oberlin College in Ohio, noted for its liberal antislavery views as well as its pioneering coeducation of women. After studying Greek and Hebrew at Oberlin, Lucy was satisfied that the Bible's teaching on the inferior position of women had been misconstrued.

In 1847, at the age of 29, Lucy Stone graduated from Oberlin with honors—the first Massachusetts woman to be granted a college degree. A few months later she accepted a position as a lecturer with the Garrison-dominated American Anti-Slavery Society. Before long, however, Lucy's strong commitment to women's rights began to clash with her responsibilities in the abolitionist cause. "I was a woman before I was an abolitionist," she explained. "I must speak for the women." Her employers finally agreed that she could lecture on women's rights on her own during the week if she would speak for the Anti-Slavery Society on the weekends. An impressive public speaker, Lucy Stone drew large audiences. Although she appeared young and innocent, she spoke with a fervor that captivated audiences that were friendly, and often neutralized those that were hostile. The notoriety gained by her public appearances, however, caused her church to expel her for conduct "inconsistent with her covenant engagements."

Although she had earlier decided against marriage so that she would never have to call any man her "master," Stone was persistently and successfully courted by Henry Browne Blackwell, a merchant who was both antislavery and profeminist. At their marriage ceremony on May 1, 1855, they both read a protest against the prevailing marriage laws, which the officiating minister, Thomas Wentworth Higginson, subsequently published. After the ceremony, Lucy announced that she would keep her own name, calling herself Mrs. Stone. A number of Lucy Stone Leagues were established in various parts of the country by sympathetic groups of feminists, and the term "Lucy Stoner" came into the American language to denote a married woman who retained her maiden name. Although Lucy decided to remain at home to care for her daughter, born in 1857, she continued to support feminist causes, praised the Emancipation Proclamation, and worked for the passage of the Thirteenth Amendment.

When the Civil War was over, Mrs. Stone helped organize the American Equal Rights Association in 1866, which agitated for both Negro and woman suffrage. The following year she resumed a full schedule on the public lecture circuit. Before long, a deep and bitter controversy among women's rights advocates arose that divided the movement for more than two decades. Mrs. Stone took the position that, in the aftermath of the Civil War, the fight for Negro suffrage should be won first, before taking up the struggle for woman suffrage. Along with her husband, Henry Blackwell, and the African American spokesman Frederick Douglass, Lucy Stone insisted that "this hour belongs to the Negro." Another group of women's rights advocates, led by Susan B. Anthony, Elizabeth Cady Stanton, and Sojourner Truth, objected to the word "male" in the Fourteenth Amendment. They were outraged that people like Lucy Stone would support suffrage for African American males while putting off suffrage for women to a later date.

In 1869 Mrs. Stone and her family returned permanently to the Boston area, settling in Dorchester, where she became the leading spirit in the New England wing of the suffrage movement. She served on the executive board of the American Woman Suffrage Association (AWSA), which was less radical than the National Woman Suffrage Association (NSWA). She made perhaps her greatest contribution in founding the weekly newspaper the *Woman's Journal*. After 1872, along with her husband, Mrs. Stone assumed editorial responsibility for the publication, and for the next forty-seven years the *Woman's Journal* was regarded as "the voice of the woman's movement," celebrated for its journalistic excellence as well as the quality of its contributors.

After 1887 Mrs. Stone's voice failed, and although she still continued to make public appearances and attend ceremonial functions, she was forced to limit her speaking to very small groups. In 1893, at the age of 75, Lucy Stone passed away at her Dorchester home. Her funeral brought great numbers of admirers from all over the country to pay their respects, and according to her wishes her body was cremated at Boston's Forest Hills Cemetery. A pioneer to the end, she was the first person to be cremated in New England.

Gilbert Stuart

A resident of Boston, the painter Gilbert Stuart went to London to live and work with the American artist Benjamin West during the Revolutionary period. He became a member of the Royal Academy, largely on the strength of his elegant painting called *Portrait of a Gentleman Skating*. Famous in London and Dublin, Stuart was also part of Boston's fashionable society, which took pleasure in his lordly airs, his use of snuff, his taste for fine Madeira wine, and his charming conversation. One story that had wide circulation on Beacon Hill was that when one of his sitters fell asleep, Stuart painted him with the ears of an ass. Local residents took pride in the way the painter reflected the sophistication of Boston in the salons and drawing rooms of Europe.

Gilbert Stuart achieved his most enduring fame through his portraits of subjects such as members of prominent mercantile families like the Appletons and distinguished political figures, most famously George Washington. Actually, he did three paintings of Washington from life. The first (called the Vaughn type) is a bust showing the right side of Washington's face; the second (called the Lansdowne type) is a full-length study; the third (unfinished), often referred to as the Athenaeum head, is now shared by Boston's Museum of Fine Arts and the National Portrait Gallery in Washington. This painting, commissioned by Martha Washington, has been immortalized by the engraving on the United States one-dollar bill.

❖

Symphony Hall

Constructed in 1900 on the corner of Massachusetts and Huntington Avenues, Symphony Hall was designed by McKim, Mead, and White, the architects who had recently designed the Boston Public Library in nearby Copley Square. Symphony Hall, and the Boston Symphony Orchestra for which it was built, are a tribute to the vision, determination, and generosity of Henry Lee Higginson.

Higginson, who was born in New York City, always insisted that the idea of creating a symphony orchestra came to him in 1854, when he was 20 years old and had traveled to Vienna to see if he had enough talent to become a professional musician. Although his European tour convinced him that he was not cut out to be a performer ("I had no talent for music," he said), the conviction that America should have "a fine orchestra" remained with him for the rest of his life.

Young Higginson returned to America in 1860, just in time to enlist in the Union army during the Civil War. After his service was over, he settled down in Boston and went into banking. As a stockholder he was made a partner in Lee, Higginson & Company, and eventually became a generous benefactor of numerous schools and colleges. But the idea of a symphony orchestra would not go away, and with the development of the fashionable Back Bay during the 1870s and the groundwork for a Museum of Fine Arts, Higginson decided that the time had come for Boston to have a symphony orchestra.

Higginson laid out a plan to form, in his own words, "an orchestra of excellent musicians under one head and devoted to a single purpose." The first conductor was Georg Henschel, whom Higginson heard conduct at a Harvard Musical Association concert in March 1881. The BSO gave its inaugural concert on October 22, 1881, in downtown Boston at the old Music Hall in Hamilton Place, where it continued to perform until the city announced plans to construct a street through the location. At that point, Higginson and his friends formed a corporation to underwrite the design and construction of a dedicated Symphony Hall. The architectural firm of McKim, Mead & White engaged Wallace Clement Sabine, a professor of physics at Harvard, as an acoustical consultant, making Symphony Hall the first auditorium designed according to scientifically derived acoustical principles. The hall's brick and steel construction, along with its original oak floors, leather seat covers, and plaster walls, all carefully preserved, contribute to the superior acoustics of the building, considered one of the two or three finest concert halls in the world. The hall, which seats some 2,600 people, opened with a gala concert on October 15, 1900. Until 1918 Henry Lee Higginson remained the sole underwriter of the Boston Symphony Orchestra, and declared himself eminently satisfied with the work he had accomplished. "The public enthusiasm for the symphony," he wrote in 1900, "showed how completely the cause of music had won its way in Boston."

Eventually Major Higginson was persuaded to share the responsibility of supporting the Symphony with other Boston families, who were expected not only to contribute to the annual deficit but also to attend concerts on a regular basis. In this respect the women of the city proved the most loyal and dedicated supporters of this civic commitment. For years, every Friday afternoon, all winter, the Proper Boston Woman dutifully attended Symphony (never "the" Symphony!). Following a morning Chilton Club lecture and a Chilton Club lunch, she would be picked up and driven down Boylston Street to Massachusetts Avenue in time to be escorted to her traditional seat at Symphony Hall for the 2:30 P.M. concert. These would be the very same seats her family has held for generations, and Lucius Beebe has described the craning of the necks to make sure that "the Hallowells and the Forbeses are in their accustomed stalls."

With that kind of support, the Boston Symphony Orchestra has become one of the finest in the world. Its music directors have included such internationally acclaimed conductors as Pierre Monteux, Serge Koussevitsky, Charles Munch, Erich Leinsdorf, and Seiji Ozawa. Major figures such as Béla Bartók, Leonard Bernstein, and Igor Stravinsky are among the numerous composers who have written works especially for the Boston Symphony Orchestra. The BSO's Pops concerts and recordings have brought music to millions, and its Tanglewood Music Center has provided essential education for thousands of young musicians. In 1952 the BSO became the first Western orchestra to play in the Soviet Union; in 1979 it was the first to play in the People's Republic of China.

Trinity Church

The "T"

Public transportation began early in Boston. As early as 1631 a colonial charter authorized a ferry service to transport residents to the various peninsulas. During the 1820s a number of horse-drawn coaches served as public conveyances in various parts of the town, and during the 1830s entrepreneurs invested in oversized carriages called omnibuses, which usually traversed their routes on regular one-hour schedules from daybreak to sunset.

The paving of dirt roads during the 1840s made it possible to begin laying steel rails for horse-drawn streetcars, and before long competing horsecar lines were operating in several localities. Late in 1856 a horsecar line belonging to the Metropolitan Railroad began to operate from downtown Scollay Square, through the city, and across the narrow part of the neck of the peninsula all the way to Roxbury. Over the next two decades, the horse-drawn railroads of Boston gradually expanded, until there were some 500 miles of streetcar lines extending about four miles beyond City Hall. In time, the narrow streets of Boston became so clogged by horse-drawn trolleys that it was said pedestrians could walk to work on the roofs of the cars.

Starting in 1889 the streetcars were electrified, provided with newfangled "trolleys" that drew their electric current from overhead power lines. The striking sight of the sparking trolley wires was playfully described in a poem titled "The Return of the Witches" by Oliver Wendell Holmes: "Since then on many a car you'll see / a broomstick plain as plain can be; / On every stick [trolley pole] there's a witch astride— / the string [trolley wire] you see to her leg is tied." To alleviate the street congestion and traffic hazards caused by so many trolley lines, the Boston Transit Commission decided to create an underground railway modeled on the subterranean trolley tunnels of Glasgow, Paris, London, and Budapest, starting at Tremont Street near Park Street. Despite angry public protests, and a Biblical admonition from Mayor Nathan

Matthews that "Thou shalt not touch the Common," construction began on March 28, 1895. For nearly three years laborers were hard at work hauling tons of dirt from the huge trench they dug along Tremont Street and dumping the soil at the Charles Street end of Boston Common. When construction was finally completed, on September 1, 1897, an estimated 100,000 people lined up to pay five cents for a sixth-tenths-of-a-mile ride from Tremont Street to Boylston Street. Boston's subway system was the first of its kind in North America.

The original subway station at Park Street was at the level of to-day's Green Line; the Red Line's "Park Street Under," one level lower, was added in 1912. The "headhouses" (called "mausoleums" in 1897), where riders entered the subway station, were designed by the architect Edmund Wheelwright with roofs of glass, walls of Maine granite, and exteriors decorated with neoclassical motifs. Two of the original headhouses are still in use today, and have been named National Historic Landmarks. The sixth largest transit system in the nation, the Massachusetts Bay Transportation Authority (MBTA) system today carries 650,000 commuters a day on its four main lines—color-coded since the 1960s as the Red, Blue, Green, and Orange lines. (The Red Line was named for the crimson of Harvard University, its original terminus; the Blue because it was the first line to travel under the ocean; the Green because it connects points on the Emerald Necklace; and the Orange for Orange Way, the original name of its Washington Street route.) Overall it comprises 64 miles of subway and trolley lines; including commuter rail and buses, the system covers more than 1,000 miles and serves a total daily ridership of more than 1.1 million. The MBTA is supported by assessments against some 79 cities and towns in the larger metropolitan areas, on the premise that the citizens of all these communities are benefited by the system. Most Bostonians refer to their transit system simply as "the T."

Three-Deckers

A tour of downtown Boston reveals a wide variety of historical architectural styles. Below Washington Street, colonial Georgian structures of red brick rub shoulders with Greek Revival buildings of gray granite. Bulfinch's stately Federal townhouses cluster under the shadow of the gilded State House dome atop Beacon Hill. Richardson's massive Romanesque Trinity Church boldly confronts the broad Renaissance palazzo of the Boston Public Library across the expanse of Copley Square.

But the city's working-class neighborhoods have also contributed their own distinctive architectural form. The three-decker house (sometimes called a triple-decker) is the most immediately recognizable structure in Boston's former immigrant communities. The three-decker, as its name implies, is a three-story wooden house, with one apartment of six or seven rooms on each floor, opening off common front and rear stairwells. Many three-deckers have front or back porches, or both, on each floor.

Irish immigrants may not have invented the three-decker (or its variant, the two-decker) but in the neighborhoods into which the Irish expanded during the latter half of the nineteenth century—Charlestown, South Boston, East Boston, Dorchester, Roxbury, West Roxbury—three-deckers became the most prevalent form of architecture housing large working-class families. The three-decker was far less expensive than the traditional single-family house, not only in the simplicity of its construction but also in the cost of its house lot. The equivalent of three houses could, in effect, be built one on top of the other on a single plot of land. The three-decker had the additional advantage of allowing the owner to finance its purchase by living on one floor while collecting rent from tenant families living on the other two floors. Or two or three related families could live together in the same building, while maintaining privacy in their own apartments. In the early years of immigration, this was considered a perfect solution for close-knit and often extended immigrant families who wanted the comfort and security of shared housing.

The precise origin of the phrase "three-decker" is not entirely clear, although the architectural historian Douglass Shand-Tucci reminds us of its naval connotation as a description of a ship with three decks, dramatized in Alfred Lord Tennyson's line: "the rushing battle-bolt sang from the three-decker out of the foam." Indeed, in one of Patrick O'Brian's novels about naval warfare in the Napoleonic era, Captain Jack Aubrey observes a line of French warships: "seventeen of the line, six of them three-deckers, and with five frigates." Standing on the front porch of one of the three-deckers along South Boston's Farragut Road, looking out beyond Castle Island to the waters of Boston Harbor, it is not too great a stretch of the imagination to feel the powerful sweep of an old sailing vessel surging out into the broad Atlantic.

In the recent real estate market, with a growing number of young professionals moving back to the city, seeking homes in old neighborhoods that border the downtown area, and raising asking prices to astronomical levels, the old three-decker has made a remarkable comeback. Once the house of choice for large working-class immigrant families who could afford little else, many three-deckers have been converted into three-story condominiums suitable for high-income professionals, either single or married with no children, who are rapidly gentrifying old neighborhoods like Charlestown and South Boston. The structure that had once been called the "people's architecture" has now taken on an entirely new and quite fashionable appearance.

Triangular Trade

As part of England's far-flung colonial empire, the American colonies were part of a mercantile system in which they would furnish such staple crops as tobacco, rice, sugar, indigo, cotton, and lumber to England, while the mother country would process and refine those products and sell them back to the colonies as finished goods.

This system was codified by Parliament in 1660 and again in 1663 in a series of Navigation Acts which stipulated that British merchants and shippers were to have a monopoly on all American goods.

Because of long distances and lax administration of the British laws, Boston virtually ignored the terms of the Navigation Acts and built up its own extensive network of transatlantic trade routes that became known as the triangular trade. Using their own ships and their own seamen, ignoring the Navigation Acts and keeping their own profits, enterprising Boston merchants participated in a series of ventures that brought them wealth and position. Perhaps the best known of the triangular routes started with the export by Boston merchants of fish, livestock, hay, flour, and lumber to various parts of the West Indies in exchange for return cargoes of sugar, coffee, cocoa, and molasses. After much of the molasses was converted into rum, the same Boston ships would carry their cargoes across the Atlantic on the second leg of the journey to the west coast of Africa; there the rum would be exchanged for slaves, who were then transported back across the ocean to be sold in the West Indies, on the third leg of the triangle.

But there were other routes which also fit into the triangular pattern. One brought ships from New England to the West Indies carrying food, horses, lumber, and fish, which were exchanged for great amounts of sugar that was then shipped across to England. There it was traded for manufactured goods, which were then brought back across the Atlantic to markets in North America. Another triangular route went from New England carrying fish, food, furs, and timber to various countries in southern Europe, where the raw materials were exchanged for such commodities as wine, silk, spices, and tropical fruit. These products were then transported to England, where they were traded for manufactured goods, which were shipped back across the Atlantic to America.

Before long there were all kinds of overlapping "triangles" marking the passage of Yankee ships back and forth from one continent to another, making many Boston merchants immensely rich. Thomas Hancock, for example, traded molasses from the West Indies for fish in Newfoundland, and also imported Dutch tea from the West Indies to Boston. By the late 1730s Hancock owned his own fleet of ships and was able to build a splendid mansion on the slope of Beacon Hill. Peter Faneuil was another Boston merchant who profited from the Caribbean trade during the same period, and who donated to the town a large building to be used as a market. Although the maritime historian Samuel Eliot Morison once stated that as slaving ports Boston and Salem were "poor rivals" to Newport, it is difficult to escape the realization that many leading families of a town that acquired the reputation of the "cradle of liberty" and the home of the abolition movement made their considerable fortunes on the trading of slaves and the profits of slave commodities.

Trinity Church

Founded in 1773, Trinity Church was the third Episcopal church in Boston, after King's Chapel and Christ Church (the Old North Church). Trinity's first two church buildings were located on Summer Street, in downtown Boston, but just three years after the Reverend Phillips Brooks became rector of the second structure it was destroyed by the Great Fire of 1872. Members of the congregation held services for the next five years at temporary locations until a new church could be constructed in the Copley Square area. A magisterial figure, six feet four inches tall and weighing nearly 300 pounds, Phillips Brooks was a spellbinding preacher whose sweeping oratorical style and rapid delivery ("he spoke like a machine gun," remarked one observer) attracted large numbers of people. He is most often remembered today as the author of the Christmas carol "O Little Town of Bethlehem," but his greatest legacy to the city of Boston was his commissioning of the architect Henry Hobson Richardson to create a suitably impressive church for his large and devoted congregation.

A native of New Orleans, Richardson came north to attend Harvard, later studied at the Ecole des Beaux Arts in Paris, and in 1874 settled in Boston. Because the new church was to be built on filled-in land in the newly created Back Bay, Richardson faced the problem of adequate stability for the building he had in mind—a massive stone structure with a single tall tower, similar to eleventh-century churches both Richardson and Brooks had seen in the Auvergne in France. Richardson's design called for the large square tower, weighing some 9,500 tons, to rest on forty 50-foot arches, which in turn were supported by four huge piers. Each pier was five feet square and made of interlocking granite blocks weighing two tons apiece. To provide an absolutely firm base in this manmade soil, a mass of gravel was filled into a depth of 30 feet, and 4,500 wooden piles were driven deep into the spongy landfill. These piles had to be kept moist to prevent them from rotting. At first this was accomplished by monitoring a small boat kept beneath the church: when the boat touched bottom, more water was pumped into the ground. Today the water level is automatically controlled, and the massive stone structure, weighing nearly 19 million pounds, is still supported on wooden piles.

The church is 103 feet high at the peak of its lofty ceilings, supported atop wide columns and intricately carved black walnut beams. It has a main tower that rises 221 feet above Copley Square. The interior of Trinity Church is even more impressive than its formidable exterior. Barrel vaults and a massive central tower carry the eyes of the viewer toward the ceiling, flanked by bold murals and bas-reliefs depicting Biblical stories and Christian saints. At the same time stained-glass windows pour patterns of brilliant colors down the walls of dull terra cotta and gold. Brooks is reported to have told the artist, John La Farge, to "put something up there that will be an inspiration to me as I stand in the pulpit to preach." Trinity Church is said to be Richardson's masterpiece, and it is regarded by the American Institute of Architects as one of the ten finest buildings in the United States.

The laying of the cornerstone of the new Trinity Church took place on November 10, 1874. Three years later, on Saturday, February 3, 1877, the final decorations were finished and the last piece of scaffolding was removed from the church. On Friday, February 9, Trinity Church was formally consecrated in an impressive ceremony attended by the governor of the Commonwealth, the mayor of Boston, scores of clergymen, and hundreds of parishioners. After Phillips Brooks died in 1893, a portico and front towers were added to the building by Richardson's successor, Hugh Shepley. In 1910 a statue of Phillips Brooks by Augustus Saint-Gaudens was placed in a ground-level niche on the Boylston side of the church, showing him with his arms outstretched in a classical oratorical pose, with the figure of Jesus Christ directly behind him.

Trinity Church provided a glorious place of worship and a permanent addition to Boston's architectural heritage. But Trinity has continued to be conscious of its moral responsibilities as well, and in recent years has expanded its various outreach programs for the poor and disadvantaged. It coordinates hospice programs for an AIDS support committee, sponsors prison prerelease programs, provides facilities for the homeless, and offers a shelter for battered women. In the 1970s the John Hancock Insurance Company erected a modernistic office tower adjacent to the church, and today the Romanesque towers of Trinity Church are reflected in its glass-sheathed sides, creating a fascinating and surprisingly harmonious composition of color and design.

William Monroe Trotter

In the late nineteenth century, Boston's small and self-contained African American community lost any chance for political self-expression when its West End neighborhood was redistricted by local Democrats. Black Bostonians, who were generally staunch Republicans—still loyal to the Great Emancipator—were thus deprived of the token number of black representatives who had been regularly elected to state and city office in the decades after the Civil War. As they now began to move from their old neighborhood on the north side of Beacon Hill to new homes in the lower South End, between Washington Street and Columbus Avenue, black residents retained political visibility only through the influence of local church leaders or the efforts of the publisher William Monroe Trotter and his newspaper *The Guardian*.

William Monroe Trotter was the son of a Mississippi slave named James Trotter, who somehow managed to move his family north to Cincinnati around 1854 and who later fought in the Civil War with the 55th Massachusetts Regiment. After the war James moved to Boston, worked at the post office, turned Democrat, and was appointed by President Grover Cleveland to a position as Recorder of Deeds in Washington, D.C. He later returned to Boston, where he started a prosperous real estate business.

Growing up in the Hyde Park section of Boston, young William Monroe Trotter proved to be an outstanding student, a popular classmate, and an active member of his local Baptist church. He attended Harvard, graduating magna cum laude in 1895, and was the first African American student elected to Phi Beta Kappa. In 1899 Trotter joined a white real estate firm, in which he prospered, and the same year married Geraldine Pindell, who became his closest friend and collaborator until her death in 1918. Over the years, Trotter and his wife became well known for their activities in Boston social circles, literary groups, and historical associations.

Despite his own financial security and his comfortable relations with members of Boston's white community, William Monroe Trotter was acutely conscious of the various forms of discrimination that most black people faced in Boston, as well as the general deterioration of race relations throughout the South. Inspired by the tradition of the black abolition movement in Boston, Trotter felt compelled to take on the responsibility of promoting civil rights. He became an active member of the Massachusetts Racial Protective Association, and in 1901 began to publish a newspaper called *The Guardian*. Using the influence of his weekly newspaper, the persuasive power of his editorials, and the effect of so-called indignation meetings, Trotter set out—somewhat in the tradition of William Lloyd Garrison and *The Liberator* some seventy years earlier—to press for greater civil rights for African Americans through increased political power and the exercise of the vote.

Like Garrison, Trotter was a difficult and demanding man to work with, and often alienated his friends and allies. He saw himself as the center of a national civil rights movement based in Boston and did not cooperate gladly with other black leaders. In 1903 he engaged in public differences with Booker T. Washington, and two years later split with W. E. B. Du Bois over the operations of the Niagara movement. In 1909 he challenged the new National Association for the Advancement of Colored People (NAACP) by putting forth his own organization, the National Independent Political

League (NIPL) as the appropriate vehicle for a successful civil rights movement. Gradually, however, the NIPL lost membership and influence to the NAACP, especially after 1913, when Trotter made headlines following an unfortunate and impolitic exchange of views with President Woodrow Wilson that was reported in the press.

William Monroe Trotter fought on, however, returning from a tour of the Midwest in 1915 to campaign against the showing of *The Birth of a Nation* in Boston. When the United States entered World War I in 1917, Trotter joined with most other black leaders in supporting the war and backing the administration, but called for greater attention to civil rights on the part of the federal government in return for black enlistment. Once the war was over Trotter became more of a local figure than a national activist, generally displaying a skepticism toward Du Bois's Pan-Africanist ideas and Marcus Garvey's black nationalist programs. Trotter favored a more integrationist approach to civil rights, insisting his people were not African but American—preferring to use such terms as "colored Americans" or "Negro Americans."

Through the columns of *The Guardian,* Trotter continued to champion the causes of local African American organizations, campaign for sympathetic political candidates, report on police brutality and racial violence, and organize old-style indignation meetings to publicize issues and events of significance to Boston's black residents. Trotter's influence and that of his newspaper declined further during the 1920s, as Boston's small black community was overshadowed by events in New York, Chicago, and Washington. In 1922 Trotter was among those who protested a decision by the president of Harvard University to exclude black freshmen from college residence halls. "If President Lowell is responsible for race exclusion in the freshman dormitory," he wrote in *The Guardian,* "he is making Harvard turn from democracy and freedom to race oppression, prejudice, and hypocrisy." After the death of his beloved wife in 1918, Trotter grew increasingly isolated and depressed, and in 1934 he either fell or jumped to his death. The passing of William Monroe Trotter deprived Boston's black community of a voice that had never ceased calling for equal rights and equal opportunities for all Americans.

U

Union Oyster House

Union Oyster House

Ye Olde Oyster House in downtown Boston has been serving shucked oysters at the same U-shaped mahogany bar just inside its front door since 1826. But the building had a fascinating existence long before that time.

Union Street, its present location, was laid out in 1636 and was later described in a 1708 broadside as "leading down from Platt's corner, passing northwesterly by the Sign of the Dragon, to the Mill Pond." The first reference to the Oyster House building itself came in 1742, when it was listed as the Union Street property of a Boston merchant named Thomas Stoddard. Some time later Thomas Capen took it over, called it "At the Sign of the Cornfields," and used it to sell silks and fancy dress goods.

From 1771 until the outbreak of the Revolution, the building housed the newspaper *Massachusetts Spy,* published by Isaiah Thomas under the motto "Open to all parties, but influenced by none." When the fighting began, however, Thomas decided that it would be wise to move his paper to Worcester. During the wartime period, the building became the headquarters of Ebenezer Hancock (John Hancock's brother), who was a paymaster for the Continental Army. Somewhat later, during the time of the French Revolution, the house became the temporary dwelling of Louis Philippe when he was in exile. He eked out a living by giving French lessons in his second-floor bedroom, until he finally returned to become ruler of France from 1830 to 1848.

The building on Union Street assumed its present role as an eatery in 1826 and is now regarded as the oldest restaurant in continuous operation in the United States. On the first floor, inside the entrance, the semicircular oyster bar is original to 1826, as are the dining booths with their high wooden backs. The great statesman and orator Senator Daniel Webster came to the oyster bar at the Union Oyster House often, washing down each half-dozen oysters (he seldom had fewer than six plates) with tall tumblers of brandy and water.

Ursuline Convent

During the early nineteenth century many native Bostonians found the increasing number of Roman Catholics, most of them Irish immigrants, in their traditionally Puritan city a matter of very serious concern. Puritans had traditionally regarded Roman Catholics as religiously heretical and politically dangerous; during the colonial period the Massachusetts Bay Colony had discriminated against Catholics individually and had passed laws that subjected their priests to imprisonment and possible execution.

One aftereffect of the American Revolution, especially the consequent improved relations with France, was a degree of toleration toward foreigners in general and Roman Catholics in particular. For a period of time in the late 1790s and the early 1800s, a small Catholic congregation developed in the town of Boston that was fairly well received and politely treated. The charm of the first bishop, Jean de Cheverus; the diligence of the immigrant workers in a variety of menial jobs; and their small and manageable numbers helped Catholics gain acceptance.

By the 1820s and 1830s, however, drastic new land policies in England and Ireland caused a substantial increase of Irish-Catholic immigrants into Boston and the early period of tolerance quickly disappeared. Fueled by traditional stories of Papist immoralities and clerical debaucheries, and further inflamed by the thunderous anti-Catholic sermons of a visiting Protestant minister named the Reverend Lyman Beecher, local residents focused on a convent in nearby Charlestown, where a group of Ursuline nuns operated a small and rather fashionable school for girls. On the night of Monday, August 11, 1834, a mob of forty or fifty laborers and truckmen broke into the convent, turned out the nuns and their students, and set fire to the building as a large crowd of people stood by and watched. By dawn, the three-story brick structure lay in smoldering ruins.

Although eight of ten ringleaders were eventually brought to trial for arson, they were all found not guilty—a verdict greeted with cheers from their friends and neighbors. Prominent Bostonians denounced the burning of the convent, leading Protestant journals deplored the use of violence, and local civic leaders tried in vain for many years to provide reparations. For many generations to come, the burning of the Ursuline Convent would remain a tragic symbol of the hatred that could be stirred up between Protestants and Catholics in Boston.

Hotel Vendome

❖

The Vault

In 1959 members of Boston's business community were seriously concerned about the economic stability of the city and their own financial future. The city's tax rate had risen alarmingly as a result of increased expenditures, ambitious bond issues, and substantial borrowing. Furthermore, census tabulations indicated that the city's population had dropped below 700,000—a loss of more than 100,000 people, or 13 percent, in only ten years. With downtown retail sales falling off, employment at an all-time low, and new commercial construction virtually nonexistent, the city's tax base in 1959 was 25 percent smaller than it had been back on the eve of the Great Depression. In 1959 Moody's Investment Service lowered the city's bond rating from A to Baa, making Boston the only American city with more than half a million people to be assigned this poor rating.

Raising the level of anxiety was the political situation. John B. Hynes, who had defeated the legendary James Michael Curley in 1949, had chosen not to run for another term as mayor. It was accepted as a foregone conclusion that his successor would be John E. Powers, a longtime political leader from South Boston who was currently serving as president of the Massachusetts Senate. The business community had experienced a period of remarkably improved relations with the city under Hynes, but feared that under a mayor they viewed as a political boss in the Curley mold that kind of relationship would not continue. This made them reluctant to participate in the building of much-needed redevelopment projects.

Concerned about their future political prospects and fearful that the city might well fall into bankruptcy and possible receivership, a number of prominent Boston businessmen decided to form an association of mutual interests as a mechanism to preserve a measure of fiscal solvency in the event of a financial disaster. Orchestrated by business leaders such as Charles A. Coolidge, a senior partner in Ropes and Gray; Gerald Blakely of Cabot, Cabot, and Forbes; Lloyd Brace, president of the First National Bank of Boston; Paul

Clark, chairman of John Hancock Insurance Company; Erskine White, president of New England Telephone Company; and Ralph Lowell, board chairman of the Boston Safe Deposit and Trust Company, the local groups formed what they called the Boston Coordinating Committee. When members of the local press learned that the committee held its meetings in utmost secrecy in a boardroom near the vault of Lowell's Safe Deposit and Trust Company, they promptly dubbed the group "the Vault."

The mayoral election in November 1959 proved to be an exciting and unexpected upset, as John E. Powers, the favorite, was defeated by the dark-horse candidate John F. Collins. A conservative, dignified man who had served several terms in the state legislature and who was determined to renew and revitalize Boston, Collins announced his intention of cooperating with the business people of the city. Every two weeks he would meet with the members of the Vault at the bank on nearby Franklin Street to discuss how political and business leaders could work together on urban renewal. The close association that developed between the mayor of Boston and the influential leaders of the city's downtown business establishment went far toward providing the stability needed to develop the "New Boston."

The Boston Coordinating Committee continued to function until 1997, when it officially announced its discontinuance. The Fleet Bank's financial chief Terrence Murray, Bank Boston chief Chad Gifford, Boston Edison head Thomas May, and others decided that the Vault no longer served its original purpose. Such Boston institutions as the New England Telephone Company, the Shawmut Bank, Beacon Properties, and Jordan Marsh had been sold, merged, or moved out of state. Even the Boston Safe Deposit and Trust Company—the home of the Vault itself—had been bought by a Pennsylvania concern.

In the past, bankers, businessmen, financiers, and insurance executives either lived in the city of Boston or else commuted from nearby suburbs and bedroom communities on the North Shore. Most of them felt a personal and individual loyalty to their city. They participated regularly in civic occasions, community programs, fundraising events, and cultural enterprises. In the current age of corporate mergers, multinational enterprises, and international headquarters, there are fewer and fewer Boston companies that are privately owned or managed by directors and executives who claim Boston as their permanent home.

Hotel Vendome

In 1871, when the Back Bay was being created and the styles of the Second French Empire were very much in vogue, the Hotel Vendome was constructed at the corner of Commonwealth Avenue and Dartmouth Street according to the designs of William G. Preston. This palatial white-stone hotel overlooking the Commonwealth Avenue Mall was executed in the French-Victorian style, in keeping with the overall theme of this fashionable residential area. A larger addition to the hotel was constructed a decade later by the firm of Ober & Rand.

The original interior of the Vendome was spacious and decorated for a well-to-do clientele in the height of fashion. The great dining hall, which seated 320 guests, was highlighted by carved mahogany and cherrywood, set with large plate-glass mirrors, and adorned with frescoes and a rich frieze. The large-scale furniture was elaborate and sumptuously upholstered, set off by drapes made of luxurious textiles richly trimmed with fringes and tassels. Colossal chandeliers, with the first incandescent lamps in New England, illuminated all this splendor. Even the elevator was heavily paneled in wood, with a built-in seat for the convenience of its passengers. Private bathrooms, ornate fireplaces, and individually controlled steam heat were some of the amenities the Vendome provided for its well-to-do guests.

On June 17, 1972, the original portion of the historic Hotel Vendome was virtually destroyed by a disastrous fire that took the lives of nine Boston firefighters when one of the weakened walls collapsed. What was left of the lower stories of the once towering building was remodeled into affordable condominiums. On the Commonwealth Avenue Mall, just off Dartmouth Street, a monu-

ment of black granite featuring a firefighter's helmet, designed by
the artist Ted Clausen, commemorates the death of the Boston
firefighters.

Vilna Shul

Before the Civil War, a small number of Jews arrived in Boston from
Germany following the failed political revolutions of 1848. Most
were middle-class merchants who settled in the South End as shopkeepers, artisans, and small businessmen. In 1852 Boston's first
synagogue, Ohabei Shalom, was established on Warrenton Street.
When some Polish Jews joined the congregation in 1858, a group of
the original German Jews left to form a new synagogue, Temple Israel.

During the late 1880s and early 1890s Jewish immigrants began
to arrive in much greater numbers, raising the total number in the
United States from 250,000 in 1880 to 3.5 million in 1920. Most
of them came from the ghettoes of Russia and Poland, escaping
the vicious pogroms that wrecked their homes and endangered
their lives. Some of the first Jewish immigrants who came to Boston
moved into the North End, which became 80 percent Jewish and
Italian by 1910. Most of the subsequent arrivals moved into the
West End, in such impressive numbers that they soon formed a
significant part of that crowded neighborhood. Many of the Jews
who had come from small towns and rural villages in Eastern Europe turned to peddling inexpensive goods from pushcarts, or operating small shops in the surrounding neighborhoods. Those who
did not work in trade or sales made a living as ragmen, junk dealers,
tailors, cobblers, or garment workers. Within their tightly knit communities they established health centers, orphanages, sewing circles, lending libraries, free-loan societies, and labor groups.

Religion, of course, was an essential ingredient of Jewish life, and
the synagogue was a central part of every community's spiritual observances. A great many of the Jews who settled in Boston
had come from the city of Vilna, located at that time near the junc-

tion of Lithuania, Poland, and Russia. Despite the pogroms which had plagued the district, Jews across Europe continued to hold Vilna in high regard as a center of literary and cultural achievement. When the Vilna Jews came to Boston, they developed a particular affection for the old Puritan city. With its winding streets, its book-stalls, its small parks, and its numerous schools, Boston reminded them of Vilna.

For nearly twenty years the Vilna Jews who lived in the West End held their religious services in various makeshift locations until finally, in 1919, they purchased two tenement buildings at 14–18 Phillips Street as the site for a permanent synagogue (a *shul,* in Yid-dish). The Boston architect David Kalman designed the Vilna Shul as an L-shaped, two-story, red-brick structure, with a small front courtyard, set back 12 feet from the street and surrounded by a wrought-iron fence. Above the arched entrance doors is a large round window with a Star of David in colored glass. While the red-brick exterior is reminiscent of an old colonial meetinghouse, the interior reflects the religious traditions of East European Jews, with the wooden pews in the second-floor sanctuary carefully sepa-rated into men's and women's sections. The centerpiece of the sanctuary is an impressive, hand-carved, dark-wooden Ark, 15 feet tall and 9 feet wide, decorated with such familiar Jewish symbols as the tablets of the Ten Commandments, the Lions of Judah, and the Star of David—all surmounted by a large bald eagle symbolizing American freedom.

As the years went by and Boston's Jews moved away from the old West End and the other crowded waterfront neighborhoods in fa-vor of larger houses in more affluent neighborhoods, they took their Torahs with them and constructed new synagogues in other parts of the city. The Vilna Shul, however, remained at its Phillips Street lo-cation, even after its own local congregation began to decline as younger Jewish families moved away to the suburbs. The final days of the old Vilna Shul came in the late 1950s and early 1960s with the destruction of the entire West End as part of the extensive urban renewal program that changed the face of the city. By 1985 Vilna Shul was down to one official member, Mendell Miller, who pro-posed to dissolve the congregation and sell off the old building.

For the next five or six years the future of the Vilna Shul was debated between realtors and planners who wanted the structure torn down to make way for modern reconstruction, and local historical and preservation groups who wanted the building retained. Finally, in 1989, with the support of Historic Boston Incorporated and the formation of the nonprofit Vilna Center for Jewish Heritage, the old synagogue was preserved as a historic site. If sufficient funding can be found, the Vilna Shul will be completely restored and made into a Jewish cultural and heritage center reflecting the historical presence of the Jews in Boston and their significant contributions to the life of the city.

W

Phillis Wheatley

The Ward Boss

By the middle of the nineteenth century, the Irish immigrants of Boston had begun to detach themselves from the crowded waterfront wards of the South End, the North End, and the West End and move out into the neighborhood wards of South Boston, East Boston, Charlestown, Dorchester, and Roxbury. By the turn of the century each of these wards was headed by a local politician—tough, shrewd, and ambitious—who became known as the "boss," and who ruled his ward with a mixture of warm generosity and ruthless power.

For many an Irish ward boss, political power was not merely a route to personal influence and social advancement. It was also an opportunity to provide assistance to the people of his district—mostly poor, uneducated, and often unable to help themselves. Their needs were basic—food and clothing, dentures and eyeglasses, jobs and pardons, medical care and legal advice—and the price of their political support was the ward boss's guarantee that he would supply these needs. "The great mass of people are interested in only three things—food, clothing, and shelter," said Martin Lomasney, the legendary boss of the West End's Ward Eight. "A politician in a district such as mine sees to it that his people get these things. If he does, then he doesn't have to worry about their loyalty and support."

In the nearby North End, young John F. Fitzgerald ("Honey Fitz") had become boss; across the harbor in East Boston, Patrick J. Kennedy controlled things; Joe Corbett ran affairs in Charlestown; Joe O'Connell was a major force in Dorchester politics; "Smiling Jim" Donovan took care of things in the South End; and a newcomer named James Michael Curley made his appearance in Roxbury. Power and patronage went hand in hand in the city's Irish wards, and in exchange for the necessities of life, a ward boss was able to turn out the votes of "his people" with machine-like precision. Only with the coming of the New Deal and federal laws or gov-

ernment agencies that provided such things as social security payments, workers' compensation, retirement benefits, and welfare
benefits would the power of the ward boss be broken in Boston and
in most other major cities.

WASPs

The term WASP was first coined during the 1960s by the Philadelphia social historian E. Digby Baltzell. In his 1964 book *The
Protestant Establishment: An Aristocracy and Class in America* he
used the term WASP as an acronym for "White Anglo-Saxon
Protestant" in describing the decidedly homogeneous leadership
establishment in Boston. The term became immediately recognizable, and eminently usable, by scholars in the various social sciences, and has been used as a form of sociological shorthand ever
since.

In a professional or academic context, the term WASP is generally accepted as simply a convenient acronym. In other circumstances, the term could be taken as an ethnic slur. In one recent
Massachusetts gubernatorial contest, for example, the Republican
candidate, William F. Weld, was referred to by his political opponent as an "orange-headed WASP." While there was undoubtedly
no malice intended in the remark, the phrase was considered a
slight to the Yankee community and reflected poorly on the rival
candidate.

It is one of the many ironies of Boston's history that when the homogeneous establishment of the city consisted almost exclusively of
White Anglo-Saxon Protestants, there was little need to identify
them in any particular way. At the present time, WASPs constitute
only one ethnic group—and a minority at that—in a city that is increasingly diverse.

Watch and Ward Society

Founded in 1878 by such leading members of Boston society as the Reverend Phillips Brooks of Trinity Church, the Episcopal Bishop of Massachusetts William Lawrence, Endicott Peabody, and Godfrey Lowell Cabot, the New England Watch and Ward Society was dedicated to "the protection of the family life in New England."

Operating out a Beacon Hill office, with an endowment fund of over a quarter of a million dollars, the Society embarked on its mission of safeguarding the public from what it regarded as indecent books. During its first year of operation the Society banned Walt Whitman's *Leaves of Grass,* which it regarded as dangerous to public morals. In 1913 the Watch and Ward Society worked out an arrangement with the Boston Board of Retail Book Merchants whereby any book the watchers found offensive the retailers would refuse to sell. The police would prosecute anyone who failed to comply. This system remained in effect through 1925, when Theodore Dreiser's *American Tragedy* was banned, and on into 1926, when H. L. Mencken got himself arrested for selling a copy of the *American Mercury* magazine that carried a story about a prostitute. When the case came before him, Judge James M. Morton, Jr., of the district court declared the arrest to be "clearly illegal."

Stunned by this setback, the Watch and Ward Society turned to the superintendent of police and the district attorney of Suffolk County for support. These two officers proved to be far less tolerant than the Society, for in the month of March 1927 they banned some nine novels, including Sinclair Lewis's Pulitzer Prize–winning novel *Elmer Gantry.* In the course of the year, some sixty to a hundred books (estimates vary) were banned in Boston. Among them were Conrad Aiken's *Blue Voyage,* John Dos Passos's *Manhattan Transfer,* Ernest Hemingway's *The Sun Also Rises,* and William Faulkner's *The Mosquitoes.*

The trend against censorship, both nationally and locally, was gaining momentum, though, and by the early 1940s the arrange-

ment between the booksellers and the police commissioner was beginning to show signs of strain. In 1945 Lillian Smith's novel
Strange Fruit, dealing with race problems in the South, was removed from public sale in Boston by Police Commissioner Thomas
F. Sullivan because of what he viewed as "certain indecent pas-
sages." Although the members of the state's Supreme Judicial Court
voted to uphold the ban, *Strange Fruit* was the last book to be
banned in Boston. According to the historian Mark Gelfand, that
eminent Bostonian Ralph Lowell thought the Watch and Ward Society's attempt to keep Kathleen Winsor's bawdy Restoration novel
Forever Amber off the bookshelves three years later was ridiculous:
"Besides being the very best advertisement for the book," he
snorted, "it is making Boston a laughingstock all over the country."

The reputation and effectiveness of the Watch and Ward Society
continued to decline, more so as it expanded its efforts from censor-
ing offensive literature to monitoring state fairs, beano parlors,
horse and dog tracks, night clubs, burlesque houses, night clubs,
and any other activities that in their view might breed vice or immo-
rality. The Watch and Ward Society continues to function, but in a
greatly diminished capacity. Modifications in the state's obscenity
laws now make it necessary to go through the legalities of due process in order to adjudge a book obscene.

Webster-Parkman Murder Case

One expected many things of the highly cultivated gentlemen who
lived in the fashionable environs of nineteenth-century Beacon Hill,
but cold-blooded murder certainly was not one of them. And yet
that is exactly what happened.

About noontime on Friday, November 23, 1849, Dr. George
Parkman stepped out of his Walnut Street home. Dr. Parkman had
graduated from Harvard Medical School, but after he failed to be
appointed superintendent of the McLean asylum, he had cut back
on his medical practice and spent most of his time managing investment properties in various parts of the city. On this day he walked
downtown, conducted some business with his brother-in-law, and

then headed toward Harvard Medical School in Cambridge. That was the last that was ever seen of Dr. George Parkman.

When Dr. Parkman did not return home that night, his wife, Elizabeth, became worried—especially after the family servant told her he had overheard a violent argument between Dr. Parkman and an unknown visitor earlier on Friday morning. The next morning, Mrs. Parkman told her brother, Robert Gould Shaw (grandfather of the Civil War hero), that the Doctor was missing, and Shaw promptly notified the police. Soon Beacon Hill was buzzing with excitement as the authorities launched a widespread search for the missing physician.

Because Dr. Parkman had last been seen walking toward Harvard Medical School, the police searched the building and interviewed Ephraim Littlefield, the custodian. A new development arose when Dr. John White Webster, a professor of chemistry at the Medical School, came to pay a condolence call on Mrs. Parkman. Webster revealed that he had been the unknown visitor on Friday morning, explaining that he had come to pay Dr. Parkman $483.64 on a personal loan, and had then left when Parkman told him he was on his way to Cambridge.

In the meantime Ephraim Littlefield, the custodian, took it upon himself to investigate a vault under the building where refuse from the dissection room was dumped. He broke through the wall of the vault, looked inside with a lantern, and saw a man's pelvis, a thigh bone, and the lower part of a human leg. Smaller bones and the remains of false teeth were later found in Dr. Webster's laboratory stove. Dr. Webster was promptly arrested.

In the spring of 1850 the Commonwealth of Massachusetts brought Dr. John White Webster to trial for murder in the first degree. Testimony showed that the two men had argued over a sizable loan that Dr. Webster had not repaid to Dr. Parkman. The false teeth and part of a jawbone found in Dr. Webster's stove were identified as belonging to Dr. Parkman. On the eleventh day of the highly publicized trial the jury found Dr. Webster guilty of murder; on the following day he was sentenced to be hanged.

On May 23, 1850, Dr. Webster made and signed a confession, admitting that he had killed Dr. Parkman in a fit of anger. When Parkman threatened to have him removed from the Harvard Medical School because he had failed to repay his loan, Webster said he grabbed a large stick of wood from the laboratory bench and killed Parkman instantly. He then dismembered and incinerated the body in an attempt to destroy the evidence.

On Monday morning, July 22, 1850, Dr. John White Webster went to the gallows in the courtyard of Boston's Leverett Street jail, and was hanged for the murder of Dr. George Parkman. Such a notorious case, involving two of Boston's most prominent and prestigious families—and two Harvard professors at that!—was the subject of considerable conversation for many years to come. The murdered man's son, George Francis Parkman, retreated with his mother and sister to the family home at 33 Beacon Street, and George continued to live there in seclusion until his death in 1908. In his will, he bequeathed to the City of Boston what is known today as the Parkman House, which has been renovated and is used by the mayor for conferences and receptions.

The West End

The West End was the designation given to that part of the Boston waterfront, located in the northwest corner of the Shawmut Peninsula, where the waters of Boston Harbor begin to flow into the Charles River. Over the course of three centuries, various waves of immigrants continued to change the ethnic composition of this district, as each newly arrived group pushed out earlier arrivals.

During the early nineteenth century, members of the town's small African American community made up a considerable portion of the population of the West End, living on the north side of Beacon Hill and down to and across Cambridge Street. As immigrants from Ireland began to arrive in increasing numbers, black Bostonians moved farther inland and left the West End area along the waterfront to the newcomers. By the late nineteenth century the West End had become a predominantly Irish district (Ward Eight), where Martin Lomasney ruled as the uncontested and legendary ward boss, exchanging political loyalty and support for the patronage and benefits he was able to dispense to his grateful immigrant constituents.

The wave of new immigration from the countries of southern and eastern Europe from 1880 to 1910 rapidly transformed the ethnic character of the West End. A polyglot mixture of Italians, Jews, Greeks, Armenians, Syrians, and African Americans joined with remnants of the old Irish residents to make the West End one of the most densely populated communities in the country. The narrow streets, the crowded tenements, the dark alleys, the babel of different tongues, the odors of exotic cooking reminded visitors of European cities.

After World War II the city began planning an ambitious program of urban renewal. Mayor John B. Hynes and other city authorities decided that hazards of fire and the danger of epidemics made the old West End so clearly "substandard" that the situation could be remedied only by "sweeping clearance of buildings." In 1958, under the direction of the Boston Redevelopment Authority, the wrecking crews began their work. Despite belated protests and organized appeals by local West Enders and their political representatives, homes were wrecked, tenements were demolished, and entire city blocks were bulldozed out of existence. Residents of the West End, most of them poor and many of them recent refugees or displaced persons from Eastern Europe who spoke little or no English, were thoughtlessly evicted from their homes without adequate provision for their relocation. Although a few important historic sites were rescued at the last minute, notably the Old West Church and the first Harrison Gray Otis House, the West End was razed to the ground. In its place went up Charles River Park, the product of the developer Jerome Rappaport, a complex of expensive high-rise apartments and luxury townhouses. This was designed to lure "quality shoppers" back from the suburbs to the city, as well as to enhance the overall appearance of the "New Boston."

The West End experience, according to the historian Walter Muir Whitehill, almost stopped urban renewal dead in its tracks. Residents of Boston's other neighborhoods, shocked by the apparently callous and insensitive treatment of poor and helpless tenants in the West End, asserted that they did not want politicians, bureaucrats, and real-estate speculators to demolish their homes, destroy their communities, and displace their people, and organized resistance to development projects that still persists. Many neighborhoods organized political-action groups and community development corporations to plan their own civic improvements and to force the city authorities to consult with neighborhood representatives before taking any action that might endanger their communities. Nearly forty years later, the story of the West End remains a source of pain and bitterness among those whose relatives' homes fell victim to the wrecker's ball and, indeed, among many Bostonians who see the West End story as an example of the human suffering that can happen in the name of progress.

Phillis Wheatley

A sickly 8-year-old African girl from Senegal arrived in Boston in July 1761 as the property of Mrs. John Wheatley. At the time of her arrival, the town's population of some 15,000 persons included about 1,000 black slaves. The young girl took the name of Phillis Wheatley, and within two years had learned English from the family with whom she lived and worked. By the age of twelve, Phillis had begun to write poetry, and in 1767 she published her first poem, "On Messrs Hunley and Coffin." After an attempt to publish a book of her poems in Boston in 1772 proved unsuccessful, efforts were made to find a publisher in London. In response to suspicions that a young slave girl could not possibly have written the poems herself, John Wheatley and seventeen other prominent Bostonians, including Governor Thomas Hutchinson, signed a public statement vouching for her authorship.

In the spring of 1773 Phillis Wheatley sailed to London with John Wheatley's son, Nathaniel, where she met a number of important people and was treated courteously. In September 1773, shortly after she had left London, her collection of poetry on religious and moral themes was published there. After Phillis was given her freedom in the fall of 1773, she continued to live with the Wheatley family for some years. She received a personal note from

General Washington, for whom she had written a complimentary piece of verse in 1776.

In 1778 Wheatley married John Peters, described as "a respectable colored man of Boston," and had three children, all of whom died young. Wheatley's own poor health continued to deteriorate, and she died in 1784 at the age of about 31. Phillis Wheatley went down in history as the first African American in North America to publish poetry.

The White Fund

George Robert White was a major property holder in Boston and president of the Potter Drug and Chemical Company, located on Columbus Avenue in the South End. During his life he gave a fine building on Longwood Avenue to the Massachusetts College of Pharmacy and was a regular contributor to the Museum of Fine Arts.

White died on January 27, 1922, and in addition to generous bequests to the Museum of Fine Arts, Massachusetts General Hospital, and Children's Hospital, he left to the City of Boston real estate with an inventory value of over $5 million, as well as a sum of cash amounting to $200,000. The net income of this legacy, worth today around $25 million, was to be used for the benefit and enjoyment of Boston residents.

Control and management of the George White Fund is in the hands of a board of five trustees, consisting of the mayor of Boston, the president of the City Council, the city auditor, the president of the Chamber of Commerce, and the president of the Boston Bar Association. The income from the fund has been used to build and equip substantial health clinics in the North End, South Boston, East Boston, and the West End, a number of boys and girls clubs throughout the city, and a playing field for school sports in Franklin Park. In 1924 a monument to the memory of George Robert White, executed by the distinguished sculptor Daniel Chester French, was placed in the northwest corner of the Public Garden near Beacon and Arlington Streets.

The White Fund is one of Boston's two largest funds; the other is the George Francis Parkman Fund. The Parkman Fund came to the city after Parkman's death in 1908, to be used for the maintenance and improvement of the city's older parks. Over the years the Boston Common and the Boston Public Garden have been beautified and protected as a result of this generous fund. In 1906 a monument commemorating Parkman, also by Daniel Chester French, was placed in the Olmsted Park near Jamaica Pond.

Roger Williams

Roger Williams arrived in Boston in 1631 and promptly established himself as a trouble-making radical separatist by refusing to join the Congregational Church. Instead he hiked north to Salem, where he earned a living as an independent preacher. Later he sailed down to Plymouth, where he finally decided to join the Church. By 1633 he was back in the pulpits in Salem again, as independent as ever, arguing that the red cross in the English flag was a symbol of the Antichrist and should be eliminated forthwith. More to the point, Williams insisted that the claims of the King of England to North America were unsound, since the English neither owned the land nor had discovered it in the first place. The land belonged to the Indians, he said, and the English colonists should have purchased it from them. Williams also questioned whether people should have to pay taxes to support ministers—something for which he said he could find no specific Scriptural justification.

This was too much for the religious authorities in Boston, who in October 1635 ordered him into court on charges of having "divers dangerous opinions." When Williams kept preaching in spite of these remonstrances, the colonial authorities sent word to Salem commanding him to come down to Boston immediately and take the next ship back to London. Williams had no intention of turning himself over to the authorities, either in Boston or in London. Instead, he took off into the forest, depending upon his friends among the Indians to keep him reasonably warm and well fed during the winter months.

By the time the summer of 1636 arrived, Williams was establishing himself as the first citizen of "Providence Plantation," where some of his equally independent followers soon joined him. Williams stayed on to lead and govern the small community for forty-five years, gradually transforming the original settlement into the colony of Rhode Island and Providence Plantations.

In 1936 the Massachusetts legislature voted to grant Roger Williams a pardon, and in the process officially revoked the order of banishment that had been passed upon him some 300 years earlier.

❖

John Winthrop

Born into a wealthy English family in 1588, John Winthrop was the son of a prominent lawyer and lord of Groton, an estate in the county of Suffolk. Winthrop attended Trinity College at Cambridge for two years, but decided to return home to marry Mary Forth, a wealthy young heiress, with whom he had three sons and three daughters. After Mary died in 1615 at the age of 31, Winthrop married Thomasine Clopton, another heiress, who died a year later. In 1618 Winthrop married Margaret Tyndal, a devout and intelligent woman, who bore him eight more children. Not long before his own death, Winthrop married a fourth time.

During his first marriage, John Winthrop began to take a serious interest in religious matters, allying himself with the Puritan dissenters who wanted to rid the Church of England of Catholic beliefs and practices. By the time he began the study of law in London in 1613, he had become a devout and committed Puritan. After receiving his law degree, Winthrop managed his family's estate, and in 1627 became a well-paid attorney at the Court of Wards and Liveries in London, managing the estates of minors.

After King Charles I succeeded James I in 1625, the English government began making it increasingly difficult for Puritans to worship freely, as well as to hold positions of government influence and trust. In 1629 Winthrop decided he would have to resign his position in the London court, and by then was already speculating about having to find "a hidinge place for us and ours." Realizing that the English authorities would never give them their own piece of land, Winthrop and his Puritan friends took over control of an existing joint-stock company which they renamed the Massachusetts Bay Colony. After Winthrop was voted in as governor of the company, the Puritans met at Cambridge, England, where they decided that only those who would actually go to America could take part in the enterprise. To make sure their colony would be free from English interference, the Puritans took the original copy of their Charter document with them to America.

John Winthrop set out from the port of Southampton, England, on March 22, 1630, aboard the flagship *Arbella,* leading four of the eleven vessels that made up the fleet. Before sailing, Winthrop spoke to the men and women about the purpose of their voyage into the wilderness and the attitude of Christian love and charity they should display toward one another. "For we must consider that we shall be as a City on a Hill," he told them. "The eyes of all people are upon us." And if they dealt "falsely" with God in this undertaking, Winthrop warned, God would withdraw his support and the failure of the colony would become "a story and a byword throughout the world."

Crossing the stormy Atlantic, the vessels first reached the coast of Maine and then moved southward along the shoreline until all the ships had put in either at Salem or Charlestown. When the water supply at Charlestown proved inadequate, Winthrop accepted the invitation of the Reverend William Blackstone to move across the river to the Shawmut Peninsula, where springs of fresh water were plentiful. Winthrop and a number of his Puritan followers made their homes on the peninsula they soon named Boston, after the town in Lincolnshire, England, from which many of the settlers had come.

For the next twenty years John Winthrop was the guiding force and moral inspiration for the Puritan commonwealth he established in the Massachusetts Bay Colony. A life of public service was not always easy for Winthrop, however, as he frequently came under fire from both political rivals and religious critics. In April 1634, for example, when the members of the Massachusetts Bay Company found that their Charter called for annual elections, they turned him out of the governor's office in favor of Thomas Dudley. Early in

1636 he was taken to task by a group of religious leaders, including John Cotton, who accused him of having been too lenient in disciplinary matters and judicial decisions. It may be that this rebuke caused him to move against the unorthodox teachings of Anne Hutchinson so vigorously.

Elected governor again in 1638, Winthrop protected the colony's Charter from attacks upon it back in England, but the following year he learned that he had suffered serious financial losses in England which left him forever without sufficient personal income. Returned to office in 1642, he engaged in the famous controversy that resulted in the division between the magistrates and the deputies as two separate houses in the Great and General Court. After being out of office for the next three years, he was brought back in 1645 and continued to be elected governor each year thereafter until his death in 1649 at the age of 61.

Women's City Club

On April 10, 1913, a group of ten Boston women met in the men's Boston City Club at 9 Beacon Street to discuss the possibility of organizing a Women's City Club. From that initial gathering, three women, Mrs. Helen Osborne Storrow, Miss Flora MacDonald, and Miss Josephine Bruorton, decided to go ahead with the venture. Each of the original three agreed to invite ten other women to form an organizational committee two weeks later. When that group of "The Thirty" met, they chose a chairperson, appointed several committees, and agreed that each of them would invite ten more women to become charter members. "The Three Hundred" held a dinner at the Boston Art Club at 211 Tremont Street and voted the Women's City Club of Boston into existence with a treasury of $3,000.

As time went on and each of "The Three Hundred" brought in ten more women, the leaders rented an office and hired a small staff. By November 1913 the organization had acquired its 3,000 members, and on December 20, 1913, the group received its charter from the Commonwealth of Massachusetts as the corporation of the

Women's City Club of Boston. Along with the charter came the personal blessing of Governor David I. Walsh, who praised the women for including members of all classes, races, and creeds in its organization. A short time later, the Club membership voted to rent for their headquarters a house at 40 Beacon Street, originally a handsome residence belonging to Nathan Appleton and his family, attributed to the architect Alexander Parris. The members of the Women's City Club turned their attention to addressing many of the social problems of the day. They pointed out the dreadful sanitary conditions of prisoners in penitentiaries and worked with Mayor Curley in 1914 to raise funds to help the homeless and unemployed in Boston. On the Club's "Bundle Day" volunteers gathered clothing and shoes for the neighborhood poor, and the annual Sale for the Blind raised funds to assist the education and employment of handicapped people. The Club set up a Domestic Service Bureau to help women learn more about home care, cooking, and sanitation, while its Cooperative Home provided a sort of early day-care center where working mothers could leave their children. The Club's services for poor immigrant women were especially important, providing newcomers not only with information regarding home care, nutrition, and basic medicine, but also with assistance in learning to speak English and attaining citizenship.

When the United States entered World War I, the Women's City Club channeled its efforts toward using the talents of women to help win the war. The Club encouraged women to do their own housework so that their housekeepers and domestics could do war work. They urged women to plant gardens, preserve fruits and vegetables, and reduce waste in the preparation of foods. Through its War Service Committee, the Club supplied directions to women for knitting socks, mittens, scarves, and sweaters for the soldiers overseas. In an attempt to promote patriotism, the Club made available to its members some 5,000 copies of "The Star Spangled Banner" and "America" on small cards so that they could teach the songs to others. The Club also created a Food Facts Bureau to furnish women with information regarding the cost, processing, preparation, and nutritional value of foods. The work of the Bureau became so well known that Herbert Hoover, the wartime Food Administrator, asked the Club to send someone to Washington to describe the program. After Miss Edith Guerrier's presentation, Mr. Hoover traveled to Boston to see for himself how a small group of Boston women could establish such a successful bureau. He subsequently used their program as a model for his own National Food Facts Bureau.

Once World War I was over, the members of the Women's City Club diverted their energies into restructuring American society. In the atmosphere of repression and "blacklisting" that followed the war, the women came out strongly against arbitrary restraints against the activities of persons suspected of voicing anti-American opinions. Club members also set out to improve the education of children both at home and at school. They supported higher salaries for teachers and encouraged the creation of opportunities for teachers to expand their educational backgrounds. They came out strongly in favor of teaching religion and morality in the schools, as well as urging objective teaching about sex in the classroom to protect children from the tragic results of ignorance. At this time women were coming into politics. On August 18, 1920, after seventy years of struggle, the Nineteenth Amendment was ratified, giving women the right to vote. Members of the Women's City Club set out immediately to emphasize to women the necessity of taking their new responsibilities seriously. "You cast your ballot," said one Club publication, "because you accept the privilege of representative government." The Club did not take a position with regard to any particular party, but set out to inform its membership about the political system and the significance of public policies. In 1924, for example, the Women's City Club organized a large open forum at Ford Hall with an assemblage of candidates who presented the political views of the Democratic, the Republican, and the Progressive parties. The Club emphasized that each individual could make a difference in society, and that the fate of America rested on each person's shoulders.

In addition to its educational and political programs, the members of the Women's City Club also wanted to improve the aesthetic appearance of Boston. They instructed women on using colored paints, attractive draperies, and gardens to improve both the interiors and exteriors of their homes. For twenty years, the Club held an annual flower show at its clubhouse at the end of May to give Boston women the incentive to plant gardens and grow attractive flowers. The Club also supported the improvement of the city's public parks and, under the leadership of Mrs. Helen Osborne Storrow, was influential in the design of the Charles River Basin, undertaken as a tribute to her husband, James Jackson Storrow, a highly respected public figure. Members of the Club also conducted protest meetings, public discussions, and newspaper campaigns against the construction of billboards and large public advertisements they felt blighted the face of the city.

As the "New Boston" emerged during the 1950s and 1960s, and as public agencies began to take over many of the city's educational, medical, and social functions, the Women's City Club became a more introspective organization. Membership, for example, became much more selective, as each potential member was required to be sponsored by two existing Club members. The Club continued to hold dances, dinners, and lectures for its own members, but no longer reached out to the general community as it had in the past. While the Women's City Club maintains an address on Beacon Street, its collection of documents, minutes, letters, bulletins, and pamphlets have been transferred to the Schlesinger Library at Harvard University, where they provide an invaluable record of a notable movement in the history of Boston women.

X Y Z

Franklin Park Zoo

The X-Way

During the 1920s and 1930s, the remarkable increase in automobile traffic was transforming cities across the country. Boston, with its notoriously narrow and crooked streets, became particularly congested. "There is probably no city in the United States," complained one city planner in the late 1920s, "where traffic conditions on the streets of the downtown business section are so near to the saturation point as here in Boston." The traffic in the confines of Boston's downtown retail district was compounded by routes connecting the North Shore to the South Shore that forced drivers to spend hours navigating the bottlenecks of inner-city traffic.

In 1927 the Boston Planning Board, after an intensive survey, produced its *Report on a Thoroughfare Plan for Boston.* Among its recommendations it called for an elevated Central Artery that would allow traffic to proceed from north to south without going through the notoriously crooked streets of the city itself. The plan, designed by Robert Whitten, president of the American City Planning Institute, proposed construction of 2 miles of six-lane highway above the city streets, carrying a capacity of 60,000 vehicles a day at an average speed of 30 miles per hour. Such a highway, said the planners, would not only remove 40 percent of the vehicles clogging the surface streets, but would also afford "enormous relief" to the flow of traffic that could now bypass the central city on its way to the North Shore or the South Shore.

Although the Great Depression deferred construction of the Central Artery for many years, in its annual reports the Boston Planning Committee continued to call for its implementation. The Central Artery became the key element in Governor Robert Bradford's master highway plan of 1948, but a series of problems and controversies delayed construction for several more years. Meat marketers in the Haymarket Square area, for example, refused to move out of their quarters; residents of the Chinatown district, along with proprietors in the nearby shoe and leather district, complained of losing their property; residents of the North End objected strenuously to having their historic community cut off from the rest of the city.

Despite protests and demonstrations, the Central Artery finally became a reality as the final link in a complex network of new expressways running north and south of the city. As construction of the last part of the highway slowly snaked its way through Boston, Mayor Hynes assured residents that temporary inconveniences would be made up by long-range gains. "When the Central Artery is fully completed," he said early in 1955, "it will tremendously accelerate traffic movement in and out of the city, and should . . . encourage building improvements and new construction along and in the vicinity of the route."

In fact, however, the Central Artery—a critical part of the "X-Way," as some residents called it—became obsolete even before it had been completed. Originally designed to handle 60,000 vehicles a day, the Fitzgerald Highway, as it was called, was soon carrying close to 200,000 vehicles a day. The resulting traffic on the 2-mile stretch of road through the city produced such horrendous backups along the expressway coming up from the South Shore that the roadway coming into Boston quickly became known as the Southeast "Distressway." One of the most anticipated features of the Big Dig transportation project is the dismantling of the old elevated Central Artery and the routing of through traffic into an underground roadway, removing the barrier between downtown Boston and the waterfront and North End and perhaps even alleviating the X-Way's epic traffic jams.

Yankees

"Yankee" is a term whose origins are uncertain and which over time has acquired applications and interpretations that have little or no relationship to its earlier meaning. During colonial times, almost anyone from New England was considered a Yankee (hence the tune "Yankee Doodle"); during the early years of the China trade, any white American merchant was categorized as a Yankee; during the Civil War, German and Irish immigrants serving in the Union army were called Yankees by the Confederates; and in the twentieth century, the term was even expropriated by a baseball team based in New York City.

In Massachusetts, the term "Yankee" seems to have appeared during the early eighteenth century. The religious Puritan aristocracy, with its strong disapproval of avarice, greed, and luxury, had given way to a mercantile aristocracy that engaged in a much more unrestrained search for wealth, profits, and individual advancement. With a growing passion for liberty, the Yankee gave personal ambition and self-interest an honorable place in the social values of America.

Merchants and sea captains who shipped out of New England seaports from Newburyport, Gloucester, and Salem to Boston, Newport, and New Bedford established the reputation of the shrewd and indefatigable Yankee trader, which carried over to their compatriots' sharp dealings ashore as shopkeepers, tradesmen, bankers, investors, and real estate speculators. "Those inhabitants of the United States, those from New England, called 'Yankees,'" wrote one European visitor in 1810, "are regarded as the most knavish, and capable of the most ingenious impositions." They carry on a large volume of business, and resort to "tricks" in order to make profits. In dealing with such people, "one needs much sagacity and an exact knowledge of their laws of trade." Sometimes the term "Swamp Yankee" was used to describe an old farmer who seldom came into the village, although there are those who believe the term referred to a landed Yankee who sold off his inherited real estate and was left with only unfarmable swamp land.

The reputation of the Yankee as a sharp, canny, and slippery trader who operated on the thin edge of the law spread during the early 1800s with the acquisition of the Ohio lands and the purchase of the Louisiana Territory. Yankee traders moved westward, taking their enterprising commercial spirit with them. Lugging wooden clocks, kitchen gadgets, pots, pans, tinware, and labor-saving devices on their backs, their horses, or their wagons, Yankee peddlers became a familiar sight in towns and villages all over the country. "Mammon has no more zealous worshipper than your true Yankee," wrote a critical English visitor in 1833. "He travels snail-like, with his shop or counting-house on his back and, like other hawkers, is always ready to open his budget of little private interests for discussion or amusement."

As the industrial revolution began to put greater emphasis on mechanization, the Yankee became less known for his sharp trading practices and more famous for the remarkable ingenuity of his numerous inventions. At London's fabulous Crystal Palace Exhibition of 1851, Yankee inventions were the talk of the town, from such relatively prosaic artifacts as picks and shovels to the more complicated intricacies of Yale locks, Seth Thomas clocks, sewing machines, and mechanical reapers. Visitors from all over the world came to London and marveled at what they called "Yankee notions," which were destined to change the basic nature of manufacturing. Merchant and trader, peddler and shopkeeper, entrepreneur and investor, tinkerer and inventor, there was no doubt that "the Yankee" had become a permanent figure not only in the legend and folklore of American history, but also in the entrepreneurial ventures of succeeding generations. The Boston Associates who diversified Boston's economy; the Lords of the Loom who managed the region's textile industry; the postwar visionaries whose electronics plants revitalized Route 128; the members of the Vault who helped manage the city's urban renewal—all took the legendary elements of Yankee shrewdness and inventiveness in new, unexpected, and highly profitable directions.

The Zoo

Frederick Law Olmsted's original plans for Franklin Park, the central link in his Emerald Necklace, included a small zoo, which became a popular favorite when the park was built. The park was named in hopes (ultimately disappointed) that money left to the city by Benjamin Franklin a century earlier might be used to finance its construction. Olmsted considered the design of the 527 acres of land that made up Franklin Park his finest achievement, and ranked it with his work on Central Park in Manhattan and Prospect Park in Brooklyn. He intended his public park to serve people of all ages and all socioeconomic backgrounds, offering a place where they could enjoy the unspoiled beauties of nature in the midst of a concrete metropolis. This was especially important at a time when few poor immigrant families had the financial means for weekend excursions in the country or pleasant recreation at home.

During the early part of the twentieth century, families from all parts of the city, but especially from the surrounding neighborhoods of Jamaica Plain, Roxbury, Dorchester, and Mattapan, came in large numbers by foot and by streetcar on the weekend to enjoy the outdoor pleasures of Franklin Park. Many would simply stroll leisurely through the winding lanes, perhaps stopping to enjoy the splendid rose garden on the Seaver Street side of the park. Others would play games on the baseball fields, the tennis courts, or the public golf course. The Franklin Park Zoo was a special treat for visitors, who would look in awe upon the huge elephants, the enormous hippos, and the ferocious lions. The children could pet the small domestic animals and then go off to watch the chimpanzees swinging from the bars in the monkey cage. The 7-acre aviary called Bird's World was a central attraction of the zoo, with an exotic Oriental Bird House, built in 1912, housing hundreds of birds flying around in all their vivid colors.

During the mid-1940s Franklin Park and its Zoo began to decline, and by the end of World War II they were in deplorable condition. Lack of city funds, the coming of the automobile, demographic shifts in the old neighborhoods, changes in tax laws—all led to municipal neglect and public indifference. Some of the open park lands were utilized for the construction of such public projects as George White Stadium in 1949 and the Shattuck Hospital in 1954.

During the 1960s and 1970s, local neighborhood volunteer groups made valiant efforts to clean up Franklin Park, provide more effective police protection, and bring visitors back to the location. It was not until the mid-1980s, however, that substantial progress was made. The city's Parks and Recreation Department, together with the state's Department of Environmental Management, joined forces with the 400-member volunteer Franklin Park Coalition to provide better funding and supervision for the park. In 1989 the Franklin Park Zoo opened its new attraction, the African Tropical Forest, with pavilions that reproduce the different African ecological zones—desert, tropical forest, veldt, and brush forest. Against these backgrounds depicting their natural environment, animals are allowed to move freely, while people are restricted to pathways along protective barriers. The free-roaming lowland gorillas draw a great deal of attention as they look out at the human visitors who have come to see them. Boston Park Rangers now patrol the park and lead free guided tours, as do the National Park Service Rangers from the Olmsted National Historic Site in nearby Brookline. The public can also visit the stables to see the horses belonging to the Boston Park Rangers' Mounted Unit that was started in 1983 to help patrol the vast acreage.

Acknowledgments

It was Aïda D. Donald, at Harvard University Press, who came up with the ingenious idea of *Boston A to Z*. With calculated charm and quiet determination, she persuaded me happily to undertake a project I was not sure I could accomplish. Her constant encouragement and patience were invaluable in keeping the work on an even keel until the various parts came together in the way she apparently knew they would from the beginning. I am very grateful.

Jennifer Snodgrass proved to be an ideal editor for this particular collection of essays, and I greatly appreciate her careful reading of the manuscript at every stage of its development. Her keen observations and wise suggestions improved the quality of the work immeasurably.

I am indebted to Aaron Schmidt of the Print Department of the Boston Public Library and to Douglas Southard, librarian of The Boston Society, who not only sought out appropriate illustrations but kindly shared with me their own insight into and knowledge of the quaint and unusual aspects of Boston's history.

And finally, to my relatives, friends, and colleagues, who helped me recall subjects long forgotten, topics unexplored, and names half-remembered, I owe a special debt of thanks for the interest they all showed in my project, and for the pleasure they took in the amusing game of seeing that the right word was placed under the right letter.

Index